The Gu
Study S

Electronic editions of:
The Guide to Learning and Study Skills: For Higher Education and at Work

Two electronic versions of the content of this book are available: Photocopy Masters edition (978-1-4094-0496-5) and Virtual Learning Environment edition (978-1-4094-0495-8).

The Photocopy Masters edition
http://www.gowerpublishing.com/isbn/9781409404965

Contains a series of pdfs, each covering a particular Skill Topic e.g. Writing Reports, Doing a Project, Dealing with Other People. Each Skill Topic has elements where users can record their thoughts and ideas. The licence for this edition entitles the purchaser to print copies of any of the pdfs for its students/learners.

You may choose to provide a complete set of Skill Topics for each individual. Alternatively, you may prefer to provide specific Skill Topics to meet specific needs. The only constraints on the usage of the photocopy masters are that (1) their distribution is limited to students/learners of your own university, college or workplace, and (2) they may only be provided in hard copy form and not as digital copies to students/learners.

The Virtual Learning Environment edition
http://www.gowerpublishing.com/isbn/9781409404958

Similarly contains a set of pdfs, each covering a particular Skill Topic e.g. Writing Reports, Doing a Project, Dealing with Other People. Each Skill Topic has elements where users can record their thoughts and ideas e.g. by printing a copy and writing on it.

The contents of the VLE edition can be posted to your learning platform(s) and be made available to all students/learners within the purchasing institution/ organisation only. This licence allows you to provide students/learners with both printed- or electronic copies of the Skill Topics.

Copies of both editions may be purchased on-line from the Gower website www. gowerpublishing.com or from bookshops or library suppliers.

If you have any queries about either edition, then please contact: Jonathan Norman, Publisher, Gower Publishing, Wey Court East, Union Road, Farnham, GU9 7PT, UK. Tel: +44(0)1252 736600 and e-mail: jnorman@gowerpublishing. com.

The Guide to Learning and Study Skills

For Higher Education and at Work

SUE DREW AND ROSIE BINGHAM

GOWER

Published by
Gower Publishing Limited
Wey Court East
Union Road
Farnham
Surrey, GU9 7PT
England

Ashgate Publishing Company
Suite 420
101 Cherry Street
Burlington,
VT 05401-4405
USA

www.gowerpublishing.com

British Library Cataloguing in Publication Data
Drew, Sue.
  The guide to learning and study skills : for higher
  education and at work.
  1. Study skills. 2. Professional education.
  I. Title II. Bingham, Rosie.
  378.1'70281-dc22

  ISBN: 978-0-566-09233-6 (pbk)

Library of Congress Cataloging-in-Publication Data

Library of Congress Control Number: 2009936942

Mixed Sources
Product group from well-managed
forests and other controlled sources
www.fsc.org Cert no. SA-COC-1565
© 1996 Forest Stewardship Council
FSC

Printed and bound in Great Britain by
MPG Books Group, UK

CONTENTS

ACKNOWLEDGEMENTS

We would like to thank the following for their comments and suggestions.

Heather and Rick Bingham, Rachel and Peter Fowerday, Mark Pettigrew and Kristina Spohr-Readman.

In memory of our friend and colleague Roger Payne,
whose ideas helped us to formulate our own.

INTRODUCTION

How can you make the most of learning activities and opportunities? What will help you succeed and achieve what you want? During higher education (HE) courses and in graduate level jobs or on placement, you'll be learning new knowledge. Alongside this, you'll be using and developing skills that are essential for success; skills that enable you to use and communicate that knowledge.

This book is based on two assumptions about what makes somebody effective in a situation. The first is that you need to be able to work out what a situation requires and what you need from it; you can then make judgements about what to do. The second assumption is that it's important to develop a base of knowledge, skills, techniques and approaches from which to select those needed for a situation.

You need both elements: to identify what's needed in a situation; to have a range of skills (etc.) you can use once you've worked this out.

WHO IS THIS BOOK FOR?

This book will help you if:

- you're on an undergraduate course;

- you're on a postgraduate course;

- you're in work, especially if it's at graduate level or leads to professional status.

This book focuses on skills needed to successfully complete assessed work in HE and that are often also needed in the workplace (e.g. handling pressure; using time effectively; communicating with peers/colleagues; presenting information).

It seems helpful to consider not just what happens on HE courses but also at work. Most students want to work at the end of their courses (paid; voluntary; self employed). Many full-time students work while they're studying. Many courses include placements. Many students study part-time, while in full-time employment.

If you're an HE student whose main concern is succeeding on a course, this book will help you. It'll also help if you're working while studying (or doing work-based learning) as well as if you've graduated and are in work. The book allows for the increasing age range and diversity of all those studying at HE level.

Each chapter is at two levels. This is based on the view that you can continue to develop skills to increasingly sophisticated levels. Each chapter:

- starts with 'Crucial Skills' needed in the early stages of HE courses (years 1 and 2 or levels 4 and 5) or at the start of graduate level jobs (including on placement);

- then considers 'Enhanced Skills' needed towards the end of undergraduate courses (years 3 or 4, or level 6) or at postgraduate level or as you get further into a graduate career.

HOW CAN YOU USE THIS BOOK?

This book is divided into chapters that consider activities you're likely to find in HE. All but one of these activities ('Writing essays and dissertations') will also be found at work.

The book is designed so you can use a chapter when you've an activity to do related to its topic. The intention is not that you work through the whole book from start to finish, but that you use chapters as and when you need them.

For any one activity, several chapters may be important. We've tried to reduce repetition, so we refer you at relevant points to other chapters you need.

For example, if your main activity is to do a project with a presentation as the outcome, you could use the chapters shown below.

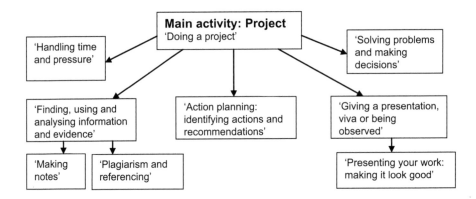

If you're doing a group project, with a report as the outcome, you could use the chapters shown below.

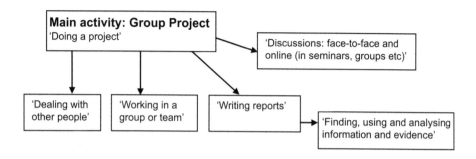

Your group project may link into other activities too: it may provide evidence for a Personal/Professional Development portfolio; you may need to keep a journal for it; you may want to reflect on your skills in working with others.

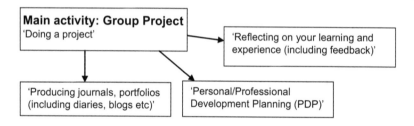

Regardless of the point you're at in your studies (beginning, middle or end of a course) or at work, we suggest you start with the 'Crucial Skills' sections of each chapter. Elements of them may be new to you and, even if not, they will act as a reminder.

WHAT APPROACH DOES THE BOOK TAKE AND HOW CAN YOU MAKE USE OF IT?

We don't have a narrow definition of 'skill'. We use the word to include not just observable behaviours but also ways of thinking and of using knowledge, and we see values and attitudes as important elements.

This book is based on the view that learning is related to a particular situation: in different situations you learn different things in different ways. It's also based on the view that effective performance is that which is appropriate for a situation. So, it aims to encourage you to identify what's needed for a particular situation, to see what will be effective and what can be learnt from it.

The book gives ideas and suggestions and encourages you to consider what might work for you in a situation. It helps you to prepare for and carry out an activity, and then to review how it went and identify what to do to improve in future. Where there are correct ways of doing things, advice is given (e.g. referencing).

You can, therefore:

- use a chapter when you have a relevant task to do (e.g. writing a report);

- use it each time you have such a task to do, until its suggestions and processes become second nature;

- even if you're experienced in the topic covered by the chapter, use it to review what you do and to remind yourself of important ideas, suggestions and processes.

There are places for you to make notes in the book, to help you think about what you'll do or have done. You can make notes directly in the book but, for your own personal use, you may copy a chapter and make notes on the copy (but **only for your own use**; tutors or others can't make multiple copies without permission from the publisher; you may not make a copy for anyone else to use other than yourself nor may you copy the whole book).

HOW DOES THE BOOK RELATE TO NATIONAL FRAMEWORKS AND REQUIREMENTS?

The start of each chapter gives the learning outcomes it covers. These are based on two main sources.

- QAA (2008) Framework for higher education qualifications in England, Wales and Northern Ireland on-line at http://www.qaa.ac.uk last accessed 26.1.10.

  This framework indicates what is to be achieved at different levels of HE awards. The framework for HE qualifications in Scotland (also from QAA) has similar specifications for levels of qualification.

- QCA (2004, since renamed QCDA) Key Skills standards and guidance, on-line at http://www.qcda.gov.uk last accessed 26.1.10.

QCDA now have 'Functional skills' but at the time of writing this book the Key Skills specifications were more appropriate for HE level.

THE 'CRUCIAL SKILLS' LEVEL OF EACH CHAPTER

Here the learning outcomes are based on level 3 of relevant Key Skills standards and level 5 of the QAA framework. Key Skills level 3 is relevant to those entering HE and level 5 of the QAA framework is that at which you'd get an HE diploma or foundation degree.

THE 'ENHANCED SKILLS' LEVEL OF EACH CHAPTER

Here the learning outcomes are based on level 4 of the relevant Key Skills standards and level 6 of the QAA framework. Level 6 of the QAA framework is that at which you get an undergraduate degree and Key Skills level 4 is relevant to this level too.

WHAT IF I'M ON A POSTGRADUATE COURSE?

In the QAA Framework for HE qualifications in England, Wales and Northern Ireland, level 7 is Masters degrees (and includes other postgraduate awards) and level 8 is doctoral. If you are studying at these levels, this book will be very helpful to you (particularly the 'Enhanced skills'), especially if you have been out of HE for some time.

1
WRITING ESSAYS AND DISSERTATIONS

HOW THIS CHAPTER CAN HELP YOU

The 'crucial skills' part of this chapter aims to help you to:

- identify the purpose of the essay and who the audience (reader) is and what's needed for both;
- choose and use language suitable for your purpose, audience and topic;
- structure your work;
- develop an argument;
- proof-read work and improve language, spelling, punctuation, grammar and style;
- review what you did and use feedback to improve your essay writing in future.

The 'enhanced skills' part of this chapter is shorter: it helps you operate to a higher level. As well as all the 'crucial skills' outcomes, you'll be able to:

- identify what you want to achieve from the essay;
- choose methods and adapt what you do to help achieve them;
- plan your work over an extended period (e.g. for a dissertation);
- use language and style to convey a particular effect;
- sustain an argument;
- make complex points in different ways, showing your own understanding/ analysis/critique, using examples or evidence your audience can understand and relate to;
- critically review what you did to improve what you do in the future.

CRUCIAL SKILLS

C1 Why is this chapter important?

Assessed essays are used across higher education (HE), many exams require answers to be written in an essay format and students often have to do a dissertation (like a long essay) at the end of courses. Being able to write good essays may be very important for your learning and your grades.

Essays are commonly used in subjects relying on words (rather than symbols or images) to communicate ideas, such as in the humanities, arts or social sciences. However, other courses (e.g. science; computing; visual arts) may include at least one essay.

Some students coming into HE are new to essay writing. They may have done courses at school or in further education that didn't require essays or it may be a long time since mature students wrote one. Even for those who've just come from courses where essays were often used, what's needed at HE is likely to be quite different.

This chapter will help anybody who needs to write an essay or a dissertation. It'll also help if you have to write in the format of an article that might be included in a journal. Use it to help you write a particular essay; use it again when you have an essay to write until, eventually, you only need to refer to it as a reminder.

C2 Other chapters you need to use together with this one

There are several other chapters that will be helpful when you're writing your essay.

Chapter	Title	How it relates to this chapter	Page
7	Finding, using and analysing information and evidence.	The content of your essay includes the information and ideas you've found, with evidence to support your argument.	147
8	Plagiarism and referencing.	You must correctly cite and reference all the works you've used in your essay. This is very important.	173
9	Making notes.	You'll be making notes on the information and ideas you're finding for your essay; good notes will help.	187
15	Handling time and pressure.	In order to get your essay written on time, you'll need to manage your time well. If you have other assignments too, you may need to manage pressure.	327

C3 Why are essays used? What are their key features?

Essays are rarely used in situations other than formal education, professional exams or for journal papers (other written communications, like reports, are more common). So why do courses use them? Essays do something very different from other ways of communicating in writing and what they do is very important for HE.

Essays allow assessors to see how much you've understood a topic, how well you can see the underlying issues and if you can make valid connections between ideas. Essays help you learn about a topic by allowing you to explore it and to think it through.

An essay doesn't have the fairly rigid structure of a report. It isn't a collection of items like a portfolio. It isn't short and snappy like a brochure. It isn't visual like a poster. It's fairly long and it flows, following a logical line of discussion. It means the writer can explore ideas in what's known as a 'discursive' style i.e. it allows you to amplify or extend what you're saying.

Essays do have a common structure: a title, an introduction, followed by a number of paragraphs and a conclusion, with a list of references or bibliography at the end (see Chapter 8 'Plagiarism and referencing'). However, this structure is fairly loose, compared with that of a report, and this both makes it valuable and makes it hard. The relatively free format of an essay gives you enough scope to either show how well you grasp something or to reveal how confused your thinking is about it. This chapter will help you see how to avoid the latter.

C4 The purpose of your essay, your audience and what's needed for both

Your purpose and audience (reader) need to be considered together. For an essay your audience will usually be the tutor who's assessing it but if in doubt, check (e.g. some dissertations are placed in libraries/learning centres for others to see).

What will the person reading your essay want from it? Rate your awareness of the following purposes: 1 very aware; 2 aware; 3 this is news to me.

Purpose	Rate your awareness of this (1–3)	Comments
To understand what you write.		Poor spelling/grammar/etc. affects how well the reader understands your work and has a huge impact on their opinion of it.
To follow the thread of what you are saying.		If they can't follow it, it has a huge impact on their opinion of your work.
For the contents to be relevant to the title.		Irrelevancies will distract and confuse the reader.

Purpose	Rate your awareness of this (1–3)	Comments
To see what you know about the topic.		Information you give needs to be accurate.
To see how well you understand the topic.		This means not just repeating information but explaining it.
To see if you grasp essential principles.		.. rather than getting bogged down in details.
To see how logically you think.		HE aims to develop reasoning skills. Logic is shown through your structure and 'argument'.
To see how you connect ideas together in a way that can be justified.		This is known as developing an 'argument'; it's a key HE skill.
To see how critical you are.		This is a key HE skill. You need to question ideas or information, not just accept them as 'true'.
To see how well you use information.		Information has to be applied to your topic, not just repeated out of context.
To see if you apply academic conventions.		To make sure you aren't plagiarising; so abbreviations you use are understandable

Which of the above do you find easy and which are more difficult? What else do you find easy or hard about essay writing? Your own purpose in writing this essay could be to focus on areas you need to improve.

My purpose for this essay

C5 What's your topic? What does the title mean?

Being clear about the topic is where students start either to go down the right or wrong track. If you include irrelevant things in your essay or if you don't put what you write in an order that helps the reader follow it (your 'structure'), it may be because you haven't thought through what the title or topic really means.

The following encourages you to analyse your title. It may seem basic, but doing this can avoid later difficulties. If you can decide on your own title, ensure that it indicates your focus (if not, the reader will be looking for something else).

If you're given a title, a good starting point is to look at any verbs in it.

Verb	What you need to do in the essay	What would get a poor grade/ fail?
Explain.	Give reasons for.	Not giving reasons or giving invalid ones.
Explore.	Look at all the aspects of something.	Only limited aspects considered.
Discuss.	Give the pros and cons, comparing and contrasting.	Gives one viewpoint only.
Describe.	Say what something is like.	Being inaccurate or incomplete.
Justify.	Give evidence for a claim.	Making statements with no evidence or invalid or irrelevant evidence.

What adverbs or pronouns are in your title?

Adverb or Pronoun	What you need to do in the essay	What would get a poor grade/ fail?
How?	Describe any methods/processes/ procedures.	Missing out stages or steps, being inaccurate.
When?	It could mean 'under what circumstances' or the timescale in which something happened.	Being vague or inaccurate.
Where?	It could mean 'in what circumstances' or it could mean a physical location.	Being vague or inaccurate.
Why?	Give reasons.	Not giving reasons or giving irrelevant or invalid reasons.
Which?	Focus on a thing or set of things.	Not referring specifically to a thing/things.
Who?	Focus on a person or group of people.	Not referring specifically to a person/persons.

Now look at the other words in the title. It helps to paraphrase (put in your own words) exactly what you think they mean and then note what you need to do to write a relevant essay. If you're unsure what the title means: check on words in a dictionary; ask what others students think it means; ask your tutor.

Your essay title

What's your title?
The title in your own words
What must you include in the essay to make it relevant to the title?

See Chapters 7 'Finding, using and analysing information and evidence' and 9 'Making notes'. Your next step is to note information needed for your essay and to ensure you have all the details needed to reference items you mention (see Chapter 8 'Plagiarism and referencing').

C6 The language you use in your essay

There are two key principles here:

1. your language must be 'correct';

2. your language must be 'appropriate'.

If it isn't, the reader may either not be able to fully understand it or could be irritated by it.

C6.1 'Correct' language

We are using 'correct' here to mean:

- words are spelt correctly;
- words are used correctly;
- grammatical rules are followed.

Spelling. If you write your essay on a computer, spellcheckers can be really helpful but only if you check what they say. A spellchecker may give you an incorrect spelling because it thinks you mean something else (e.g. it might give you 'their' when you mean 'there'). If in doubt, use a dictionary (paper or on-line).

Using words correctly. If you have any doubt about using a word correctly, check it out. Wrongly used words can cause either misunderstanding or great amusement. People may get it wrong when they use words they don't normally use, either technical terms that are new to them or when they're trying to use 'clever' academic language.

In this book we use some casual language, like 'don't'. This is **not** generally acceptable in a formal essay.

Grammar. Grammatical rules exist because without them meaning would be unclear. If you write using a computer, the grammar-checker is not very helpful, as it may think you are trying to say something you don't intend.

What often makes work unclear is punctuation. Here's an example from a (very entertaining) book on grammar on how punctuation can change meaning.

> 'A woman, without her man, is nothing.
>
> A woman: without her, man is nothing.'

> (Truss, 2003, p. 9)

There are some simple rules that many people get wrong and that often irritate assessors. The use of the apostrophe is one of these.

Examples

Its – always means 'of it'.

It's – always means 'it is'.

Dog's – always means 'of a/the dog'.

Dogs' – always means 'of more than one dog'.

Punctuation isn't the only thing that needs to be used correctly. A sentence must always have a main verb.

Example

> 'On my way to the library.' This is not a sentence.
>
> 'I was on my way to the library.' This is a sentence.

The tense of the verbs you use needs to be consistent or it'll confuse the reader.

Example

> 'The dogs were barking and the noise is distracting me.' This has inconsistent tenses.
>
> 'The dogs were barking and the noise was distracting me.' This has consistent tenses.

There's not enough space here to do more than suggest general things you need to give attention to. There are many books on grammar, dictionaries (including on-line ones) and thesauruses (which give you alternatives for a word e.g. Roget 1988).

When you proof-read work, check your spelling, use of words, punctuation and grammar.

C6.2 'Appropriate' language

Formality. An essay needs formal language. This means avoiding writing as people speak. It also means **not** using texting abbreviations, slang ('I can't get my head around'; 'This is just, so, totally uncool'), sports commentator verbs ('She's going across the road and she's falling over') and, of course, swearing. It also means not using regional dialect that might not mean something to others outside the region ('The child was mardy' means something to one author of this book but not to the other).

First or third person. Check with your tutor if you have to write in the first ('I think') or third ('It is thought') person.

Inclusivity. All written work must be non-discriminatory. This means not using 'he' or 'man' when referring to a generalised individual and **not** assuming that people in specific groupings have the same characteristics (e.g. gender; race; culture; age; disabilities).

Example

> 'A nurse wears her uniform with pride' is discriminatory.

'A nurse wears her/his uniform with pride' or *'Nurses wear their uniforms with pride'* are not discriminatory.

This principle applies to using examples. Do your examples include a variety of people (e.g. different cultures; ethnicities)?

The vocabulary you use must be appropriate for the subject area, using words that are normally used in it (e.g. technical or specialist). However, your assessor may want to know that you understand a term, so you may need to explain it. You'll need to use your knowledge of the subject area to judge which words need explanation and which don't.

C7 Planning your essay

You need to find a way of planning your essay that works for you. There's no one best way to do it (tutors may advise one, possibly one that works for them, but you need one that's OK for you).

Here are some suggestions:

- you could start by identifying the outcomes for your essay or the key ideas you want to get across (we planned this chapter by first identifying the learning outcomes for it and then having a section on each outcome);

- you could brainstorm ideas on the topic and then sort them into a logical order;

- you could do a first draft off the top of your head, then revise it and add in information or evidence (one of the authors of this book likes to work in that way);

- you could identify some key texts (e.g. books; journals; websites) and make notes on crucial information, then structure your thinking around your notes;

- if you like to think in a visual way, you could draw a diagram, a picture or a flow chart to help sort out your ideas, see example below.

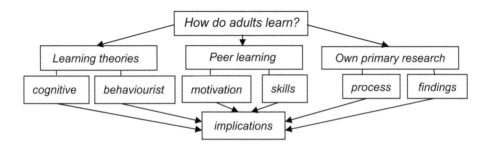

What do you usually do?	What's helpful/unhelpful about this?	What could you try instead?

C8 Structuring your essay

In this context, 'structure' means that each paragraph in an essay is about one main idea or piece of information and that the paragraphs are in an order that helps the reader understand the line of reasoning (the 'argument').

If you use several different ideas in one paragraph and then repeat some of the ideas in later paragraphs without saying why you're referring to them again, you'll confuse the reader.

If you create a line of reasoning but miss out a crucial bit of information, then the reader will be confused. They'll be confused if you mention something in one paragraph but don't explain it until several paragraphs later.

A rough guide to structure is:

- the introductory paragraph says what you'll cover in the rest of the essay;

- the last paragraph (or last few paragraphs) gives what you conclude from what you've written. Rather than thinking of the word 'conclusion', if you see it as 'what do I conclude' you may end up with a better final paragraph;

- the paragraphs in the middle take the reader from the introduction to what you conclude.

The following checklist will help you think about your structure.

Question	✓
Does your introduction clearly say what you'll cover in the essay and clearly relate to the essay title?	
Is each sentence about one thing i.e. one main idea or piece of information, closely connected?	
Are all the sentences in a paragraph about the same thing i.e. a main idea/piece of information? Are the connections between the sentences (ideas and information) clear?	
Have you put your paragraphs in a helpful order and have you been consistent? Possibilities are: • in date order or the order in which something happened • by stages or steps • by causality (i.e. one thing led to another) • by theme (e.g. paintings; drawings; sculptures) • by importance to your subject • what else?	
Have you made the connections between the paragraphs clear?	
Have you given essential information needed to understand something at the point it is first mentioned?	
Have you avoided having paragraphs about the same thing dotted around with no logical order?	

Because you know what you mean, it's hard to see it as somebody who's reading your essay for the first time does. Ways of checking if your structure makes sense include:

- identify a key word or phrase that indicates what a paragraph is about. Now check if everything in the paragraph is about that; if not you may need to move something from it. List your key words/phrases in the order in which your paragraphs appear and ask if that's a logical order; if not, move paragraphs;

- jot down (briefly) the main points that somebody who knows nothing about the topic would need to know in order to understand what you've written; look at your draft essay to see if you've included them;

- ask somebody else to read it to see if they can follow it;

- if the tutor offers to look at a draft, take full advantage of this and act on the feedback;

- draft it, leave it for a few days, then re-read it;

- if you have written it on the computer, print it off and read it;

- read it aloud.

Using a computer makes structuring your work much easier than handwriting it, as it allows you to move things around (don't forget to back it up when you save it and give successive drafts a number, so you don't forget which version is the latest one).

The layout of your essay helps make the structure clear (e.g. making clear where your paragraphs start and end). This means (if you use a computer) a line space between paragraphs and it means 'running lines on', i.e. not starting each new sentence on a new line (see Chapter 10 'Presenting your work; making it look good').

Look at the last two paragraphs. Now look at them below without line spaces and without 'running on'. Which is clearer?

Example of poor layout

Using a computer makes structuring your work much easier than handwriting it, as it allows you to move things around (don't forget to back it up when you save it and give successive drafts a number, so you don't forget which version is your latest one).
The layout of your essay helps make the structure clear (e.g. making clear where your paragraphs start and end).
This means (if you use a computer) a line space between paragraphs and it means 'running lines on', i.e. not starting each new sentence on a new line (see Chapter 10 'Presenting your work; making it look good').

C9 Developing an argument: putting the 'soul' into the essay

Writing an essay is a bit like telling a story: you work out an 'angle' that gets across the main point and appeals to the reader. You're creating a line of thinking and your reader is following a thread leading them somewhere. You need enough detail for your 'story' to make sense but not so much that your reader gets bogged down, so you need to include details that add to the 'story' and to exclude anything detracting from it.

There are different approaches to creating your essay. There's no 'right' way, no one correct line of argument. It's up to you to choose one that suits you and the topic. Readers want to see what your argument is (and that you've got one that you've worked out for yourself), how you construct it and what connections you make along the way.

For example, to answer the essay question 'Should airport provision in the UK be expanded', here are two possibilities.

Possibility 1

Line of argument	Examples
1. Provide an overview of the current provision.	*Number of airports/passengers/flights (perhaps compared with other countries).*
2. Identify all the factors to consider in expanding them, and provide information/evidence about each.	*Projected passenger needs; airport capacity needed for this; expand current/build new; costs; impacts on residents; impact on environment.*
3. Discuss the different factors.	*Which factors will most affect the economy and the environment.*
4. Finally, make a judgement.	*Decide if impact on environment is outweighed by the economic benefits.*

Possibility 2

Line of argument	Examples
1. Explore why it's an issue.	*Tension between environmental concerns and need to increase capacity. Short term as opposed to long term interests.*
2. Look at the different viewpoints about this issue.	*Government; employers; passenger airlines; freight airlines; local residents; pressure groups ; the planet.*
3. Provide and weigh up the evidence in relation to the viewpoints and issue.	*Current capacity; projected demand; impact on economy/local residents/environment; costs/ benefits of alternative transport.*
4. Finally, make a judgement.	*Decide if better to invest in alternative transport.*

Which of the following alternative approaches would suit your 'story'?

Possible approaches	✓
Start by making a claim/statement, then justify it.	
Start by identifying the evidence, then say what it proves at the end.	
Start by stating key themes, then explore them one by one, then show how they're connected.	
Use a chronological order (e.g. start with the final conclusion then say what led to it; or start at the beginning and go through the stages to reach the conclusion).	
Start with a statement of existing knowledge.	
Start with a statement of new knowledge and tell the 'story' of how it was created (e.g. 'here's something wonderful we now know; how did we get here?)'	
What else?	

C10 Drafting, editing and proof reading

C10.1 Drafting

It's highly unlikely that your first draft will be good enough to hand in. Most writers do several drafts of a piece of work and computers really help here. If you're not using a computer but are handwriting, it's helpful to write your first draft on every other line. This will help you do amendments before your final version. If you use a computer, you can cut, paste and move things around easily.

An essay is often seen as a final product but it's the drafting of it that's the learning experience. Through thinking about the structure, you'll be sorting out and forming your ideas about the topic: you learn as you write. Putting an idea in writing can make you see it in a new way and question it. If you leave writing your essay till the last minute, you'll miss out on this and your work won't be as good or get as good a mark.

C10.2 Editing

Editing means amending a draft to make it better. This checklist can help.

Item	✓
Can you say the same thing in fewer words (you get marks for quality, not bulk)?	
Can you use more appropriate words or better examples?	
Have you got the best order for the paragraphs?	
Have you got the best order for the sentences in each paragraph?	
Are the connections/links between your sentences/paragraphs/ideas clear?	
Is everything relevant to the title (if not, take it out)?	
Have you checked the assessment criteria for the work? Are you meeting them?	
What else would make the work better?	

Example: saying the same thing in fewer words

FIRST VERSION

It is very unlikely that your first draft will be good enough to hand in. Most writers do several drafts of a piece of work and computers really help you do this. If you're not using a computer but are handwriting your work, then it's helpful to write your first draft on every other line. This will help you do amendments before your final version. If you use a computer you can cut and paste and move things around at will.

SHORTER VERSION

Your first draft is unlikely to be good enough to hand in. Most writers do several drafts of a piece and computers help here: you can cut, paste and move things. For handwritten work, write a draft on alternate lines so you can insert amendments before making a final version.

Linking words and phrases

How can you link sentences and paragraphs? Here are some linking words and phrases.

however	in addition	as a consequence	a different perspective is
on the other hand	bearing in mind the former	following on from	another example is
in spite of	turning to	as a result of	an alternative way of seeing this is
whereas	after considering	a further idea/ concept is	instead of
having looked at the positives, the negatives might be addressed	*What else?*		

Such linking words act as 'signposts' i.e. they tell the reader where they are in the work. Other ways of signposting include:

- telling the reader what you will cover;

- providing summaries at various points in the essay of key things covered so far;

- making explicit the relationship between information or ideas.

In some sorts of essays you can't use subheadings, which are a way of signposting used in reports, so it's even more important to use your wording to signpost.

C10.3 Proof-reading

Proof-reading is checking your draft for accuracy. It helps to:

- leave if for a few days then look at it again;

- print it out to look at it if you've produced it on a computer;

- ask somebody to do a final check (but ensure the final version is still your own work).

Here's a checklist to help.

Have you checked...	✓
spelling?	
the meaning of the words you've used?	
punctuation?	
that all your sentences have a main verb?	
any details are correct?	
all other work referred to is cited (see Chapter 8)?	
your list of references follows the correct conventions (see Chapter 8)?	
your paragraphs are clearly separated?	

C11 Reviewing and improving what you do

How can you improve your essay writing next time round?

Activity	This is what I'll repeat/do the same in future	This is what I'll do differently
Being clear about the essay's purpose, audience, requirements.		
Clarifying the title.		

Activity	This is what I'll repeat/do the same in future	This is what I'll do differently
Using 'correct' language.		
Using 'appropriate' language.		
Planning the essay.		
Structuring and developing an argument.		
Drafting work.		
Editing work.		
Proof-reading work.		

ENHANCED SKILLS

E1 What do you want to achieve?

Working this out in advance can be helpful.

Your aims	✓	You need to …
To get the essay done quickly.		find efficient ways of doing things.
To get a good a mark/grade.		ensure you meet the assessment criteria.
To impress the assessor.		ask what they are looking for (explicit and implicit; different tutors may have different emphases).
To improve my use of language.		read more in your subject, practice writing and use feedback on it.
To improve my structuring.		read published work in your subject and explicitly look at how they structure it.
To construct better arguments.		read published work in your subject and explicitly look at how they structure it.
To show how widely read I am.		see Chapter 7 'Finding, using and analysing information and evidence'.
To show how critical I am.		look at Chapter 7.
What else?		

Some more ideas

For more efficient ways of doing things, see Chapters 15 'Handling time and pressure', 9 'Making notes' and 7 'Finding, using and analysing information and evidence'.

Keep all the feedback you get on your essays and look at what it says you did well and what you need to improve.

E2 Doing an extended piece of work

You may need to do a long essay or dissertation taking a whole semester, a year or longer (for postgraduate work). You need to plan carefully. Chapter 7 'Finding, using and analysing information and evidence' gives ideas about this for information gathering and Chapter 9 'Making notes' considers keeping notes for an extended piece of work.

The actual writing also needs planning. You need to allow enough time and most of us underestimate this: do an estimate and double it! You also need to add time for things you can't anticipate, like computer systems going down. See Chapter 15 'Handling time and pressure'.

Here's an example for a 5,000 word essay/dissertation.

Action	Time
First draft after pulling together most of your information.	4 days
Search for further information this reveals you need.	Depends what's needed. 2/3 days?
Second draft.	3 days
Editing.	2 days
Making list of references or bibliography.	1 day
Proof-reading.	1 day
Total.	14/15 days

You'll also need to add in time for other things such as:

- other course work;
- domestic or family tasks;
- socialising/leisure.

So, you need to start writing several weeks before the deadline.

It may feel less daunting if you write sections as you go along. If you do this, allow enough time at the end to put it all together and re-order it, if need be.

E3 Creating effects with your language

The style you write in will create an impression. What impression do you want to create?

Look at different styles of writing to see what the differences are. They include:

- the length of sentences (e.g. longer, complex sentences create a 'weightier' effect);
- the types of words used (e.g. short; common; longer; specialist);
- formality (e.g. first or third person; use of slang);
- the format (bulleted lists highlight points but are often frowned on for essays).

Have a look at the work of others in your subject area (e.g. journal articles; books) and make notes on the language features they use.

There's a danger here. Students may think that flowery, academic language is needed and try to write in a way that's alien to them. If you do this you may end up using words wrongly. It's better to write simply than to write wrongly.

What sort of impression do you think the following make?

Feature	Your notes on this
Using only very long paragraphs.	
Using only very short paragraphs.	
Having pages full of quotes.	
Having pages with no quotes.	
Using mainly short sentences.	
Using mainly long sentences.	

E4 Sustaining an argument

Your essay needs to flow logically from one point to another, to show you can use and connect ideas and information. You need to show how well you've made your discussion/argument and how well you develop it.

To help your reader follow your thinking/'storyline', you could:

- have one strong thread running throughout your work, with everything linking and referring to it;

- have several threads that you bring together, cross-referring to each other, with your essay built around connections between them. To avoid the reader getting lost, you need a strong focus on the connections and may need to limit the number of threads.

Example 'Should airport provision in the UK be expanded?'

- One approach might be to have a main thread (e.g. about increased demand).

- Another approach might be to identify a number of threads, all pulled together by a deciding factor (e.g. environmental considerations).

Whichever approach you adopt, the key aspects are:

- signposting;
- making connections between sections;
- maintaining the thread of the discussion/argument.

Signposting is essential to help the reader see how you've connected ideas and information, and showing a logical progression (e.g. 'Chapter 3 has already considered... and in Chapter 7, the issues raised in relation to... will be explored').

Making connections between sections in a long piece of work involves linking ideas and information throughout the work (e.g. in an essay on how students adjust to HE, you might have an initial section on the importance of students making friends in the first week, a later section might refer to the importance of peer support throughout the first year, and here you might refer back to your initial section).

Maintaining a thread involves relating ideas and information back to the main thread to help the reader follow your line of thought (for the 'airport' example, the main thread might be the environment e.g. for a section on the importance of freight traffic... 'there are also environmental implications here, as freight has to be moved from the airport to its destination and that may mean roads and the use of fossil fuels').

E5 Getting your point across

You'll need to make complex points and there are different ways of doing so, showing your own understanding/analysis/critique of information and ideas.

Ways of trying to help the reader see what you mean include:

- using an analogy ('it is rather like...');
- showing what the opposite would be;
- using a quote that supports what you are saying;
- using examples that are relevant to the topic and that the reader can understand and relate to (this is one reason why it's important to be aware of who your reader is);
- expressing it in more than one way;
- returning to an idea ('earlier, we considered...');
- using a visual image (if that's acceptable in your subject area).

If you're trying to explain something complex, it might help to:

- break the idea/information down into its parts and explain each one;
- identify the essential feature and explain it first before going on to say more;
- avoid getting bogged down in detail;
- see if there are stages or steps that have to be explained in a logical order.

If you're trying to critique something you might (see Chapter 7 'Finding, using and analysing information and evidence'):

- look at what different authors have said about it;
- refer to both positives and negatives about it;
- discuss research that gives an alternative picture;
- identify possible vested interests;
- consider how good the evidence is;
- look at the context in which it was written/developed.

E6 Review: improving things for next time

What could make your future essay/dissertation writing even better?

Activity	This is what I'll repeat/do the same in future	This is what I'll do differently
Identifying what I want from the essay and a strategy for getting it.		
Planning for an extended piece of work.		
Creating effects with language.		

Activity	This is what I'll repeat/do the same in future	This is what I'll do differently
Sustaining an argument.		
Getting points across.		
What else?		

REFERENCES

Roget, P. M. (1988) *Roget's Thesaurus of synonyms and antonyms*, London: Ramboro
Truss, L. (2003) *Eats, shoots and leaves: the zero tolerance approach to punctuation*, London: Profile Books

2
WRITING REPORTS

HOW THIS CHAPTER CAN HELP YOU

The 'crucial skills' part of this chapter aims to help you to:

- identify the purpose and subject of the report and its audience;
- choose and use a format and style suitable for your audience, subject and purpose;
- identify the key information your report must convey and structure its contents to ensure these points are clearly and coherently made;
- make judgements about your material in order to draw conclusions;
- where appropriate, make specific recommendations;
- choose and use an appropriate way of presenting your report, including visuals;
- edit your report to improve accuracy, language, spelling, punctuation and grammar and presentation;
- review what you did and use feedback to improve your report writing in future.

The 'enhanced skills' part of this chapter is shorter: it helps you operate to a higher level. As well as all the 'crucial skills' outcomes, you'll be able to:

- identify what you most want to achieve from the report and how to do so;
- plan your work over an extended period (e.g. for a project or work placement report);
- use language, style and presentation to convey a particular effect;
- make complex points in different ways;
- be critical in your approach to your content, identifying any uncertainties or ambiguities;
- identify any new or original perspectives and conclusions;
- critically review what you did to improve what you do in the future.

CRUCIAL SKILLS

C1 Why is this chapter important?

Whereas essays and dissertations tend to be used only in education, reports are common in many settings. In most professional jobs, you'll use and produce reports (sometimes for a client). Being able to write one is an important professional skill, so courses set reports as assessed tasks to provide you with experience.

This chapter will help you whether or not you have written reports before. Use it to help write a report you need to produce now, and then to help you with future ones.

C2 Why are reports used? What are their key features?

They're used to 'report' on something; it's a way of presenting the findings of an investigation to people who need to know about an issue or topic.

For example, they may be used to report on:

- a scientific experiment or investigation (e.g. a laboratory report);

- an investigation of a building (e.g. a surveyor's report);

- an environmental investigation (e.g. in relation to planning permission);

- a piece of social or educational research;

- a legal issue;

- an issue that an organisation wishes to investigate before making a decision (e.g. government reports that lead to the development of new legislation).

Reports need to be easily understood by the people who need them. They're real, living, used documents. They follow set formats which may vary with the type of report, the subject area and whom it's for. Having a format that is common for a subject area for a particular type of investigation, means that anybody using such a report knows exactly where to look for what (e.g. those familiar with the format for surveyors' reports on houses can quickly skip to the section they need).

By 'format' we mean:

- the section headings used;

- the numbering system used for the section headings;

- the order in which headings appear;

- the overall length of the report and the length of each section in it;

- the layout and presentation.

C3 Other chapters you need to use together with this one

It will help to refer to several other chapters in this book as you work through this one.

This chapter is about writing the report, not about doing the investigating leading to a report or about finding, using and critically analysing the information you need for it.

Chapter	Title	How it relates to this chapter	Page
7	Finding, using and analysing information and evidence.	This will help you identify, select and analyse information needed for your report.	147
9	Making notes.	You'll need to keep notes of your ideas and information.	187
14	Action planning: identifying actions and recommendations.	Many reports end in recommendations.	301
8	Plagiarism and referencing.	You must be sure work is either your own or is fully cited and referenced, so you can't be accused of cheating.	173
10	Presenting your work: making it look good.	You'll want to present your work as well as possible; people are influenced by appearance.	205

C4 Your starting point: format and style needed

Reports vary for different groups in different subject areas and for different purposes. You need to start by finding out what your report needs to be like. It also has to be written in a style (including the sorts of words you use) that's appropriate for the readers.

You could start by thinking about the following.

Item	Example	Your own report: notes
What's the subject area of this report?	Education	
What's the purpose of this report?	To report on an evaluation I carried out and to make recommendations	
What's the topic or focus of this report?	Assessment	
Who'll read it (your audience)?	Tutors and students in my department	

It helps to look at similar reports. Where? How? Possibilities are:

- ask your lecturer (or manager) for an example;

- ask your lecturer (or manager or client) what's required;

- look at published reports in a library/learning centre;

- look on the web;

- ask other students (or colleagues) if they have examples (but don't look at only one, in case it's a poor example);

- what else could you do?

You now need to think about the following.

Item	Your notes
How long should your report be?	
What section headings are needed?	
How long should each section be?	
How is the numbering of sections to be done?	
What sort of content goes in each section?	
Should it be written in the first person (I) or third person (one/ they/he or she)?	
What language is needed (e.g. common/technical/specialist words; short/long sentences)?	
How should it be laid out?	
Will charts, graphs, images be required/useful?	
What else is needed?	

Here's an example of section headings and the numbering system for a research report in the social science or education areas. Check what reports in your subject or professional area are like.

Example

Main headings	Possible sub-headings (example only)	Comments
Title and author		Usually on a separate covering page.
Contents list		This gives section numbers/headings and the page numbers for them. It doesn't have a section number itself.
Executive summary		This section isn't normally numbered.

1 Introduction	1.1 Context
	1.2 Aims and objectives
	  1.2.1 Aims
	  1.2.2 Objectives
		Numbering of sections normally starts here.

2 Methods	2.1 Methods used 2.2 Target group 2.3 Review of methods	

3 Findings	3.1 Response rate
	3.2 Theme (e.g. 'mature students in higher education')
	  3.2.1 Sub theme (e.g. 'motivations of mature students')
	  3.2.2 Sub theme
	3.3 Theme
		Further sub headings under a sub theme would be numbered (e.g. 3.2.1; 3.2.1.2).
		However it's seen as too tedious to go down to that level and most writers would stop at 3.2.1.

4 Discussion		Optional.
5 Conclusions		If there's no discussion section, this would be 4.
6 Recommendations		Optional.
References		This section isn't numbered.
Appendices		Each appendix is numbered, often using a different type of numbering from your main text e.g. Roman numerals (Appendix i, Appendix ii, Appendix iii).

In some reports (e.g. government reports) each paragraph is numbered.

If you're likely to use a similar format repeatedly, you could save an outline format on your computer and adapt it each time you write a report, to save you starting from scratch. You may find electronic report 'wizards' (for help here, ask an ICT support department or technician in your university/college/workplace).

C5 Your contents

Your report must clearly convey information to the reader. What would help someone follow what you're writing? This may relate to your purpose and focus.

Which of the following might help?

Item	✓	Comments
Putting points in time order.		If time order isn't important, you may bog the reader down by saying what happened when.
Sorting information into key themes or issues that are important to the reader.		Often, this very important.
Putting themes or issues in a particular order (e.g. logical for the information presented).		Often, this very important.
Putting points in an order that helps you prove something.		You're leading your reader through a process.
Including all essential information.		You may be so familiar with the topic you can't see it as the reader will and may miss out key information or stages.
Including essential detail.		Too much detail can bog down the reader; too little can mean s/he can't follow what you say.
Including detail that's helpful rather than essential in an appendix (e.g. an example of a questionnaire used).		Try not to have too many appendices or you'll outface your reader.

Some guidance on what might be needed in sections

Executive summary. Long reports (e.g. government reports) often have an executive summary. This means the reader doesn't need to read the whole report but can see what's important from the summary and then go to the sections s/he thinks they need. An executive summary gives the main points from each section and is short (e.g. for a 2,500 word report it might be 500 words long) and might be in bullet points. It's not the same as an abstract, which is much shorter (about 60 words) and just indicates the main focus of a piece of work rather than summarising points.

Discussion. Sometimes there'll be a 'Discussion' section. Here, you'd discuss what you've discovered (e.g. giving possible explanations for the findings; alternative perspectives).

Conclusions. This shouldn't contain any new information. People are often unsure what to put in this section and it helps to ask yourself 'what do I conclude from what I've found?' Your answer to this question goes in the conclusions section. It should be directly based on the findings section (e.g. your conclusions might summarise key points from the findings). You might conclude that your information did/didn't adequately explore the issue you set out to explore. In your conclusions, you're making judgements about what's important in the findings.

Recommendations. These should be based on the conclusions (which, in turn, are based on the findings). Recommendations that aren't connected to what's gone before will prompt the reader to ask 'where's the evidence that this recommendation is needed?' When the purpose of a report is to make recommendations (i.e. what you think should happen next), they need to be specific enough for the reader to act on (e.g. 'working relationships should be improved' is more of a wish than a recommendation; a specific recommendation would suggest how working relationships should be improved, for example 'a conflict resolution process should be developed'). See Chapter 14 'Action planning: identifying actions and recommendations'.

References. You need to give citations and references to any work you mention in your report. See Chapter 8 'Plagiarism and referencing'.

Appendices. These should contain information that's not essential within the main report. They are for information that's helpful in explaining sections of the report. You need to refer to your appendices in the body of the report or the reader won't look at them (e.g. 'see Appendix ii for the interview questions').

Throughout, use whatever conventions are required for your subject area (e.g. in presenting numerical, scientific, engineering information etc).

But...

The above advice is general only. The report you need to write in your subject, for your purpose and audience may need something different. Check with your lecturer (or manager or client)!

C6 Presenting your report

How will you lay out your report? Sections C4 and C5 considered section headings and content, but you also need to think about what it'll look like. This not only affects the impression gained by the reader but how well they can follow it. How are other reports of this type presented? Which do you like and would suit your report?

Here's a checklist to help you think about this (but see also Chapter 10 'Presenting your work: making it look good').

Item	✓
Have you got different font sizes or styles for different levels of headings to make them stand out?	
Have you included page numbers?	
Is it clear where paragraphs start and end?	
Do you have sufficient 'white space' around your text/images?	
Are any visual images or diagrams clear?	
Are any tables or charts clear?	
Have you followed conventions for presenting images, diagrams, tables, charts (e.g. labelling; giving base numbers; giving scale)?	
If it's in some form of binding, how easy is it for the reader to use?	

C7 Drafting, editing and proof-reading

Drafting

As with any piece of written work, you'll have more than one draft. Word processing your report will really help, as it makes it easy to amend work.

The report may be the end point of another activity (e.g. you may be reporting on a project) so you need to estimate how long it'll take to write it and include this in planning.

How long will it take to write your first draft and so by when do you need to have completed the preliminary work? How many redrafts will you need and how long will they take? Having a plan of work with timescales and deadlines (working back from the deadline) helps: it always takes longer to write a report than you think. See Chapter 15 'Handling time and pressure'.

Be careful about version control. Whether word processing or handwriting, number each draft to avoid getting muddled with different versions (and include the number of the draft in the file name, if you're word-processing it).

Editing

Check and amend your work to make sure it does what you want it to do. It's helpful to use techniques which allow you to 'stand back' or see your work afresh, for example:

- print it off and read it on paper rather than on screen;
- read it aloud;

- leave a draft for a few days before looking at it again;
- ask somebody else to read it and get feedback from them.

Here's an editing checklist.

Item	✓
Have you cited and referenced all work mentioned in your report?	
Have you included all the information the reader needs to make sense of it?	
Have you removed anything that is not relevant to your topic?	
Is it concise enough (could you express it in fewer words)?	
Have you used words and terms correctly?	
Are the points in the best order?	
Is each paragraph about one main idea?	
Have you got information about something in several different places rather than grouping it all together (if so, it needs reorganising)?	
Have you included any key stages where a process or sequence is important?	
Do your conclusions follow on from your findings?	
Do your conclusions include new material not already covered in the report (if so, it's best to remove it)?	
Are your recommendations specific and related to the conclusions and findings?	
If you have appendices, have you directed the reader to them?	
Have you complied with any word limits?	

Proof-reading

This is checking the report for accuracy.

Item	✓
Is your punctuation correct?	
Is your grammar correct?	
Is your spelling correct?	
Is numerical information correct?	
Are images, tables, charts, diagrams labelled correctly?	
Is all work cited and referenced, following the correct conventions?	
Are page numbers given in your contents list correct?	
Are the numbers and titles given in your contents list correct?	

Item	✓
Are the section numbers in your text correct (do they follow on from each other)?	
Does the layout help the reader follow the work?	
Have you been consistent in your layout (e.g. always putting quotations in quotation marks; always using italics in the same way)?	

C8 Reviewing and improving what you do

How can you improve your report writing next time round?

Activity	This is what I'll repeat/do the same in future	This is what I'll do differently
Being clear about the purpose, topic and audience.		
Identifying the appropriate format to use.		
Using the appropriate format.		
Content being organised to help the reader.		
Language used to help the reader.		
Presenting and laying out the report to make it clearer.		
Drafting work.		
Editing work.		
Proof-reading work.		

ENHANCED SKILLS

E1 What do you want to achieve?

What do you want the end result of the report to be? Your task may be to produce a report for a particular person/group, as well as or instead of your assessor (e.g. a placement report may also be for your work-based mentor). Tutors may ask you to write a report 'as if' it were directed at a particular group or person.

You may want to think about the following.

Key question	Further questions	Suggestions
If your report were directed at somebody other than an assessor and for a non-assessment purpose, what would you want it to achieve?	Could your audience find what they need easily?	Signposting (see Section E3), format, logical order of contents, layout.
	Would your audience understand it?	Grammar, punctuation, appropriate use of words.
	Would it convince your audience? Would it seem trustworthy and valid?	Language style, use of evidence/ information, references to other work, logical structure.
	What would your audience want it for and would it meet that need?	Put yourself in their position; look at what's happened after similar reports were produced.
What, in an educational setting, will get a good mark?	Will it meet the learning outcomes and assessment criteria?	Check what they are. If there aren't any, ask the tutor what s/he is looking for.
	What else might influence the assessor's view of your report?	Look at previous feedback from the tutor; listen to their advice/ comments; ask them.
	Have you followed academic conventions (e.g. referencing)?	Proof-read; check what's required (e.g. in a library or learning centre).
What do you want to learn about report writing for the future?	What does previous feedback suggest you do well? What do you think you do well?	Keep doing it and build on it.
	What does feedback suggest you need to improve? What do you think you need to do better?	Seek advice (use this book; use other books; on-line advice; ask tutors/managers; use central university/college support).
	What do(es) your employer/ future employers want?	Ask them; look at examples of reports.

E2 Planning work over an extended period

You may need to write a report on a long-term activity over a semester/few months, year or even longer (e.g. on a long project; a piece of research; during a placement). Many published reports are the results of several years' work, with interim reports throughout.

What would be the issues for you in doing such a report over an extended period?

How could you allow for these issues? What could you do about them?

Here are some issues we can think of.

Issue	Suggestion
Staying motivated.	Make a plan and keep referring to it; tick things off when done; write sections as you go along to give you less to do at the end.
Keeping records of all the material you gather for the report.	See Chapter 9 'Making notes'. Have a simple and effective system.
Making sure you have all the information needed.	See Chapter 7 'Finding, using and analysing information and evidence'.
Allowing enough time for each stage of the work.	See Chapters 7 'Finding, using and analysing information and evidence' and 15 'Handling time and pressure'.
Finding efficient ways of doing things.	See Chapters 7 'Finding, using and analysing information and evidence', 9 'Making notes' and 15 'Handling time and pressure'.
Leaving enough time to draft, edit and proof-read the report.	Work back from the deadline to set a date to start drafting. Allow time for at least 3 drafts/editing; double it. Allow time for proof-reading; double it. Aim to finish well before the deadline (what if computer systems go down at the last minute?).

E3 Getting the effect you want

This assumes you're clear about what you want from the report (see Sections C4 and E2). It may help to make a summary of what the report needs to achieve. You can then think about how to get the effects you want from your report.

Here are some suggestions.

Signposting. This means making clear where to find things. You can do this partly via: your contents list; having page and section numbers; your layout. You can also do it by the words used. You can: refer the reader to other sections of the report ('As can be seen in Section 3.2...'; 'Please see Appendix iv for...'); remind the reader of what has gone before in the report or tell them what's coming up ('The issue of discrimination will be addressed in the discussion section'); summarise key points at the end of each section; if you have an executive summary, ensure it highlights points you want the reader to spot.

Language. The 'Crucial Skills' part above looked at ensuring the language used is appropriate for the readers. You can also ensure that it engages them. How? Get ideas from looking at three very different publications (a 'serious' daily newspaper; a tabloid daily; a magazine). How does the language used differ between them (sentence length; word length; use of slang; emotive or non-emotive words)? What ideas does this give for using language differently? What will engage your readers, for your topic (e.g. what might be the differences for academics reading a research report or managers reading a marketing report)? What language will impress your readers, for your topic and purpose?

Appearance of the report. We're all influenced by what things look like. What might annoy the reader? It might be how you 'bind' the work. Imagine being a tutor marking 100 reports, where for each report each sheet is in a separate plastic pocket, so you need remove each one to write comments on it. Reports without page numbers will irritate. Anything that looks scruffy won't create a good impression. See Section C6 above for what's helpful. You might consider using images (e.g. diagrams) to make connections between things clearer or to illustrate something. Consider readers with disabilities: Arial 12 is easier to read; avoid underlining; use matt paper (pale yellow for visually impaired people and pastels for those who are dyslexic); leave plenty of white space; avoid long unwieldy sentences.

E4 Making complex points

The more you progress up the levels of higher education (or at work), the more complex will be the ideas and information you have to work with. You may need to convey such complexity to your readers.

What makes something complex? It might be a difficult concept to grasp or it might have several different implications; there could be lots of connections to other ideas; it may be that there's ambiguity or uncertainty about it or conflicting ideas or information.

What helps you to understand difficult or complex ideas?

Which of these could you use in your report and how?

Here are some suggestions:

- give examples that the reader can relate to;

- give scenarios or case studies that the reader can relate to;

- break the idea/information down and explain one part at a time;

- identify the key, basic idea and explain that, and then give more information about it;

- images often help people understand (e.g. flow diagrams; charts; models; photographs; illustrations/animations);

- factual information, especially if it 'shocks' (e.g. in 2007, 41059 people died in motor vehicle accidents in the USA – National Highway Traffic Safety Administration);

- paraphrase information or ideas using simple language;

- use metaphors ('it's rather like...').

E5 Being critical

See Chapter 7 'Finding, using and analysing information and evidence' for more on this. By their very nature, reports tend to be questioning something (i.e. are critical). At higher levels in university/college or at work, you need to be critical. This doesn't mean focusing on what's wrong with something, but, rather, questioning it, looking at reasons why something might be like it is, looking at alternatives, identifying what's uncertain, where there might be ambiguities, what new thinking is around.

When your report is supposed to question and be critical...	Your notes
what proportion of your draft report is descriptive rather than questioning?	
in your draft, have you explicitly drawn the readers' attention to any unfounded assumptions, inaccuracies, ambiguities?	
is your own information accurate? Have you explicitly questioned your own information?	
have you explicitly identified other possible perspectives or views on the matter?	
have you included up-to-date ideas and information?	

E6 Original interpretations, conclusions and recommendations

At higher levels, you're increasingly expected to be perceptive in interpreting information and ideas and to see things in new ways. This doesn't mean being totally innovative! This is rare: most ideas build on those that have gone before. It does mean though, trying to see things in different ways and not just seeing what's obvious.

In many types of report you need to interpret information for the readers, making judgements about what's important and explaining how you arrived at that view. Seeing things in a new way isn't the same thing as having ideas with no basis.

For example

A report may be needed as the basis for deciding whether to build a new airport runway. There's likely to be conflicting information (e.g. environmental damage; job creation; security risks) and you'll need to weigh this up to draw conclusions and make recommendations about whether the runway should be built. There probably won't be a 'right' answer, so you need to make a judgement and it needs to be clear how you arrived at it. How could you be original or see things in a new way here? Possibilities might be: a completely different transport solution; an alternative runway location; a proposal for new vertical take-off planes.

What could help you see things in new ways? Here are some suggestions:

- think what the opposite would be;

- think what the ideal would be;

- think what somebody in the next or last century would suggest;

- think what a five-year-old would suggest;

- think what the daftest possible idea would be;

- draw pictures, doodle.

E7 Review: improving things for next time

What could make your future reports even better?

Activity	This is what I'll repeat/do the same in future	This is what I'll do differently
Identifying what I want to achieve and how to do so.		
Planning for an extended piece of work.		
Getting the effect I want.		
Getting complex points over.		
Original interpretations, conclusions (and recommendations).		

3
PRODUCING PORTFOLIOS AND JOURNALS (INCLUDING DIARIES, BLOGS, ETC.)

HOW THIS CHAPTER CAN HELP YOU

The 'crucial skills' part of this chapter aims to help you to:

- identify what your journal or portfolio, diary or blog aims to do and who will use it;
- use an appropriate format;
- identify the key points you want to demonstrate;
- choose appropriate contents (evidence);
- organise contents in a way that's helpful to the user;
- edit and proof read contents;
- review what you did in order to improve your portfolios or journals, diaries or blogs in future.

The 'enhanced skills' part of this chapter is shorter: it helps you operate to a higher level. As well as all the 'crucial skills' outcomes, you will be able to:

- identify what you would like to achieve from your portfolio or journal, diary or blog;
- use methods to get the effect you want;
- use ways of getting across complex ideas and information;
- critique the contents of your portfolio or journal, diary or blog;
- plan to use it over an extended period of time, including for Personal Development Planning (PDP) or Continuing Professional Development (CPD);
- critically review what you did and use feedback to improve what you do in the future.

CRUCIAL SKILLS

C1 Why is this chapter important and how can it help you?

This chapter will help you produce any type of portfolio or journal, diary or blog: written, visual, electronic.

Some subject areas (e.g. art; design; architecture) have always used portfolios or journals to show examples of work, for learning and assessment. Other subject areas are newer to the idea. Journals have been used for specific activities (e.g. placements), but are now more widely used.

There are key reasons why such types of work are becoming more common.

- Assessment in HE is changing, moving towards methods that assess a wider range of skills and abilities than did traditional methods such as examinations and essays. This has included a shift towards students providing evidence of what they've done, often through creating portfolios and journals.

- Views on how people learn have developed. Learning is seen as related to an ability to reflect: thinking about and making sense of what you've seen, heard, read or done. Journals (including diaries and blogs) and portfolios encourage reflection.

- There is an increasing focus on students 'taking responsibility for' their learning, setting targets, identifying actions needed and monitoring these actions. Portfolios and journals (including diaries, logs and blogs) are useful tools here. Portfolios are often used in Personal Development Planning (PDP).

In the workplace, there's now a focus on Continuous Professional Development (CPD), that is, ongoing training and updating. People may be asked to keep a portfolio to monitor their CPD and plan actions for the future. Many courses require students to start a portfolio that can be taken into employment and used for CPD.

This chapter helps you consider what to include and how to present portfolios or journals. Increasingly, these are electronic (e.g. e-portfolios). For any technical aspects, you could seek help from your university/college/workplace IT support or from colleagues or other students.

C2 What are journals (including diaries and blogs) and portfolios? What are their key features?

The journal (also a diary, log or blog)

These record what happened by date, time or activity period (e.g. daily journal; placement blog). They can be paper-based, audio/video and/or electronic.

What do the different terms mean? A diary usually records things (actions, thoughts, feelings etc) on a daily basis; a journal could be for any time interval (weekly, monthly); a log records what happened; a blog is short for 'web log' and it's an electronic record that's on the web.

From here on, we'll use 'journal' to include a diary, log or blog, as they all use a similar process.

A journal used during a course or at work has a specific purpose. It's meant to demonstrate or provide evidence for something. You may not be recording everything that happened, but you must record things that are important for whatever it is you're demonstrating or proving. This is a very important principle.

Sometimes students are asked to produce a reflective journal. Here you not only record what happened but you also review and make sense of it (e.g. what went well, didn't go well, what you've learnt from it).

The portfolio

This is a collection of pieces of evidence for something. Its purpose is to demonstrate what you can do or know about something and it must contain evidence. This is another very important principle.

It would be unusual for a portfolio not to have a reflective element. You're normally asked to include a commentary on the evidence.

C3 Other chapters you could use with this one

There are several other chapters that could be helpful.

Chapter	Title	How it relates to this chapter	Page
17	Reflecting on your learning and experience (including feedback).	How to identify what the evidence shows about you; making sense of it for the user (e.g. showing what you can do or need to improve or what you've learnt).	379
7	Finding, using and analysing information and evidence.	Journals are a form of evidence; portfolios are made up of evidence.	147

Chapter	Title	How it relates to this chapter	Page
14	Action planning: identifying actions; making recommendations.	You may be required to identify what you need to do next (e.g. to build on strengths/successes or to improve).	301
18	Personal/Professional Development Planning (PDP).	Portfolios and journals are commonly used in PDP and CPD schemes.	401
8	Plagiarism and referencing.	You must give references to anyone else's work you mention or that influenced your thinking.	173
10	Presenting your work: making it look good.	How you present a portfolio or journal is important in making your meaning clear.	205

C4 What do you need to demonstrate?

Here are some possibilities. You may have to demonstrate more than one thing.

Item	✓	Item	✓
What you did on placement.		Activities needed by a professional body (license to practice).	
What you learnt on placement.		Your contribution to a group task.	
If you met a set of competences or learning outcomes.		Your activity during a project or research task.	
Your specific skills (e.g. technical skills; writing skills).		Your observations of something.	
Your achievements during your life/or over a specified period.		What you have noticed in a specific situation.	
How your work/thinking has changed and developed.		To meet some criteria.	
What else?			

A good journal or portfolio is directed at what it's supposed to demonstrate or prove and a poor one has irrelevant or unclear content. You should:

- only include relevant information;

- include the best information or evidence you can (see Section C5);

- put it in a format that helps the reader/user to use it;

- make clear to the reader/user what it demonstrates or proves.

If you aren't clear what you're trying to demonstrate or prove, you'll find it difficult to produce any journal or portfolio, let alone a good one.

So check out first what you need to demonstrate/prove. Sometimes something is self evident to a tutor or manager but not to a student or employee. If your tutor (or manager or professional body) doesn't make it clear what you should be demonstrating, ask them!

Here are some things that would help clarify what your journal/portfolio should show (NB: not all courses/CPD schemes will have all these items).

- Learning outcomes.

- Assessment criteria.

- A list of competences.

- A professional framework.

- Specifications by a professional or regulatory body.

- Module or course handbook.

- Assignment brief or instructions.

- Examples of other journals/portfolios in your subject area.

Who will use your journal or portfolio?

This may affect what you need it to show and what it needs to be like.

Who will use it?	Implications
Your own private use to record what you've done.	You can be open and honest; use personal abbreviations; short-hand; arrows to link ideas; circle important items; make notes in margins. Organise it so you can find things easily (e.g. for CV).
Your peers (e.g. other students; colleagues).	You might be more careful in what you say or show, considering the effect on others. Can use commonly understood shorthand, abbreviations and words. Needs to be clear/organised for others to understand.
Anybody with internet access (e.g. open blog).	As above. May need to be more careful about protecting privacy and confidentiality for yourself and others mentioned.
A tutor/manager/mentor who's assessing it.	Look at assessment criteria for layout and conventions (e.g. spelling; referencing). Use appropriate language. Consider the effect of what/how you say/show things. Make it easy to use.
An employer or client or somebody who may exhibit your work.	Use appropriate professional language and conventions. Choose content to show off your work/ideas. Keep to any guidelines. Make it easy to use.
A professional or regulatory body.	As above.

What does your journal or portfolio need to demonstrate?

What it needs to demonstrate	Implications

C5 Selecting what to include (your evidence)

What does 'evidence' mean? It's information that shows something is true or valid. It's what you might produce if somebody said 'prove it'.

How might you prove something?

Often journals and portfolios are used to show tutors/managers/mentors something they can't directly see for themselves, for example: how you operate in groups; how you spend your time away from the course; they don't know what went on in your head (e.g. how your ideas developed).

Here are some idea starters for common things you might have to prove in portfolios and journals and possible types of evidence.

Item to demonstrate	Possible types of evidence
Ability to work in a group.	Your notes on what happened; minutes of meetings; statements by other group members; a written contract of what each group member agreed to do; end results showing what was done.
Ability to solve a problem.	Notes on the process you used; successive drafts/images showing how you tried to solve it; items/images showing stages of the process, including end results.
How you've developed.	Your notes on what you did over time; successive drafts of a piece of work; images showing how your work has changed over time; feedback from others showing your development.
Ability to do something.	A recording (audio/video) of you performing a task; a reference; a mentor's validation statement; photographs; plans; designs; images.

Here's a checklist to help you identify good evidence (i.e. it proves what you want it to).

Item	Notes	✓
Does it really show what you think it shows (i.e. is it valid)?	'Valid' means it shows what you say it shows. What would really 'prove it'? For example, describing a building in words may not be as valid as having an image (photo; floor plan), but describing your **reaction** to the building might be written or an audio/video of you talking about it.	
Is it relevant to what you need to demonstrate?	Irrelevant content will confuse and irritate the user.	
Is it recent or current enough?	Where you have to show your development or any changes, you may need older, as well as current, evidence.	
Have you got enough evidence to show something?	This is very important. You need enough evidence to show what you need to show, but no more than that (it'll be unnecessary work and may confuse the user). If you aren't selective, your portfolio will be too big to assess.	
Is it authentic evidence about you?	Evidence must show something about you, not someone else.	

Evidence in a portfolio doesn't have to be written. It can include, for example, visual images (still or moving), sound (electronic/tape) and CD/DVDs.

For more guidance, see Chapter 7 'Finding, using and analysing information and evidence' (Section C8) and Chapter 17 ' Reflecting on your learning and experience (including feedback)' (Section C4).

What are the key things you want to demonstrate?

For some journals or portfolios it may help to focus on key things, rather than trying to cover everything (however, check what's needed as journals that record fieldwork or logs of experimental work may need to include all relevant details).

For each of the following:

- think about the requirements for the journal/portfolio suggest;

- if you had to choose five things, what would they be and in what order?

Do you need to demonstrate?	Key points/your focus	Your notes
What you did.	What are the most important things you did or produced, for yourself and for the situation?	
What you're good at.	What were you most pleased about and did well in the situation? What did others think you did well?	
What you need to improve.	What things were you least pleased with and went least well in the situation. What did others think?	
What you've learnt.	What are the most important things you learnt?	

C6 Planning

If you identify right at the start what you need to demonstrate or prove, you can ensure you keep the right sort of information or evidence. It's probably better to keep too much and discard what you don't need than find you haven't got enough. Going back to find it again can be difficult or impossible.

Here are some tips.

- Keep a diary up to date. If you miss a day, by tomorrow you'll have forgotten some of what happened, by next week most of it and in a month all of it. This also applies to journals and logs.

- Keep your evidence in a format similar to the one in which you'll finally present it (e.g. electronic form for an e-portfolio).

- If you're going to use an item in a physical ('hard') portfolio, store it where it won't get damaged.

- Keep all the information needed with each piece of evidence (e.g. with photos of art work, keep information on the size, materials).

- If you refer to somebody else's work in your journal or portfolio, keep the details you need to reference it, as you would with any piece of work (see Chapter 8 'Plagiarism and referencing').

- Keep the journal or portfolio somewhere safe. If it's on a computer, back it up.

C7 Organising it: your format

The commonly accepted structure of a report or essay helps the reader follow it, but a journal or portfolio only has the structure you give it. You could end up with an unconnected set of items, where the user has no idea about relationships between them.

Your need to help the user see almost immediately what the journal or portfolio is trying to tell them. For paper based work (i.e. a 'hard' journal or portfolio), this means a contents page, page numbers and numbered sections; for electronic work, it means having a clear menu that takes the user where they need to go.

What section headings might make most sense? The following gives some ideas.

Journals

Will the user find it most helpful for it to be organised by:

- day;
- week;
- some other time period;
- topic or issue?

Within this, will they find it helpful to:

- have common section headings (e.g. for each day or each week);
- just see how your ideas flowed (i.e. without structured headings);
- have different section headings (e.g. for different time periods)?

What sort of section headings might be useful? Here's an example.

1.   *Week ending 7.11.08*

2.   *Activities carried out*

3.   *Difficulties encountered*

4.   *Positives/things that worked well*

5.   *Negative/things that did not work well*

6.   *Main learning points*

If you're producing a blog, a good one is short and punchy, can be read/seen very quickly (think of a blog of somebody's trip; you don't want to see long descriptions or hundreds of photos; you'd want a few really good photos and a few entertaining descriptions).

How might the layout/format help? Here are some examples.

- A page divided into two columns with the first for what happened and the right for your reflections on it.

Example

Events (description)	My thoughts (reflections)
My presentation:	
Introduction went smoothly.	*I felt very nervous but think I handled the nerves well.*
Lasted 15 minutes, instead of 20.	*I should have practiced it to check how long it lasted. Will do next time.*

- Use colours, dividers or different fonts.
- If electronic, create links from the text (e.g. links might be 'reflections': or you could have the key learning points as the main text with links to 'evidence').

How will you 'bind it'?

- If it's in a hard back note book, it'll be hard to remove or replace a page.
- If it's electronic, you need it divided into files you can easily sort and replace, or amend.
- What will make it look good (assessors are influenced by appearances)?
- What will be easy for the assessor to handle or access?

See Chapter 10 'Presenting your work: making it look good'.

Your notes on the format for your work

Portfolios

It's important to help the user find what they need easily. Imagine looking at 100! Any assessor will be more kindly disposed towards those that make it easy. If you're using a portfolio to get a job (or exhibition etc) it needs to be eye-catching and easy to use.

Whether it's a 'hard' or electronic portfolio you need sections. Look back to C4: matching your section headings to what you have to demonstrate makes it easier for the user to find their way through it. You need to organise it in a way that gets across your main message: for example , if you want it to show your development, you might put it in time order; if you want to show the range of things you can do, you might have sections for each of those; if you want to show you have certain skills, have those as section headings.

It also helps to have a standard format in each section. For example:

- for an image, always put information about it below it, or above it, or on the reverse – wherever, but always in the same place;

- either start each section with a reflective commentary telling the user what the section shows, followed by evidence, or visa versa.

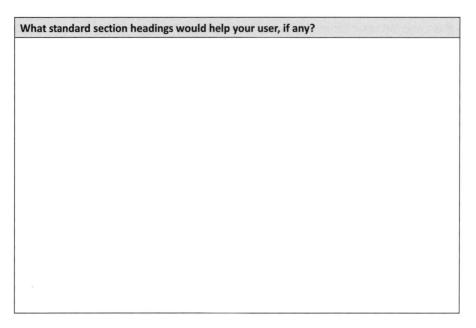

Apart from section headings, other aspects of your format can help or hinder the user.

- If you have slides in a 'hard' portfolio, the user needs access to a slide projector. Holding them up to the light won't look as good.

- Electronic images may take the user a long time to download. Will they have the software needed?

- How have you bound it? Has the reader got to take it apart to see things? Putting each item in a plastic pocket means the user must take it out to look at it (imagine doing that for 100 portfolios!).

- If you handwrite your work, it must be legible.

Here are things that make it **really hard** for a user (try to avoid them).

- No contents list/menu on a home page, page numbers or section numbers.

- No labeling of images or information about them.

- No titles for items.

- No dates, if dates are important.

- No obvious order for items.

- Something very big to physically handle or to download.

- Very small typeface or illegible items.

If you were the user of your portfolio, what would make it easy to use?

What would make it hard to use?

See Chapter 10 'Presenting your work: making it look good'. This is **very** important for portfolios (including e-portfolios) that will be assessed or will be used to apply for jobs.

C8 Reflective narratives and commentaries

Although not all journals and portfolios explicitly ask for a reflective element, by their very nature they are reflective. In sorting information (including images) into sections you're reflecting; you're making sense of the information for the user by deciding which bits of it belong together.

You may, however, be asked to produce a written or recorded (audio/video) summary of your learning from your experiences during the time you kept the journal or portfolio. This is likely to include a reflection on the development of new understandings, knowledge and skills, and a plan to build on strengths and how to improve.

It's important, here, to look at Chapter 17 'Reflecting on your learning and experience (including feedback)' for further guidance.

C9 Editing and proof-reading

This is just as important for these sorts of pieces of work as for any work.

You may decide to edit and proof-read as you go along (e.g. check journal entries after a short time lapse; check portfolio items as you store them), but you also need to allow enough time to go through it all at the end.

Editing checklist

Item	✓
Is your content relevant, valid, current (or for an appropriate timescale) and sufficient? Is it 'your' evidence, about you?	
Could somebody who has never seen your journal or portfolio before find their way through it?	
Could somebody who has never seen your journal or portfolio before know what it's about or what main points it's making?	
Could somebody who has never seen your journal or portfolio before identify the key points you want to get over?	
Will the user be able to handle it, physically, or be able to access it and the contents if it is electronic?	
Will it take the user a reasonable amount of time to see its key meaning?	

Proof-reading checklist

Item	✓
Is it all legible/readable/visuals clear?	
Is everything that needs to be labelled, labelled?	
Have you been consistent throughout (e.g. labelling; section headings)?	
Is your spelling correct?	
Have you used words correctly?	
Is your grammar/punctuation correct?	
Have you cited and correctly referenced everything you've mentioned that somebody else has written or produced?	

C10 Reviewing and improving what you do

How can you improve your journals and portfolios next time round?

Activity	This is what I'll repeat/do the same in future	This is what I'll do differently
Being clear about what I need to demonstrate.		
Selecting what to include.		
Planning.		
Reflecting on the contents.		
Action planning (if needed).		
Organising it (the format).		
Editing.		
Proof-reading.		

ENHANCED SKILLS

E1 What do you want to achieve?

Here are some things you might like to achieve from the journal or portfolio, with possible implications for what you might then do. You'll be able to think of more.

What you may want to achieve	Implications
A good grade.	Know what's expected and the assessment criteria; follow the guidance in Section C above and use this Section E to further improve.
To show employers (or clients) when I'm job hunting/seeking outlets for my work.	Find out what employers/clients want and build it into what you're doing. How do employers or clients want to access an electronic portfolio (e.g. on-line; via a CD)?
To monitor how I'm progressing or see how far I've developed.	Keep the journal/portfolio updated and look at it frequently. Regularly summarise main positives/needs for improvement/actions.
To use as a store for information from which I can draw (e.g. for a CV; interview).	Store it in a way that means you can access contents easily and won't lose things; keep it updated.
What else? Your notes.	*What else? Your notes.*

E2 Getting the effect you want and communicating complex ideas

Getting the effect you want might be divided into three main areas:

1. making it look as good as possible;

2. making the clearest possible links between the point you're making and the evidence you're providing;

3. communicating your thoughts in the best way possible.

This relates to whatever your thoughts are after looking at Section C4 and E1: to identify the effects you want, you need to be very clear about the outcome you want. You may need to create effects about quite complex ideas.

Making it look good

In some cases you may be using a portfolio in a competitive situation (e.g. in a job application). Even where it's judged against criteria (rather than in comparison to others), the assessor or user may be impressed by work that stands out in appearance from the rest.

Section C covers the basics. Look at Chapter 10 'Presenting your work; making it look good' for further ideas but here are a few to consider:

- attractive and easily readable typeface;
- for a 'hard' portfolio/journal, most handwriting is hard to read and rarely looks as good as well laid-out typeface;
- being consistent (e.g. what you indent; what's bold; what's in italics);
- breaking it up (e.g. sections; including images in text) and doing it in a way that relates to key points you need to get across;
- having 'white space' around sections, with small blocks of text;
- avoiding 'naff' images (e.g. badly drawn cartoons);
- use of colour;
- attractive front cover/homepage.

Making clear connections between your claims and your evidence

Here are some suggestions (you may want to use some, not necessarily all):

- signposting (i.e. tell the user what they are about to look at);
- being explicit (tell them what x is evidence for);
- diagrams to show connections (e.g. flow charts);
- use of links, if electronic;
- use of examples;
- explaining the connections;
- writing a flowing narrative that pulls together your 'story', cross-referenced to your evidence.

Communicating your thoughts in the best possible way

This relates to:

- appropriate use of language (e.g. for the subject area; 'standard English');

- being concise (too much detail can confuse the user); bulk just makes unnecessary work for the user;

- clarity of visuals (including labelling);

- ensuring only relevant items are included;

- the logical order of your information/ideas/evidence;

- validity of your evidence/content for the point you're trying to make;

- using quotes to make something 'come alive';

- using visuals/sound to show something that's hard to show in writing;

- explaining why you've included the evidence that's in your journal or portfolio.

E3 Planning for a journal or portfolio over an extended period of time (including for PDP or CPD)

By their very nature, journals and portfolios are developed over a period of time. You need to avoid getting to the end and finding you didn't keep essential information.

You may need to keep a journal or build a portfolio:

- over a year's placement or over a series of short placements;

- over a whole year of a course or over the whole course;

- throughout your professional life.

Here are some key issues and you may want to jot some notes about what they mean for you, in your situation.

Issue	Things to consider	Your notes on what you could do
The needs of the situation may change or your role/work may change.	You need a flexible format/way of recording/storing information. What would/wouldn't be easy to change?	

Issue	Things to consider	Your notes on what you could do
It may be evidence for a research process (e.g. a project; dissertation; thesis).	Your examiners must see an 'audit trail', proof that you did what you did. What will you need to note in order to have a full audit trail?	
You need to avoid getting to the end of the period and finding you are missing information/ material.	Be clear from the start what you need to demonstrate/prove. It's better to keep too much than too little (you don't have to use it all). At the start, check if you need a portfolio by the end. If so, start saving items.	
You need to store it and not lose it.	How much will you have? Will it be physical or electronic and what space do you need for it? How can you keep it safe and undamaged? How might you lose it? Can you avoid this? See Chapter 9 'Making notes'.	
After you graduate, an employer or professional body may need it in a different format or you may only need bits of it.	How could you keep it to allow you to put it in another format if needed? How can you use it to select and use bits of it?	
You may need to show it to others, at different stages.	Who? Other students, family, tutors? Why? What will they expect to see/not see? What's confidential about it?	

E4 Critiquing your journal or portfolio

You may be expected not only to present a journal or portfolio but to critique it; to identify what was good or useful about it, what was not good about it and what its limitations were. This can be very important. If, for example, a journal records work as part of a research process, how and what you recorded might affect your findings.

Interpreting the findings may depend on your critique of the effectiveness of your journal.

Particularly for an ongoing, long-term portfolio, you need to continually critique it to see if you're keeping information needed (an author of this book failed to record her conference presentations and publications at the start of her career, so her list of publications is much shorter than it should be!). If you find you're missing important evidence, you can start keeping it (she now has a list of publications, albeit incomplete).

It's important here to look at Chapter 17 'Reflecting on your learning and experience (including feeback)' for guidance.

E5 Review: improving things for next time

What could improve your future journals and portfolios?

Activity	Feedback I've received on this	How will I respond to this feedback?
Identifying what I want from to achieve and how to do so.		
Getting the effect you want and getting complex points over.		
Planning to keep a journal or portfolio over an extended time.		
Critiquing your journal or portfolio.		

4
GIVING A PRESENTATION, VIVA OR BEING OBSERVED

HOW THIS CHAPTER CAN HELP YOU

The 'crucial' skills part of this chapter aims to help you:

- be clear about the purpose of your presentation, viva or observation and the needs of your audience;
- identify factors that affect the outcomes of your presentation, viva or observation;
- prepare for the presentation (individual or group), viva or observation;
- structure your content for your subject, purpose and audience;
- match your language, style and approach to the subject, purpose and audience;
- develop appropriate visuals;
- engage your audience;
- plan to improve.

The 'enhanced' skills part of this chapter is shorter: it helps you operate to a higher level. As well as the 'crucial' skills' outcomes, you'll be able to:

- identify the outcomes you want from the presentation (individual or group), viva or observation;
- choose techniques to get them and adapt what you do to achieve what you want;
- make points effectively by using structure, language, tone and emphasis, including making complex points and presenting arguments;
- respond perceptively to your audience, being aware of the effect of your style and approach;
- plan for where you need to give presentations or be observed over an extended time;
- evaluate your effectiveness;
- identify how you can further develop your skills.

CRUCIAL SKILLS

C1 Why is this chapter important and how can it help you?

In higher education (HE) there are four main ways you may be assessed:

- writing about something;
- providing evidence about something;
- talking about something;
- being observed demonstrating something.

This chapter is about the last two.

Presenting or demonstrating something are key activities in education, at work and in many other contexts. Most people feel nervous in such situations. They're often one-off events: you have to get them right first time. We may feel more judged by others when facing them than when giving them something written to take away. 'Why did I say/do that?' is a common cry!

The (very good) news is that you can learn ways of being effective that also help you handle nerves. This isn't a skill you are born with: it's about knowing useful techniques and when to use them, and good planning.

This chapter helps you prepare for a particular presentation, viva or observation. You can use it again for future events until the processes it suggests become second nature.

C2 What sort of activities does this chapter consider?

As a student, you may be asked to:

- present a topic or the results of project work as a group presentation;
- do an individual presentation (e.g. for a seminar; to present what you know about a topic);
- be videoed doing a presentation;
- do on-line presentations (e.g. using a specific application; video; sound presentation via a podcast);
- be in a viva (i.e. an interview with a small group of experts: PhD students have one to discuss their thesis; there may be one for undergraduate dissertations; if work is assessed as borderline, a viva can help examiners make a decision);
- be observed (e.g. Teaching Practice observations; drama, dance or musical performances; health care students working with patients).

At work you may be asked to:

- do a presentation as part of an interview, as well as being interviewed;

- do presentations to clients, sales pitches, and so on;

- promote your work or that of your employer, face-to-face or on-line.

In this chapter, 'audience' is used to mean whoever you are presenting to, or whoever is conducting the viva or the observation, whether one person or more.

C3 Other chapters you need to use together with this one

There are several other chapters you need to look at. Some relate to skills and approaches needed in a presentation/observation/viva and others relate to situations where you commonly have to present something.

Chapter	Title	How it relates to this chapter	Page
10	Presenting your work: making it look good.	Important in helping you prepare good visual aids.	205
15	Handling time and pressure.	Helpful if you feel stressed about a presentation, viva or observation.	327
7	Finding, using and analysing information and evidence.	Useful if you need to gather information for your presentation/viva/observation.	147
11	Discussions: face-to-face and on-line (in seminars, groups, etc).	Useful if you have to lead or engage in discussion as part of a presentation/observation/viva. You may need to give a presentation as part of discussions.	229
12	Working in a group or team.	You may need to give a presentation of the results of such work.	253
5	Doing a project.	Helpful for doing a presentation of the results of such work.	97

C4 Your starting point: what and whom is it for?

This is a key question. A good presentation, viva or observation is one that meets the needs of the situation and the audience. You need to do different things in different situations. It won't go down well if you use technical language with people who don't understand it or if you treat people who know a lot about something as if they know little.

A tutor may ask you to do a presentation 'as if' it were to a particular group (e.g. a group of professionals). The target audience may be self evident (e.g. other students; colleagues; a client). Check the assignment brief, learning outcomes or assessment criteria for the purpose and audience. If you're in any doubt, ask your tutor (or manager, if at work).

Which might be your purpose or purposes? Here are some possibilities.

Purpose	✓	Implications
To explain a topic.		The focus is on the topic, how clearly you structure your explanation, the reasons and explanations you give and the relevance of your examples.
To show what you know about a topic.		As above. Prepare well, so you know as much as possible and can answer questions.
To share information with others.		The focus is on the quality of information you give, how clearly you structure your explanation and how helpful it is for the audience.
To give the findings of a project or investigation.		As above. Your structure needs to show what you did and what you found out.
To demonstrate your presentation skills.		How you give the presentation will be more important than (or as important as) the content.
To practice using presentation skills.		The focus will be on trying out presentation skills. It's better to try and make mistakes than not to try.
To persuade others/to 'sell' something.		Use language and examples the audience can relate to and target it at their needs and interests.
To publicise something.		Identify the 'unique selling point': what will most appeal to the audience? Avoid detail that distracts from main points.
To demonstrate your professional skills.		You need to be accurate in what you do. It must be obvious and very visible (e.g. exaggerate to make things clear).
To demonstrate how to do something.		Any steps or stages must be very clear. Go at a speed that others can follow, repeat things and recap.

Who might your audience be and what are the implications? Here are some possibilities.

Audience	✓	Implications
Tutor.		They'll be sympathetic and allow for nerves. They'll judge what you say and do and probably know more than you about the topic.
Other students.		They'll be on your side. They'll share your interests/experiences and use your language. Avoid being over familiar with them in what may be a formal situation.
Learners who you are informing or teaching.		You'll need to identify their level of knowledge and interest so you can pitch things at their level. You may need to 'work' to get their attention and interest.

Audience	✓	Implications
Employers.		They may allow for nerves. They will put their organisation's interests first and expect you to look and act professionally.
Clients (including agencies or exhibitors).		You'll be competing with others who also want the client's attention or work. They'll expect you to look and act professionally.
The public.		What will their interest be in your topic or situation? You must target that and pitch it at a level most people can engage with.
Professionals in your area.		They'll share your interests/values and use your language. They'll expect you to look and act professionally. They may know more than you about the topic.

What does 'look and act professionally' mean?

It means different things in different situations: you need to find out what the norm is in your professional area (it doesn't necessarily mean dressing formally or having a formal manner).

Even where it seems informal, there may be implicit rules that are followed. You may be able to work it out from observation, but if in doubt, ask. Here are things to look out for.

- What clothes do they wear usually and in formal situations?

- What are their values? What sort of throwaway remarks would they accept or challenge?

- What sort of language is used? Would certain terms offend them?

- Is there a code of ethics (e.g. naming a person involved in research may be breaching codes of confidentiality)?

Just think about the differences between what might be expected from a group of barristers in court as opposed to the same group in the pub. What do you immediately think of when you hear the word 'nurse' or 'artist'? Our aim here is not to encourage stereotyping but to alert you to the sorts of norms groups have.

For your presentation, viva or observation:

...what is its purpose and what are the implications for what you need to do?

...who is the audience and what are the implications for what you need to do?

C5 What might affect your presentation, viva or observation?

What sorts of things might affect what happens and what could you do about them?

Item	Suggestion
Inappropriate room.	Check in advance and prepare accordingly (e.g. change the seating arrangements, move equipment).
Lack of equipment/facilities.	Check in advance and prepare accordingly (e.g. no internet access, don't use web links; no projector, use handouts or Flip Chart).
Others not doing in advance what they are supposed to do.	Make clear what you need; write it down; be assertive; have Plan B (i.e. do it yourself or do something different). Look at Chapter 13 'Dealing with other people'.
People not cooperating during the event (e.g. your audience or participants).	Work out in advance what will encourage them to cooperate and plan for this. Look at Chapter 13 'Dealing with other people'.

Item	Suggestion
Not being able to find the information you need to prepare for it.	Start early; discuss with the tutor (or manager). Look at Chapter 7 'Finding, using and analysing information and evidence'.
Not having enough time to prepare; leaving it too late.	Start early; limit what you do according to the time you have. Look at Chapter 15 'Handling time and pressure'.
Never having done one before.	Practice on friends and family. Rehearse in front of a mirror.
Being very nervous.	This chapter will help; talk to others (you'll find they are nervous too); use visual aids.
Having a very quiet voice.	Imagine you are speaking to somebody on the back row and project your voice at them. Use visual aids.
Being afraid of the audience.	What is the worst they can do? Imagine they're cardboard cutouts. Imagine they're friends. Prepare well so you are less worried about what they might ask. See Chapter 13 'Dealing with other people'.
Antagonistic audience.	This is unusual. If you know who they'll be, plan to avoid offence. During the event find out why they're antagonistic ('you seem a bit unhappy and I'm wondering why'): it may have nothing to do with you. See Chapter 13 'Dealing with other people'.
What else might affect it?	

C6 Preparing for your presentation, viva or observation

Whether people can follow what you are trying to communicate will be determined by how you structure it and by your communication skills.

C6.1 Structure

No matter how good a communicator you are, if what you're trying to communicate is in a muddle the audience will not understand.

Your first task is to collect your material (see Chapter 7 'Finding, using and analysing information and evidence'). This chapter assumes that you already have any information, designs, images and so on needed: it is only concerned with how you present it.

How does structuring material for a presentation, viva or observation differ from doing so for a written piece of work?

With written work you can go back and re-read something as often as you want. With a presentation/viva/observation, your audience has to 'get it' on the spot; there's no going back to it (unless it's on-line or recorded). This means that simple is good: you can only cover a limited number of points and have to express the essence of each point. Too much information can mean your audience gets lost.

For an example, think about TV documentaries. They tend to:

- start with a punchy question/statement which shows what the programme is about (e.g. 'so where does our money system come from?' 'our earth was created from disasters');

- give one idea and then give examples or evidence for it;

- repeat the idea before giving the next idea and evidence for that one;

- repeat both ideas and then give the next idea and evidence for that one;

- briefly repeat all the ideas;

- finally, they usually repeat the punchy statement or question and give a punchy conclusion (e.g. 'so it was one big collision that led to earth being as it is').

This is not to say it's the right or only structure for a presentation/viva/observation, but it indicates some principles you might follow.

- Have a very clear introduction.

- Have a few very clear ideas that are closely related to the introduction.

- Give each clear idea followed by an explanation of it.

- Keep recapping and repeating what you have said.

- Pull it together at the end.

Example

Viva about a project.	*Summarise the project at the start. What you say influences what they then ask you.*	*If asked a question, start with an idea or concept and then go on to the detail.*	*Try to get them onto things you want to cover by reminding them of items, 'as I said in my introduction'.*
Observation of you carrying out a work task.	*Make clear what you are doing at the start.*	*Make each main step or stage clear and then make each sub step or stage clear.*	*Summarise what you did.*

So, for a presentation/viva/observation you have to do now or soon...

...what's the key focus for this presentation, viva or observation (in one sentence)?

...what are the (few) key ideas/concepts you want to get across?

...what order would make most sense to your audience (e.g. time/date/order in which something happened; causes followed by effects or effects followed by causes)?

...which details are essential to back up each idea/concept? What's helpful but not essential?

...what's the best order for the details? What order would demonstrate the idea?

...what one big thing could you conclude from the information/ideas/concepts covered?

Once you've done this you can create a structure.

For example (note these are suggestions only)

	On-line presentation	*Group presentation*
Introduction	*1st slide gives what it is about.*	*One person says what it's about.*
Key ideas followed by detail.	*One slide per idea, followed by 1 or 2 slides with detail.*	*One person per key idea, and then follows it up with detail.*
Recapping of key ideas.	*Slide that recaps what covered so far.*	*Link person introduces each person and, between presenters, recaps what's been covered so far.*
Conclusion.	*Last slide has conclusion.*	*One person does the conclusion.*

Your notes, to use during the presentation, viva or observation

You need notes to use during the event: it is unlikely that you can 'wing it'. Your notes should follow your structure (see above) or you'll get confused.

Here are some suggestions.

- You should be able to read your notes at a glance (avoid badly handwritten ones).

- The better prepared you are, the fewer notes you need, just reminders.

- The more nervous you are, the greater the possibility of getting muddled; minimise it by having well organised notes (e.g. numbered pages; highlighted words).

- Whatever you use must be easy to handle (artists and designers could think about how easy their artefacts will be to handle).

- Have your notes in a format with essentials highlighted but with more detail if needed (e.g. a page with two columns, first column has few words, second has backup detail).

- Use numbered cards, one idea per card.

- Use PowerPoint slides as speaker's notes. Print them and add notes of more detail.

- If you have a viva based on a piece of work, take it with you, with yellow 'stickies' marking pages you may want to look at.

- See Section C7 on engaging the audience. It's a **really** bad idea to just read notes. It's boring and looks as if you don't know your material. Notes are to refer to, not to read.

- See Chapter 9 'Making notes'.

C6.2 Communication skills

Once you've sorted out the structure, you need to decide how to get your 'messages' over. Check Section C4: what's your purpose and who's your audience?

What sort of language will your audience expect and understand? Note these general principles, regardless of the audience.

- Avoid gender stereotyping (e.g. say 'she or he' or 'they', other than when referring to actual individuals).

- Avoid racism or racist stereotyping (e.g. assuming all UK citizens are white).

- Avoid being aggressive, swearing or obscenities.

- Use language than can include everybody (e.g. allow for people who may be disabled, from other cultures).

- Use correct language (e.g. words used appropriately; correct spelling and punctuation in handouts or visual aids). Bad spelling on visual aids shouts out!

- What sort of language will be good for your purpose and your audience?

Language features	✓	Examples/suggestions
Technical or specialist words.		Scientific terms; subject specific terms (e.g. in English 'iambic pentameter'; in Education 'constructivism').
Words that non-specialists/non-technical people can understand.		Use terms in general use (e.g. in English 'a poem with 5 beats to a line'; in Education 'a theory that people construct their own meaning through learning activities').
Short, simple words.		See Gower's *Plain Words* (reference at the end of this chapter).
Longer or more unusual words.		See Roget's *Thesaurus* (reference at the end of this chapter).
Words that imply emotions.		For example: 'overjoyed'; 'shocked'; 'dreadful'.
Words/phrases that are very objective.		Short; precise and descriptive; no waffle; impersonal.
Words/phrases that will have a particular effect.		For example: 'failure' evokes memories and feelings; some TV catch phrases conjure up an image.
Short punchy sentences.		'Normally, they worked hard '.
Longer, more elaborate sentences.		'In the normal run of events, unusual events notwithstanding, they expended considerable effort on the work'.

What style and approach might be appropriate?

Style	✓	Examples
Informal.		Casual (but smart) clothes; relaxed, familiar manner; use accepted abbreviations and shorthand language; use anecdotes.
Formal.		Formal dress; formal posture; use 'sir'/'madam', 'ladies and gentlemen'; define terms precisely.
You the expert.		Use a confident tone; give evidence (e.g. report on your research and findings).
You're one of them.		Use 'we' instead of 'you'; 'as we know…'
You deferring to them.		Use questioning and checking strategies; use pauses; refer to the expertise in the room.
You in the lead.		Use an authoritative tone; be positive (not 'we think we might…' but 'Let's do…'); use techniques like building up the picture piece by piece, only revealing the whole at the end.
You persuading.		'I think you'll agree that…'; use evidence (e.g. statistics); appeal to their interests; use their language.
You offering ideas but with no fixed views.		'You might see this as x or y….'; 'On one hand…. on the other hand.'

Visual aids and handouts

Visual aids are very important, whether for a presentation, viva or if you're being observed.

- People tend to look at the visual aid rather than at you, so they help if you're nervous.

- Just listening to somebody is hard; your audience needs variety to keep their interest.

- Visual aids reinforce or highlight what you say.

- They can explain what you say.

- Handouts can be taken away as a reminder of what you said.

- Handouts can have detail that might clutter up your presentation, viva or demonstration.

- In some cases visual aids are essential (e.g. with a visual topic such as buildings).

- Good visual aids and handouts impress people: it looks as if you've put in effort.

What do we mean by 'visual aids', what are they useful for and what might you consider about them?

Type of visual aid	Uses	Issues
A projected still image (e.g. PowerPoint, Overhead Projector Slide; photographic slide).	To summarise/highlight points, recap/remind the audience, give information. Slides need 'labels' (e.g. location of original; scale).	You need: a computer/ projector; to check it works in advance and have Plan B in case it doesn't.
Projected web or intranet site (e.g. e-learning environment).	To give information. People won't be able to read lots of words.	You need: to check the room has working internet/intranet access; a working computer/ projector; to have Plan B in case it doesn't.
A projected moving image (e.g. video or film).	Shows how something works or what happened; may be a film clip; may have a lot of impact.	You need: equipment to show it; to check it works in advance; Plan B in case it doesn't. 'Cue up' in advance the bit you want to show.
A model.	Shows something that's hard to describe. Scale needs to be clear, as do materials of the 'real thing'. What else might matter?	Can you transport it without breaking it? Is it big enough for them to see it?
Actual photographs.	Shows something that's hard to describe. Needs 'labeling' (e.g. scale; material).	If you display them, are they big enough to see? If you hand one round: people won't listen while it's going round; they need time to look; you may not get it back.
Designs on paper.	Shows something that is hard to describe. Needs 'labeling'. What else might matter?	As above.
Actual pieces of art (e.g. paintings).	Shows something that's hard to describe. Needs to be a size/format that allows for transporting/showing. May need 'labeling'.	Can you transport it without damaging it? Is it big enough for them to see it? Will handling it cause damage?

Do you hold the copyright of a 'visual'; if so how will you protect your copyright? Do you need to get copyright permission for any item (if in doubt, ask a specialist such as somebody in a library/learning centre or a professional)?

What are 'handouts', what are their uses and what might you consider about them?

Type of handout	Uses	Issues
Paper copies of slides.	A reminder of what you covered. Can be printed with space to make notes.	Give out at the start not at the end when people have already made notes (they'll be irritated).
Printed/written summary of what you have said.	A reminder of what you covered.	If you don't want to 'pre-empt' what you'll say, say at the start that you'll hand out a summary at the end.
Printed diagrams/charts/tables	Can ask audience during the event to refer to them	Allow time to hand them round and study them
Full version of whatever you are presenting (e.g. a report).	In case they want to go into more detail about what you covered.	If you give it out at the start, they'll read instead of listening; only do so if you want them to refer to it during the event. Otherwise, say at the start it'll be available later.
Copies of photographs.	Can ask audience during the event to refer to them.	Allow time to hand them round as people don't listen while this is happening.
Printed/written instructions for activities or exercises.	For an observation, can help the observer see what you intend (e.g. a lesson plan for a teaching session).	For an observation, give out before it starts.
	In a presentation, use if you want the audience to do something.	For a presentation, give out at the point when it's needed or people will be confused.
Feedback form for the audience to complete about your presentation.	To tell you what went well and what to do in future.	Make it short; ask them to complete it before they leave, or you won't get them back.

Is there anything on the handout that is copyright to yourself; if so, how will you protect it? Do you need to get copyright permission for any item (if unsure, ask a specialist, e.g. somebody in a library/learning centre or a professional)?

What visual aids will you use? What will you need to consider when preparing them?

What handouts will you use? What will you need to consider when preparing them?

What if your presentation is recorded (e.g. video, audio, on-line presentation)?

A recorded presentation doesn't have the same effect as a live one. Section C7 looks at this in more detail, but if a recording (video/audio/on-line) is being assessed you need to adapt your plans accordingly.

Here are some implications

Videoed presentation or observed performance	Sound recording of presentation or observed performance	On-line presentation
It will show what you do but not audience reaction.	Other sounds that intrude may confuse.	The focus is not on interaction but on what you provide.
The viewer will have difficulty in seeing visual aids unless they are shown close up.	Visual aids can't be seen; body language can't be seen; what happens can't be seen.	Totally visual (text and images); no voice or body language to moderate what you communicate.
TV presenters/performers talk to the camera, not to the audience.	The focus is on what you say and how (e.g. too quiet; pauses; 'ers' and 'ums').	They can return to your presentation to look at it again.

If your presentation or observation will be videoed or on-line, what will you need to do to allow for this?

Making your visual aids look good.

See Chapter 10 'Presenting your work; making it look good'. This looks at how to layout work (e.g. PowerPoint; handouts) and how to label items. Audiences can be critical of poor visual aids and handouts.

C7 Engaging your audience (whether one person or many)

What makes you bored when somebody is presenting something to you?

What makes a presentation interesting to you?

What makes it difficult to follow something that you are observing?

When you ask somebody a question, what helps you follow their answer?

What do your answers suggest about what **you** could do in your presentation, viva or observation to engage your audience?

The key thing to consider here is the nature of your audience (go back to Section C4).

- Is your audience one person, a few people or lot of people?
- Will you see them face-to-face or will they see a video or hear a sound recording or see an on-line presentation or performance by you?
- What will they be interested in?

Which of the following suggestions make sense for your situation?

✓	Suggestions
	Have a very clear structure so they won't be confused (see Section C5).
	Ensure people are sitting where they can see and hear you. Ask if they can see/hear.
	Don't turn your back on them while you're talking (e.g. while looking at a projected image or flip chart).
	Ask the audience questions or give them an activity (e.g. make a list; vote on something).
	Check they've understood, see if they need you to clarify something.
	Make sure you include everybody. If someone has a disability, allow for it (e.g. for deaf people, speak slowly and ensure they can see you; for people with a visual disability, describe things).
	If you have a disability, plan so you can allow for it (use support in your university/college/workplace, e.g. from student services).
	Use humour, but be careful as it can be misunderstood.
	Avoid telling jokes unless you're very confident and the jokes are inoffensive.
	Avoid anything that makes you more nervous (e.g. wear comfortable clothes; have well-organised notes; visual aids/handouts that are easily handled).
	For a group presentation, stick to what you planned or you'll confuse your colleagues.
	For a group presentation, allocate tasks according to strengths, but give everybody an opportunity to present, even if they're scared (they need the practice).
	Practice in advance; it may take more or less time than you think.
	Stick to time. Your audience will appreciate it.
	Vary the tone and volume of your voice to keep interest.
	Have an attention-grabbing opening (e.g. controversial statement; dramatic story).

For face-to-face situations, what about your body language?

Body language can distract people from what you are saying. Being nervous makes you more likely to use habits that distract (one of the authors of this book sways while she's presenting, and paces!). People can bite their nails, twiddle with things, sniff, cough. What sorts of behaviours distract or irritate you? In group presentations it looks bad if those who aren't presenting chat to each other giggle or look bored.

If you have distracting habits, find a way of controlling them. Hold your hands behind your back or hold a sheet of paper so you can't fiddle.

Body language can encourage people to listen to what you are saying. These things engage other people.

- Smiling.

- Leaning towards them when they are speaking.

- Looking them in the eye.

- Standing up to do a presentation (it gives you 'authority' and helps project your voice).

- Moving in a natural way (standing totally still is distracting; use hand gestures).

How will you engage your audience? Which suggestions will you try?

Ask for feedback about what you did after the event.

C8 Reviewing and improving what you do

How can you improve your skills in presenting, being in a viva or being observed?

Activity	This is what I'll repeat/do the same in future	This is what I'll do differently
Being clear about the purpose and the audience.		
Identifying the implications of what the purpose is and who is the audience.		
Identifying what might affect it and planning for this.		
Structuring it.		
Using appropriate language and style.		
Using visual aids and handouts.		
Engaging the audience.		
Using appropriate body languages.		
Note anything else here that was important for you in what you did.		

ENHANCED SKILLS

E1 What do you most want to achieve from the event?

Section C4 looked at the needs of the situation and the audience, but what about you? What do you want to get from the event?

This could relate to your starting point and your personal aims. If you're very nervous about such events, your aim may be to feel more comfortable with them. If you envisage a career where such events are important, you may want to develop your skills to a high level. What you want may depend on whether or not the activity is assessed.

What you want to achieve will determine where you put your effort. For example:

- if you want to feel more comfortable in such activities, focus on techniques that will reduce nervousness;

- if you want a high grade, find out the assessment criteria (these might be implied rather than explicit) and put in effort to meet them;

- if your future career will involve this sort of event, talk to employers, clients or others 'in the know' to find out what they're looking out for and then focus on improving that;

- if you need more practice, could somebody give you a mock viva, or listen to you practising your presentation?

In relation to doing presentations/observations or taking part in a viva...

...what do you most want to achieve?

...what will you need to focus on for that? What will you give most attention to or most improve?

...which of the previous sections in C do you need to revisit?

...who or what else could help you?

E2 Getting your point across

It doesn't matter if it's a presentation, viva or observation; the important thing is to get your points across to your audience. If you aren't clear about this, see Section C6.

As you get to higher levels, you're likely to deal with increasingly complex situations and information, which could be interpreted in different ways. There may be more ambiguity and uncertainty. How can you deal with this effectively?

Firstly, identify a point you would like to get across (preferably one that is complex or where there are uncertainties)

How could you use the following ideas to make your point as effectively as possible?

Item	Your notes
Structure Where, in your structure, would you introduce this point for most effect or understanding? What essential detail is needed to explain it and what's the best order for the details? Is there any information that if you miss it out, the rest won't make sense?	
Language What sort of words will help (e.g. objective or subjective, cool or impassioned)? Where would short punchy sentences help and where do you need longer, more elaborate sentences?	
Examples What examples will the audience best relate to? What might bring it home to them? What's familiar to them and how can you relate that to your topic? What anecdotes would help?	
Tone What tone do you want to set? Cheery? Serious? Weighty? Considered? Persuasive? What would create that effect?	
Voice and body language What tone of voice would reinforce the point? Would a slower pace emphasise it? What body language would send the right message?	
What helps you understand or appreciate other people's points?	

E3 Responding to your audience

The more experienced you become in these events, the more it becomes an interaction between you and the audience, not just one way.

Interaction doesn't just mean both parties speak. It also means that in your role as presenter/performer/viva interviewee you're taking note of your effect on the audience, so you can adapt things on the spot.

Things to look out for in your audience include:

- looking bored, yawning, slumped;

- looking alert, interested;

- facial expressions (concentrating, puzzled, amused);

- trying to say something (sitting forward, hand up, mouth open);

- reading things you've given them rather than listening to you;

- reading something else that you haven't given them, texting.

If they look engaged, that's great. If not, what can you do?

Firstly, you need to be confident enough with your material to be able to notice what the audience is doing. That means being comfortable with the things covered in Section C. If you lose your thread you'll be too flustered to see what's happening to the audience.

Here are some ideas.

- Don't give people things to read unless you want them to read rather than listen to you.

- If they're reading something else or texting, politely ask them not to (just because they're being rude doesn't mean you should be).

- Check if there's a problem (can they all hear you or see things?).

- Check if they've understood you or if you need to cover it again.

- Move on quickly to another section or item.

- Speed up (it may be a bit tedious) or slow down (you may have lost them)

- Ask them a question.

- Do something they don't expect.

Here's what not to do.

- Blame them; you need to accept that if they're not engaged it's likely to be because of something you are/are not doing.

- Grumble at them for not being interested.

- Be aggressive with them.

- Be sarcastic.

You'll have experienced ways others (e.g. tutors; teachers) have tried to involve you, so should already have ideas about what works and what doesn't. If you want to generate discussion, here are some ideas:

- Ask people to discuss in 2s or 3s for a minute, then share with the group.

- Ask them to spend a minute noting something down prior to discussing it.

- Make discussion points or activities clear; have handouts, or project a slide, with the instructions.

- Thank people for contributions; don't discourage them by putting them down.

- Have a prepared list of questions to ask them.

- If they ask you questions and you don't know the answer, say so (it's better than waffling); offer to find out the answer for them.

How will you engage your audience?

E4 Planning for where you keep encountering these events

You may find you need to do many such events (e.g. in teacher training and health courses, students are regularly observed). Courses have presentations every year. Presentations or demonstrations may be part of your job. A viva is more likely to be more one-off.

If you find yourself doing such activities where the same people are involved (e.g. tutors; students; managers; colleagues), they may have given you feedback or you could ask them for it. It's important to act on that feedback, so you need to make sure you've understood what you could do to improve. Ask those giving the feedback for suggestions.

If different people are involved, you might get different feedback from them, as nobody sees things quite the same. If you get conflicting feedback, discuss it with those who gave it to avoid being confused. See Section C4 in Chapter 17 'Reflecting on your learning and experience (including feedback)' for suggestions about making sense of feedback.

Being in a situation where you have to do many presentations or observations means you can use the experience to improve. You could keep a record/diary of what happened each time, with what you plan to do differently and then how it worked out next time. If you improve, that's great. If you get stuck, you can seek help from tutors or managers or by looking at books or resources.

Great presenters weren't born like that. They've just had a lot of practice.

E5 Review: improving things for next time

What feedback have you had about your presentations or observations or a viva and who from?
Do you agree or disagree with this feedback?

If you'd been a fly on the wall, what would you have thought?

What could improve your skills here?

Activity	This is what I'll repeat/do the same in future	This is what I'll do differently
Identifying what I want to achieve and how to do so.		
Getting my points across.		
Responding to my audience.		
Being aware of the effect I have on others in such situations.		
Planning to take part in such events on an ongoing basis.		

REFERENCES AND SUGGESTED READING

Gowers, E. (revised by Greenbaum, S. and Whitcut, J.), (1987), *The complete plain words*, London: Penguin.

Roget, M. (revised by Roget, J.L.and Roget, S.R.), (1988), *Roget's thesaurus of synonyms and antonyms*, London: Ramboro.

Roget, P. and Kirkpatrick, E.M., (2000), *Roget's thesaurus of English words*, London: Penguin.

5
DOING A PROJECT

HOW THIS CHAPTER CAN HELP YOU

The 'crucial' skills part of this chapter aims to help you:

- be clear about the purpose of your project;
- explore your project and choose how to tackle it;
- plan your project including time, skills and resources needed to work efficiently;
- use methods of enquiry relevant to your topic, purpose and audience;
- identify factors that affect the outcomes of your work;
- prepare to ensure you have the skills and resources needed to help you succeed;
- use support and feedback to help tackle the project;
- check your progress and revise plans as needed;
- choose an appropriate format and structure for presenting it;
- plan to improve.

The 'enhanced' skills part of this chapter is shorter: it helps you operate to a higher level. As well as the 'crucial' skills' outcomes, you'll be able to:

- identify the outcomes you want from your project and choose ways of achieving them;
- plan for an extended project;
- consider different ways of tackling your project;
- make and use opportunities for using and developing your skills over an extended project period;
- identify and use methods and materials at the forefront of your subject;
- deal effectively with the uncertain, ambiguous, complex and unpredictable in projects;
- evaluate your effectiveness by getting feedback and making judgements about your choices.

CRUCIAL SKILLS

C1 Why is this chapter important and how can it help you?

The process of doing a project is similar no matter how big the project or its topic. This chapter takes you through that process, helping you think about what you need to do for a current project.

This chapter can help you:

- on a one-off basis, if you have a project to do (e.g. that's important for assessment);

- carry out a work-based project;

- present your project (e.g. in job interviews, to show how you can work independently);

- build on your project skills and improve them (e.g. for use later in a course or at work).

The sections in this chapter cover issues that are interconnected, so throughout it, you'll see suggestions that you move back and forwards between its sections.

Terms used in this chapter

We use 'audience' to refer to any end-user of your project outcomes (e.g. the reader of a written piece; the observer of a visual piece; the user of a design).

We use 'methods' to mean processes or procedures used in your subject area to explore or make things. 'Methods of inquiry' are those that help you investigate, research or evaluate something. You may use other methods too (e.g. design or production methods).

C2 What's a 'project'? Why do courses include them?

In higher education (HE), a project is an activity to investigate (and learn about) something (as opposed to a tutor telling you about it). You plan and carry it out and you may be able to decide on the topic. Usually you work independently, with support from a tutor.

At work, any activity where you need to develop or implement something new could be seen as a project (e.g. new administrative systems; new products; new designs). Your project may be for a client. At work, many projects are group ones or involve working closely with others.

If you're involved with others in a group project, on a course or at work, look both at this chapter and at Chapter 12 'Working in a group or team'.

A report, a presentation, a poster, a design or a creative item are some possible outcomes of a project. The project is the activity you engage in that enables you to produce the finished product. Often activities that are called something else are really projects (e.g. a dissertation or PhD thesis is the written presentation of a project).

HE courses often have projects towards their end, when students have developed the skills and knowledge to work independently; they often aim to assess how well you can apply such skills and knowledge. Some courses operate from a view that students learn best by finding out for themselves (sometimes called inquiry-based or problem-based learning) and have projects at earlier stages; some courses do projects from day one (e.g. art and design).

Some projects are very short and small (you can do them in a class session or a day), while others are much longer and take a semester, a year or even longer.

C3 Other chapters you need to use together with this one

There are several other chapters you'll need. The guidance in them is not repeated here to avoid overlap, so it's really important you look at them. Some relate to skills and approaches needed to do a project and others refer to ways of presenting it.

Chapter	Title	How it relates to this chapter	Page
7	Finding, using and analysing information and evidence.	Most projects (HE and work) involve finding, using and analysing information and evidence.	147
15	Handling time and pressure.	A key feature of projects is that you plan and carry them out yourself. How you plan and use time is crucial.	327
16	Solving problems and making decisions.	Most projects involve solving a problem, even if the project isn't presented in that way.	357
13	Dealing with other people.	It's very likely you'll need other people (e.g. to help; to provide information; as 'subjects' of a research project).	275
12	Working in a group or team.	You may need to do a group project where work is divided between a small group and success depends on all of you.	253
1	Writing essays and dissertations.	These are ways in which you might be asked to present the results of a project. You need to look at the chapter that's relevant to your current project.	7
2	Writing reports.		31
3	Producing portfolios and journals (including diaries, blogs, etc.).		49

Chapter	Title	How it relates to this chapter	Page
4	Giving a presentation, viva or being observed.		69
10	Presenting your work; making it look good.		205

C4 Your starting point: what's your focus and purpose?

When people have problems with projects or get low grades/marks, they're often not clear enough about what they're trying to do; this can mean doing unnecessary work or producing something that's confused. It's surprisingly common for student project work to have an introduction saying it's about one thing and for the rest of it to be about something else. How would you mark that? It certainly won't get as good a grade/mark as if it all tied together.

Once you're clear about your focus and purpose, you need to keep them at the front of your mind. Write them large and put them on your wall. Make them a screen saver for your computer or put them on every page in your diary. Whatever you do in your project should relate to that focus, or you may waste time and confuse yourself and others.

A simple technique is to turn your topic into a key question you need to answer (you may have quite a lot of leeway to decide the 'angle' to cover). Your question should be specific, to ensure it's answerable. NB Check with your tutor (or manager) that this approach is OK.

Example: how a differently worded question can change what you do

This is for the topic of 'Airport security'

Possible question	Implications for the project
What are the key issues in airport security and how might they be addressed?	Very broad, big topic (What sort of airports? International? Private? Every country?). May not be manageable. Suggests equal balance between considering issues and solutions.
How effective is airport security at Stanstead Airport and how might it be improved?	Specific (about one airport), more manageable, but can you get the information? Will it be confidential? Whose approval would you need?
What might be an effective security system for a UK-located international airport?	Specific (about a type of airport), more manageable. Focus is on solutions rather than issues (though you'd need to identify the issues to identify the solutions).
What are the security issues in controlling access to airport land and how might they be addressed?	Specific (about one aspect of airport security), more manageable. Suggests equal balance between considering issues and solutions.

Possible question	Implications for the project
What are the security issues in baggage handling in airports and how might they be addressed?	Specific (about one aspect of airport security), more manageable. Suggests equal balance between considering issues and solutions.

Turning your topic into a key question could work with any subject area. For example:

- Architecture – what would be an environmentally friendly design for a bungalow?

- Fine Art – how can colour be used to create mood in portraiture?

- Education – what helps students develop study skills?

- Science – what materials are best suited to a light-weight footbridge?

What's the topic for your project?	How might you word this as a question?

If turning the topic into a question doesn't work (it usually does!), how else can you give it a really clear focus?

It might help to use this SMART acronym in thinking about your question (or focus)

		Yes	Maybe	No
S	Is your question Specific?			
M	Is your question Measurable, i.e. will you know when you have answered it?			
A	Is your question Achievable? Can it be answered in the time you have and with your skills, knowledge and resources?			
R	Is your question Realistic? Is it something reasonable for you, in your situation, to consider? Can you find information about it?			
T	Can you deal with it in the Time you have available?			

If you answer no to any of the previous questions, perhaps you need to rethink your question/focus.

What else should you consider? Here are some thoughts about possible requirements.

Issue to consider	Your notes
Who's the project for?	
How might the results of the project be used?	
Who else might read it other than the target audience and why might they find it helpful?	
What do the assignment instructions say about what's needed?	
What do assessment criteria suggest is needed? If none, ask your tutor what will get a good mark.	

Here are some thoughts about the **possible purpose** for it.

Purpose to consider	Your notes
To find out about a topic.	
To investigate an issue.	
To evaluate something.	
To provide evidence for something.	
To make recommendations about something.	
To design or create something.	

Purpose to consider	Your notes
To use or demonstrate knowledge gained.	
To practise or demonstrate skills/ methods learned.	
To practice working independently.	
To allow you to follow your interests; a motivator (e.g. rather than all students working on the same thing).	

In order to work out **the focus** for your project (i.e. the question you need to answer) you may need to read about your topic: see Section C6. This will help you see the main issues and decide what's important to investigate or explore.

What was your draft key question (or focus)?	Do you need to amend this?

Here are some examples of projects where the end result didn't match the focus.

- The focus was supposed to be what makes students successful on a course. The project was actually about which assessment methods were useful.

- The focus was supposed to be how portfolio assessment helps students learn. The project was actually about a computerised test that was a small part of a portfolio.

C5 Planning, planning and more planning; starting point

The key to a successful project is its planning. You're likely to be busy: full-time or part-time students may be doing paid work; you may have family responsibilities; you have a social life (we hope); you may have work for other modules. You'll have to do this project by a deadline.

If you don't plan, you may not finish it on time and if you do manage to complete it, it won't be as good as it could have been.

Section C10 will help you make a plan, but before you can do this you need to consider what's needed for its elements. We have already covered the first elements (focus and purpose). The following sections look at others. We then return to planning as an issue.

Which of the following elements are needed in your project? These are the things to plan for:

Element	✓
Working out what's needed (purpose, focus, assessment criteria; see Section C4).	
Finding information about the topic.	
Using/analysing this information.	
Finding information about the methods you'll use in your project.	
Designing methods to use in your project.	
Trying out/piloting the methods of inquiry you wish to use.	
Amending methods in the light of your trial/pilot.	
Using the methods.	
Collecting together the findings/results/information.	
Analysing/interpreting the findings/results/information collected.	
Identifying how to present the findings/results/information collected.	
Drawing conclusions from your work.	
Making recommendations.	
Designing or creating something.	
Presenting the project (e.g. in a report; on a poster; in a presentation or viva).	

C6 Finding the information needed on your topic and on your methods

Look back to Section C4. What's the purpose and focus of this project? You need to be clear about this to identify the information needed. It may be that the whole purpose of your project is to review existing literature. If this isn't the case and your project aims to investigate, evaluate, produce or create something, then you may need information for two purposes, as indicated below.

To gather information about your topic	To gather information about methods you'll use
Why do you need this? Reasons include to: • set the context for your project • see what others have already discovered (so you don't start from scratch) • find the main issues relating to your topic, to help you decide on your question/ focus • show what you know about the topic.	Why do you need this? Reasons include to: • see which methods might best answers your key question/focus • identify how to best use that method • identify any issues in using that method (e.g. ethical) • Help you design the method(s) • show that you've carefully planned what you do • help avoid using an inappropriate method that doesn't give the results needed.
Example of items you might use: • books on the topic • journal articles on the topic • internet articles on the topic.	Example of items you might use: • books on research methods in your subject area • books on particular methods (e.g. questionnaire design) • journal articles giving results of research that describe the method used to collect data/information.

Advice!

Although you may need to keep looking at literature (on your topic or methods) throughout your project, it's best to look at key items before you carry out an investigation, to make sure you're not missing important issues or aren't using an inappropriate method of inquiry.

Look at Chapter 7 'Finding, using and analysing information and evidence' for help.

C7 Designing and using methods

This section may not apply to you if your project is only about reviewing published literature. In all other cases it will be applicable. Here are some key principles.

Principle	Examples and issues
Your method must be relevant to the focus of your project (i.e. it must be capable of answering your key question).	If you want to know: For example, if people with good A level results get good degrees, you'd compare A level results with degree results. For example, what lecturers think affects degree results, you'd ask them (e.g. interview; questionnaire).
You must be able to carry out the method.	Do you have the equipment or resources? Can you have access to people for information?
You must be able to carry out the method in the time you have available.	How long will it take, e.g. for people to reply to a questionnaire? If you need to evaluate something that's happened, will it happen in time for you to do so?
You must adapt the method to your situation.	Can you adapt it to the size of your project, or the time you have available?
You must follow ethical guidelines.	Falsifying information/results is seen as a dreadful 'sin' by academics, regardless of subject. In some subjects (e.g. Health) you may need approval from an ethics committee Do you need permission ('informed consent')? Will you need to protect anonymity or confidentiality?
You need to follow your method accurately and consistently.	If you don't, you may not be able to trust your results.
You must review and evaluate how well your methods worked.	How well you used a method may influence the results and your interpretation of them.
You need to try it out (trial or pilot it) and amend it before you use it 'for real'.	A method may not work first time (e.g. people don't answer a questionnaire as you expected). It's best to identify any problems so you can amend your method before you use it in the main part of your project.

What are the methods of inquiry and what are they useful for? They fall into two main groups:

- **quantitative** (also called positivist): methods that collect factual or numerical information; there is often a hypothesis you're testing; the aim is to generalise (i.e. people who do x tend to do y);

- **qualitative**: methods that collect perceptions or look at what happened; the aim isn't to generalise but to explore (and try to understand) one situation or one person/group.

When you analyse and interpret the results of the methods, you need to be aware of these differences. For example, it's probably not appropriate to turn qualitative information into numbers. If you want numbers, use a method that collects numbers.

It's not appropriate to generalise from qualitative methods. If you want to generalise, use quantitative methods.

You can use both sorts of methods in one project, to collect different sorts of information (e.g. use quantitative methods to find factual information and qualitative methods to help you understand situations).

Here are some common methods of inquiry.

Method	Useful for	Issues
Analysing existing data.	Seeing patterns and relationships.	Can you access the data? Confidentiality? Intellectual property?
Analysing existing documents.	Identifying what happened or what was said.	Some sources may be confidential. Availability?
Analysing situations.	Identifying the factors that affect something.	Must have all the information about the situation. Avoid your own bias when interpreting.
Analysing sound or visual records.	Identifying what happened or what was said.	Can be time consuming. Must evaluate the material and the source carefully.
Experiments or testing.	Trying something out to see what happens (e.g. testing a hypothesis).	Must be certain the experiment isn't affected by other things. May be ethical issues (e.g. if using people or animals)
Control groups.	Exploring cause and effect.	There may be ethical issues (e.g. in withholding something from the control group).
Questionnaires.	Gathering factual information from large groups or where you have no direct access to them.	Return rates can be poor. Need careful wording. Any qualitative information can be hard to analyse (e.g. rating scales are easier).
Interviews.	Exploring perceptions with a few people.	The purpose is to explore what some individuals think and you can't generalise from that. Beware of 'leading' questions.
Focus groups.	Exploring shared perceptions with groups of people.	Individuals might not reveal their thoughts. It's the perceptions of one group so can't generalise.
Structured observations.	Seeing if/how often something you thought would happen does happen.	You can't observe many people (or animals/items) at once. Getting the categories right is important. Something unanticipated might happen.

Method	Useful for	Issues
Unstructured observations.	Seeing what happens.	You can't observe many people (or animals/items) at once. Recording what happened can be difficult.
Field notes.	Recording what happens.	You need to record/note it at the time or you forget. If you don't have records, you can't use it as evidence.
Journals/logs/blogs.	Recording what happens.	As above.
Case studies.	Exploring one situation/person/ group in depth.	You can't generalise from one case (this isn't the aim).

You need to consider which method(s) might best answer your question and then look for information on it/them. There's insufficient space here for more on methods, but you'll find detailed information relevant to your subject in many books and other resources.

What method(s) do you think you could use?

What do you need to know about it/them and how are you going to find this out?

C8 Factors that affect the outcomes of your work

What sorts of things might affect your project? You need to build those into your plan (see Section C10). Here are some possibilities.

Items	✓	Our notes	Your notes
I don't have the knowledge to do it.		Can you develop it? Can your tutor or the library/learning centre help?	
I don't have the skills to do it.		Can you develop them (see Section C9)? Can you get round this (i.e. amend your plans)?	
I don't have the resources to do it.		Could you borrow them? Use library/learning centres; ICT/audio visual support; sound/video/film studios. You may need to change your focus/question.	
The books/ journals needed aren't available.		Start your search early. Ask advice from your library/learning centre. Can you change your focus/ question?	
'They' won't give me permission to do it.		Ask permission early on, so you can change direction if need be.	
'They' won't give me the information.		Ask early on so you can change direction if need be. Would other information help? Should you change your focus/question?	
My computer or the university/ college network breaks down.		Allow enough time in your plan for the possibility.	
I lose my work.		Back it up and keep separate from the computer. Have good recording systems. Copy everything.	
I become ill.		Get a doctor's note in case you need to prove it. Build time into your plan.	
There's a family problem.		Get a doctor's note/evidence in case you need to prove it. Build time into your plan.	
Other course work takes longer than expected.		Allow time in your plan for this to happen.	
What else?			

C9 Developing the skills (and techniques) you need to do it

It's unlikely you'll start with all the skills needed for your project. In HE, tutors will have set this as a learning activity; they'll expect you to develop knowledge and skills through it, not to necessarily already have them.

Firstly, you need to think about which skills or techniques you'll need to use. Some will be common to any work (e.g. for academic work: referencing; using databases; word-processing; using the internet), some will be particular to your subject (e.g. medical procedures) and some will be particular to your topic (e.g. analysing data).

Now you might consider some questions.

- Have you been taught this? If so, your tutor/manager may expect that you can do it. Look through your notes or ask others.

- Is there a specialist section in your college/university/workplace that could help you (e.g. library, learning centre, ICT, audio visual, study skills or academic advisers)?

- Is there guidance about it on the university/college e-learning environment? Often such environments have support and information sections.

- Are there specialists in your department (e.g. technicians; postgraduate students; lab assistants)?

- Could other students/colleagues help? But beware – any assessed work needs to be yours or you may be accused of cheating.

- Can any chapters in this book help? Other books/on-line resources?

Skills/techniques I need to use	Actions I'll take to learn these	By (deadline)	Progress

C10 Making your plan

The previous sections should have given ideas on the tasks needed for your project.

Start with your deadline and work back. You'll want some time at the end to check, edit and proof-read and you should allow for 'computer malfunction'.

- For example, if your hand-in time is week 14 and the final draft is to be finished by week 13, when do you need to have completed each of the other stages?

- Is there anything you have to do before you do something else?

- Is there anything you must do that depends on other people (start this early in case they let you down)?

- How long will each task take? Add at least half on again (it always takes longer then you think).

- You need to build in an allowance for things going wrong or for the unexpected.

- If your plan indicates it'll take more time than you have, what can you change? Can your topic be more focused or specific? Which stages could be more efficient?

What format for a plan will best help you?

Example: you could have one in table form

Task	Actions needed	Resources needed	By (deadline)	Progress made

Example: you could have a visual timeline

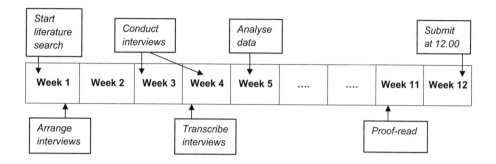

Monitoring and revising your plan

Your plan needs to be a living document. You need to use it and amend it. Projects rarely go to plan and you need to revise them. You might need to change:

- your whole focus or key question (e.g. if the information isn't available);

- your methods;

- your target 'population' (i.e. the people or things you're studying).

C11 Who can help and how?

Section C9 has already suggested some sources of help.

With projects you may be dependent on the goodwill of others: your supervisor/tutor; other tutors; colleagues; library/learning centre staff; technicians; your 'research subjects'. You need to keep their cooperation: see Chapter 13 'Dealing with other people'.

One way others can help is by giving feedback (e.g. on stages of the project; tasks; a final written draft or prototype). When asking for feedback you might consider:

- giving the person a reasonable time to provide the feedback;

- telling the person what you'd like feedback on (e.g. aspects you're worried about);

- if you don't understand the feedback, asking for clarification;

- considering if you agree with the feedback (but we suggest feedback from an assessor/manager is taken seriously!).

C12 Presenting your project

Section C3 suggests other chapters of this book of help in presenting your project, but below are some general principles.

- Start by making the focus clear.

- Explain what you did (your methods).

- If stages are important, include them all in an order that helps the audience understand.

- Put raw data or raw information in an appendix. In the main piece of work you interpret the data or information for the audience: tell them what they/it says (note: the word 'data' is plural). How you present your findings is very important (see Chapter 10 'Presenting your work: making it look good').

- Make sure you've made the key outcomes of your project clear.

- Include a review/evaluation of how you went about it.

- A 'conclusions' section should only refer to what you found from your project (not new information).

- Any recommendations should be based on what you found and on your conclusions.

- Use conventions (e.g. referencing; spelling) correctly (it influences the audience's view of your work).

C13 Reviewing and improving what you do

How can you improve your skills in doing project work?

Activity	This is what I'll repeat/do the same in future	This is what I'll do differently
Making my focus and my purpose clear right at the start.		
Making a plan.		

Activity	This is what I'll repeat/do the same in future	This is what I'll do differently
Monitoring and revising my plan.		
Finding information on my topic.		
Finding information on my methods.		
Designing and using methods.		
Developing my skills.		
Getting the resources needed.		
Using support and feedback.		
Presenting the results or outcomes of my project.		

ENHANCED SKILLS

E1 What do you most want to achieve from the project?

Here are some possibilities. What do you want from a project you need to do now?

Possible aim	✓	Implications for what you need to do
To get a high mark or grade.		Check the assessment criteria. Find out what will get a good mark and focus on that.
To find out about a topic that might help me get a job.		Check what would be a useful topic for employers. What would show off your abilities to the best advantage?
To find out about a topic that might help me in my current job/to help me in my career.		Discuss with your employer what they'd like you to focus on (if assessed in HE, check if your tutor is happy with that). Use appraisal meetings to see what projects are viewed highly (see Chapter 18 'Personal/ Professional Development Planning').
To provide a basis for postgraduate study.		Identify the sort of postgraduate course you're interested in. What skills, techniques, interests will they expect? What sort of project could include these?
Just to get it done as easily as possible.		Check the assessment criteria. Find out what's needed for a pass. Choose a topic that has lots of information on it and methods that are easy to use.
It is a topic I've always been interested in.		Make sure you don't get so carried away by the topic that you lose sight of your focus and the time available.
I think this topic really matters.		As above.
What else?		

E2 Long or large projects

If your project is very large or long (e.g. the whole of the final year of a course; over a year), there are two main issues: planning and staying motivated.

Planning

The same principles given in Sections C5 and C10 apply here, but more so. If a project is very large or long it can become increasingly complex, with more things that might affect it. Lack of planning will have a greater effect: if a project is supposed to last a week and it goes wrong, you could just about recoup the situation if you stayed up all night working on it. A large project will be much more difficult to patch up at the last minute.

The advantage of a large or long project is that you probably have more time to devote to it and you can spread the work out (although the danger is that you think the deadline is a long way off, you may leave it too long before starting).

It may help to divide the work into stages and do detailed plans for each stage. If you produce something by the end of each stage you'll see progress and will feel more positive. The less you can leave until the end, the better.

You may need to build relationships with people with whom you'll have frequent contact in the project: see Chapter 13 'Dealing with other people'.

Staying motivated

What helps you get on with things and what's likely to stall you?

Staying motivated is an issue for many people. Common points at which it's difficult to keep moving with a project are:

- right at the start (deciding what to do and getting going);

- if you hit a point of having to process lots of information;

- at the end, when the work is done but the presentation (e.g. report) needs preparing.

Here are some suggestions to help you stay motivated. Which might work for you?

	✓		✓
Pick a topic that interests you.		Be prepared to get things wrong.	
Pick a topic that'll be useful to you.		Be willing to try again.	
Use your project plan: follow it; if you get too far behind it may seem overwhelming.		Work at the time of day that suits you best.	
Set small targets (make lists) and tick them off when done.		Set aside a certain amount of time each day to work on it and stick to it.	
Ask somebody (friend, relative) to act as a 'progress chaser' for you.		Give yourself rewards when you've done something.	
Just decide! Don't spend so long deciding on your topic that you start late.		Work in a setting that you find comfortable.	
Give yourself a break. Don't work nonstop or you'll get fed up of it.		Prepare bits of the final presentation as you go along, so there's less to do at the end.	

E3 Extend the methods you use

Be careful. You don't want to try new things if they damage your project. You need to make good use of methods with which you're confident. However, that may limit you and new approaches might help. Any methods will depend on the subject area and topic, so this section aims to help you think about issues rather than suggesting methods. Don't forget that it's important to try or pilot things.

Suggestion	Examples
Could you use ICT to make things more efficient?	A clear file structure for notes and other work. Good 'version control' (e.g. put date on title or 'draft 2'). Word-processed documents are easier to amend. Word-processed notes can be copied into drafts (e.g. referencing details).
Are there any ways of using ICT to help you do things you couldn't otherwise do?	Spreadsheets can sort or calculate information. The 'find' 'replace' and 'select' functions are useful. Can you use the symbols in a word-processor? What about using graphics programs (e.g. for cropping photos; creating tables/charts).
Are there any specialist calculators to help you with techniques?	Scientific or financial calculators.
Could you use a digital recorder for sound recordings (e.g. interviews)?	Download files from a digital recorder on to your computer.
Is there anywhere (in your college/university/ workplace/locally) where you can borrow equipment?	Possibilities include an ICT support section; an audio visual section; a library or learning centre.
Could friends help?	Somebody we know asked friends and tutors to be 'extras' in a film created for a project.
Could your tutor or other specialists at college/ university/work help?	They might have ideas or be able to help you develop skills. They might even be able to do something for you. Are there drop-ins (e.g. 'maths help') for quick advice?
Would making physical models help you think about it?	Somebody we know uses play dough to make models of how she feels about something.
Would diagrams or sketches help?	They can help show connections between ideas. Doodling may free up your mind to think of new ideas.
Would any mathematical techniques help interpret or explain information?	Find out which techniques help (e.g. when it's better to use a percentage; when to use a median or mode).
Who might have done it before? Could you get ideas from them?	Your literature review might tell you this. Chat to people about your project (one of the authors found out about freely downloadable software to use for a project). Use an internet search engine.

E4 Being at the forefront of your subject

If your project is at the end of an undergraduate course or for a postgraduate course, it's important to use literature and methods that are 'at the forefront' of your subject. This can also be important at work: by their very nature, work projects are likely to be 'at the forefront'.

What does this mean? It could mean you need to look at key literature in your subject area, no matter when it was produced. It won't look good if you miss out the key person who's written about or produced something on your topic. It may mean you need to know about current issues and thinking on a topic. You want to avoid being unaware of some recent discovery or change of thinking.

To find out what information or knowledge is currently important (and that can include 'old' knowledge), you could:

- read around the topic; articles and books (especially recent ones) will tell you who or what is 'in' or 'out';

- ask tutor or others 'in the know' (e.g. PhD students in your subject area);

- ask professionals in the area;

- keep an eye on the news and media;

- look at relevant web sites.

It also means using methods or technologies currently seen as important. A few years ago, one of the authors was embarrassed to turn up to do a presentation with an electronic presentation on a floppy disc, to find they only had facilities for a memory stick. Fashions change; technology advances; laws change (e.g. health and safety; data protection). How can you find out what methods are currently seen as important? You could:

- read books and articles on methods of inquiry;

- ask your tutor or other specialists (e.g. technicians; ICT advisers);

- ask professionals in the area;

- look at recent work done in your subject area and at the methods used (e.g. go to exhibitions, read recently published journal articles);

- look at relevant web sites.

Generally, the higher the level of your work, the more likely you are to need to use reputable sources of information and ideas. You might get away with referring to web sites in a project at the start of an undergraduate course, but by the end (and at postgraduate level), you'll be expected to deal with scholarly material (e.g. journal articles) and 'primary' information (i.e. original material that hasn't been analysed or interpreted): see Chapter 7 'Finding, using and analysing information and evidence'.

E5 Dealing with uncertainty

Projects at the end of undergraduate courses or at postgraduate level or at work are unlikely to deal with simple and straightforward ideas, information, methods or situations. The mere fact that it is worth investigating suggests complexity. It's almost certain there won't be simple questions or clear cut answers.

This isn't something to be concerned about. Indeed, an assessor (or manager) may expect you to identify the uncertainties and to deal with them. This doesn't necessarily mean 'solve them': a project could be concerned with identifying what is uncertain, or ambiguous or unpredictable and looking at what effect that has on the topic. In planning your project, you'll need to allow for the unexpected (e.g. illness; computers crashing; snow).

How can you deal with these things? You could:

- identify what's uncertain, ambiguous and the effect it has;

- identify the key elements of a complex situation and analyse those most important for your topic;

- avoid forcing things to fit where they don't. There may be no cause and effect, for example. If you claim there's a cause and effect where there isn't, your assessor (or manager or client) won't be impressed;

- identify in advance the complexities, ambiguities and possibilities: allow for them;

- explain any complexities, ambiguities or uncertainties in your final presentation (e.g. in a report). How can you do so effectively? Possibilities include: use examples; make any steps clear; pick out key issues; avoid getting bogged down with detail; explain the same idea in different ways; use stories, analogies, diagrams or photographs;

- look at Chapters 15 'Handling time and pressure' and 16 'Solving problems and making decisions'.

E6 Develop your skills

The above 'enhanced skills' sections refer to developing new skills and ways of doing things. A project is a great opportunity for this and it's worth making the most of it. Once you work out what you need to develop, you can:

- look at guidance on it;

- ask somebody for guidance on it;

- try it out, then reflect on what worked and what didn't and see what to do next time.

However, it might be best not to bite off more than you can chew. If you have a topic and methods in which you're already confident, or have some of the skills, it will give you a base 'comfort level' from which it'll feel easier to develop new skills than if everything is new.

E7 Review: improving things for next time

What feedback have you had on how you do projects?

What do you think of the choices you made throughout the project (or that you have made so far in the project)

What could improve your skills in doing projects?

Activity	This is what I'll repeat/do the same in future	This is what I'll do differently
Identifying what I want to achieve and how to do so.		
Planning for long or large projects.		
Staying motivated.		
Extending the methods you use.		
Being at the forefront of your subject.		
Dealing with uncertainty.		
Developing your skills further.		

6
SUCCEEDING WITH EXAMS (OR TESTS)

HOW THIS CHAPTER CAN HELP YOU

The 'crucial' skills part of this chapter aims to help you:

- identify the type of exams/tests you're likely to experience;
- review your current strategies for both revising and taking exams/tests, and identify factors that might influence your success;
- find a range of different revision techniques and strategies to use during exams/tests;
- compare possible methods and choose those that might suit you best;
- develop plans for both revising and taking exams/tests, using relevant support, feedback, resources and timescales;
- carry out, monitor and revise your plans as necessary;
- reflect on the effectiveness of both your revising strategies and your performance during exams/tests and consider whether other strategies could be more effective;
- identify ways to improve and develop your skills.

The 'enhanced' skills part of this chapter is shorter: it helps you operate to a higher level. As well as the 'crucial' skills' outcomes, you'll be able to:

- identify your aims for the future and how exams might affect them;
- choose appropriate techniques and strategies for revising and taking exams to help you achieve those aims, allowing for your personal style and issues;
- plan an implementation strategy, using relevant methods, identifying opportunities and constraints and allowing for unpredictable events;
- evaluate your strategies and their effectiveness, including how your decisions and other factors affect the result;
- identify how to further develop your skills in this area.

CRUCIAL SKILLS

C1 Why is this chapter important and how can it help you?

Examinations (and tests) are the traditional way of assessing students in higher education (HE). Your degree or award result may be totally or partly dependent on exams, or you may not have them at all. You may have long or short exams or 'phase tests' (i.e. tests of your knowledge at points in the course where the purpose is to identify how well you're doing).

The end of your course may not be the end of exams. You may need to take more to get graduate level jobs or for promotion. Some public, statutory and regulatory bodies (PSRBs) have exams: you may need to pass them to gain professional membership.

Why do courses (or PSRBs) have exams or tests?

Different assessment methods test different things: usually exams test knowledge rather than how to use or apply it. Some exams, however, give 'cases' where you apply what you know and some test professional skills (e.g. report writing). Often, answers will be in an essay format. Exams may be used where you need to have a wide knowledge: where you don't know exactly what will come up it encourages you to revise a wide range of material.

Some also see exams as fair: it's more possible to anonymise work; examiners can be sure that **you** did them (as opposed to somebody else doing the work for you or stealing it from the web). Some think that since exams only test knowledge they're less biased than other methods, as they don't test personal skills that students may not have developed because of background or experience. However, we (the authors) are dubious about this last claim. Exams are not 'skill free'. Like other assessment methods, they depend on communication skills, use of language/notation, ability to analyse what's needed, estimate time, work fast and keep cool. Without such skills, you may not do well, even if you have the knowledge.

This chapter is about those skills needed for exams/tests. Use it when you have an exam/test coming up, to see how to prepare for it. This chapter will first consider how to deal with exams/tests and secondly how to deal with revision; the sort of revision you need to do may depend on the sort of exam/test you have to take.

Please note that if you have a disability, it's very important to declare this well in advance, as special arrangements may be made for you in exams (e.g. you may get extra time; any mistakes in written English may be discounted).

C2 Other chapters you need to use together with this one

It's important to look at other chapters in this book together with this one.

Chapter	Title	How it relates to this chapter	Page
7	Finding, using and analysing information and evidence.	Most exams are based on the knowledge you gain from the material you use.	147
9	Making notes.	An essential part of revising is note taking; some exams allow you to take in notes with you.	187
15	Handling time and pressure.	These are critical skills for revising and taking exams.	327
14	Action planning; identifying actions; making recommendations.	You need to make plans to help you revise.	301
1	Writing essays and dissertations.	If your exam requires longish written answers, this will help you see how to structure them.	7
10	Presenting your work; making it look good.	How you present work in an exam may be key for the assessor to understand what you mean.	205

C3 What sort of exams/tests might you have and what's wanted? This is your starting point!

Here's a list of possible types of exams/tests you might come across, with some implications for what you need to be able to do.

Given the different implications, it's important to find out what sort of exam or test you'll have as soon as possible, so you can start preparing: if in doubt, ask your tutor/mentor. Also ask for any assessment criteria; find out what they're looking for in a pass or a high mark/grade (e.g. knowledge; how you express it; accuracy; the breadth or depth of what you cover).

In the following, 'under exam conditions' also applies to tests. It means you take it in a room at a specified time and that it's 'invigilated'; that is, somebody watches to check you don't cheat; there are rules about what you can or can't do (you'll need to check what the rules are).

Type of exam or test	Implications
Multiple choice.	'Answers' provided and you choose between them. There'll be one correct answer. It may be to test your knowledge or your ability to analyse statements about it. This can be harder than you think and practising such tests is a good idea.
Quiz.	Often done via an e-learning environment, this is usually a formative activity to help you see what you do or don't know. You can use the result to see where you need to improve.

Type of exam or test	Implications
Phase test.	This will be before the end of a module/course and aims to give the tutor and you an indication of your progress. You can take advantage of it to see where you need to improve and how much effort to put in, so it's good to take it seriously.
Self marked tests or marking each others.	This may aim to help you learn what's 'right' or 'wrong' and may be for formative purposes, i.e. to help you learn, so if you cheat you'll only cheat yourself.
Marked by a computer.	There'll be no leeway: the answer will be right or wrong.
An exam/test on a computer done under exam conditions.	This is to ensure it's your own work. You'll need to take your ID and log-in with you. You need to be familiar with using computers and the program used, as there won't be time to get to grips with it on the spot.
An exam/test on a computer but done in your own time.	There'll be less pressure and you'll have more time to get to grips with the program used. In some cases you may be able to keep trying until you get it right.
Oral examination such as a viva under exam conditions.	This is covered by Chapter 4 'Giving a presentation, viva or being observed'. 2/3 people will ask you questions, on your own. You need to think on your feet, so you must be well prepared.
Observation of your performance under exam conditions.	See Chapter 4 'Giving a presentation, viva or being observed'. Somebody will observe and assess you and may ask questions. They may be checking if you follow a process accurately or safely.
Objective Structured Clinical Examination (OSCE), often in health sciences (e.g. nursing; medicine).	As above. Somebody will observe you at each 'station' (i.e. different type of patient or medical issue) against a checklist of specific things they're looking for (e.g. communication; clinical examination; joint manipulation techniques).
Unseen exam, under exam conditions, where you can only take in writing tools.	You're unlikely to know what will come up. You need to spend the first few minutes of the exam reading the whole paper to see which questions you can best answer. They often require essays.
Unseen exam, under exam conditions where you can take in specific equipment (e.g. calculator).	As above.
Unseen exam, under exam conditions, where you can take in notes.	You may have a better idea of what may come up. Your notes must be usable quickly so you don't spend ages finding the right ones (see Chapter 9 'Making notes'). Often essay answers.
Seen exam, where you can use books and other resources.	You may be able to go away and do this within a specified time. It's similar to a coursework assignment but done under pressure. See relevant chapters for guidance (e.g. Chapter 7 'Finding, using and analysing information and evidence'; Chapter 1 'Writing essays and dissertations).

Type of exam or test	Implications
Seen exam, under exam conditions, where you can use books and resources.	Time provides the pressure. You'll need to be very familiar with the books/materials you take in, so you can find exactly what you need quickly (e.g. mark pages you may need; have a list of useful page numbers). Often essay answers.
Exams where you have to solve problems.	The assessor will want to see how you solved the problem not just the solution (e.g. with maths exams). Also see Chapter 16 'Solving problems and making decisions'.
Exam/test set by your tutors.	They may give hints as to what might come up, or you may be able to work it out from the topics covered in class. Beware: cover your bases in case your guesses are wrong by also revising other possible topics.
Exam/test set by people external to your course (e.g. an examining or professional body).	You'll have little idea what might come up. This is what makes such exams hard. Professional exams differ in that you may be working as well; this can make time management more difficult (although you'll have more knowledge from your practice).
Aptitude or reasoning tests or simulations (e.g. in-tray exercise).	May be part of selection procedures for jobs. May be: multiple choice; problem solving; comprehension; 'in-tray' (deciding what to do with items). Usually very tight in time allowed so must work fast.

C4 Some exam techniques

The techniques needed will vary with the type of exam/test. Section C3 gives the implications of each sort, from which you can see which techniques might be needed. What have you done in the past?

What ways of dealing with exams have you used in the past?	What's worked well about this?	What hasn't worked very well about this?

What might affect your success in exams/tests that you are facing soon?

Item	✓	What impact might this have? What do you want to do about that? Your notes
My own motivation to do well in whatever I do.		
I must do well so I can achieve something important to me.		
The outcome isn't important to me.		
I like doing exams/tests.		
I don't like doing exams/tests.		
I neither like nor dislike exams/tests.		
How well I do is important to other people in my life.		
Other people or things are more important to me than how well I do.		
I only need to pass; there's no extra credit for getting a high mark.		
What else?		

Deciding what to answer

This is the critical skill in many exams and tests, especially those taken under exam conditions where you have limited time. There's a danger of spending a long time on one question, only to discover a better one to answer but to have run out of time.

There are two issues here:

1.   identifying which questions to answer;

2.   identifying the order in which to answer them.

Carefully read all the questions first (there are exceptions, this may not be possible if: the exam/test is computer based; there are lots of short questions and a very short timescale). Keep calm and spend the first 5 minutes identifying those you can answer. It may help to jot down key information for each, as a reminder for later on. If you can't answer enough, pick the best option from the rest but don't let this panic you.

Check if some questions are worth more marks than others. Make sure you know this right at the start: it may influence which questions you answer.

Which order will you do them in (unless it's computer based, where the order may be pre-determined)? There are two approaches:

1.   do first those you can best answer: you'll have enough time and you'll feel better;

2.   do first those you can answer least well, to get them out of the way (but this may panic you if you don't know the answers).

Do not, under any circumstances, leave your best question till last and run out of time.

The implication here is that you must manage your time well.

Managing your time

This is the second crucial skill in exams/tests done under exam conditions. Passing or getting the mark/grade you deserve may depend on it.

You need to identify how long the exam will take, the questions you need to answer, how many marks each is worth and then divide up your time. For example:

- in a 2 hour exam, if there are 4 questions each worth 25 per cent of the marks, each should get 30 minutes of your time;

- in a 2 hour exam, if 4 questions are each worth 10 per cent and 2 are worth 30 per cent, the 4 each get 12 minutes and the 2 each get 36 minutes;

- if a 3 hour exam is worth 100 marks, then you need to be scoring a mark every 1.8 minutes. Knowing this helps you focus on making points quickly and succinctly.

You could ask your tutor/mentor which marks are 'easy wins' (e.g. in calculations, getting the basics set out, even if some more difficult bits are left out; in professional accountancy exams, doing executive summaries and setting out structures for case study presentation).

It's unlikely that you'll pick up enough extra marks to make it worth spending extra time on questions you know well. You'll probably pick up more marks by trying to answer all the questions equally. The worst case scenario is to leave your best question until last and run out of time. When you've used up the time on a question, move on, even if you haven't finished it. If you've time left at the end, you can go back and finish it then.

If you're running out of time, you could indicate what you were going to cover, rather than do nothing (e.g. a bullet point list of information/ideas; notes covering the main issues; set out a plan for answering the remaining question).

It it's an exam/test with lots of short questions, each may attract only a few marks. The more you answer, the more you'll increase your chances of good marks. It's best not to spend ages on a question you can't answer but to move on and return to it later, if you have time.

Keep your watch in front of you, all the time!

Matching the answer to what's needed

This is why you need to find out, if possible, what will get a good mark or grade.

Research suggests that some students think factual information will get a good mark, while others think it's underlying concepts (Marton and Saljo, 1984). If you think one is needed and it's the other, you may have a problem. What else might matter in getting a good grade?

For example

- *If knowledge (facts or underlying concepts) will get good marks/grades, you need to get as much of it down as possible.*

- *In HE and professional exams, this may not be what's needed. It may also be important to develop an argument and write in an appropriate style. In this case, writing as many facts as possible in a random order will get you nowhere. You'll need to use the same writing skills as for written course work (e.g. for an essay or report).*

Here are some other questions you need the answer to, in advance.

Questions	✓
Will you need to give examples?	
Will you need to show 'working out' (e.g. for maths questions)?	
Will you need to show how you arrived at a solution (e.g. for problem solving)?	
Will you need to follow a set procedure (e.g. for observation/lab type exams)?	
Will you need to give references to literature, using academic conventions?	
Will you need to know formulae (e.g. chemical; statistical)?	
Will you need to use notation correctly (e.g. musical; mathematical)?	
Will you have to draw anything?	
What equipment can you take in with you (shows what you'll have to do in the exam)?	
Have you checked what format the examiners want (e.g. reasoned theoretical essay; short memos; business report)?	

Two essential questions, regardless of the type of exam/test, are:

1. have you fully understood each question? If your answer is wonderful but it doesn't address the question, you'll get no marks at all;

2. what will help the examiner understand your answer?

To help examiners understand your answers, regardless of the type of exam/test:

*   your work must be legible;

*   it must be in an order the assessor can follow;

*   vocabulary you use must be correct;

*   follow the main conventions of written English (punctuation; grammar; spelling);

*   follow the conventions of the subject (e.g. mathematical notation; symbols; labelling);

*   leave plenty of 'white space' so your work is easy to read and your answers are clear.

Taking notes (or books, etc) into an exam

NB Only do this if it's clear you're allowed to. Otherwise it's cheating. Check the rules as they may change from year to year.

If time is tight and you're under pressure, you want to use the material you take in with you as easily as possible.

- What might be important in the exam? Find this out first.

- Identify what's essential to take with you. If you take too much you may be confused.

- Don't rely on being able to read texts in an exam. If time is tight, you need to spend it getting down or thinking through your answer. Think of the texts just as reminders. You're unlikely to get credit for quoting from them.

- You could have a different way of marking what's essential and what's 'extra' (e.g. different coloured paper, post-its or pens; coloured dividers).

- Make sure any markings used won't come adrift (e.g. post-its) and that they'll mean something to you when under pressure. If you turn down the corner of pages, when faced with 20 turned down corners, how will you know where to find something?

- Have a layout for your notes that'll help you find things (e.g. margins; bold; highlighters).

- Use diagrams to remind you of connections.

- If you know a topic well, have a list of words to act as a reminder.

- Take with you a list of your material and where to find each item.

- See Chapter 9 'Making notes'.

- *What else could you do?*

Practice

Once you've found out what's needed in the exam, you need to practice doing it. How?

- Practise answering previous questions and time yourself.

- Can practice answers be marked (e.g. by tutor; mentor; colleague; student from a higher level)?

- This also applies to on-line or computer tests.

- Use your course work to practise (e.g. for essay-type answers, do the first draft of it off the top of your head, then amend it using your notes and information).

- If you can take notes or books into the exam/test, practise using them in advance.

- Try to get an idea of important topics that often come up.

- 6 months before the exam, start looking for relevant topical issues (e.g. new medical advances; economic climate changes; new technical developments).

- Practise your skills (e.g. for an oral exam; a debate; an in-tray exercise).

Keep calm

What do exams do to you?

Your possible reaction	✓	What do you actually do? (e.g. write fast; hands shake; can't focus)
Find them exhilarating: I perform well.		
Make me a bit nervous.		
Depends on the topic: if I know it I'm OK, if not I can panic.		
I panic even if I know the topic, but I get through it somehow.		
I get so nervous I can't operate at all.		

The techniques you use will vary according to your answers above. If you react so badly that you can't operate, look for some help (e.g. student services; medical services; colleagues).

Here are some suggestions.

- Have a plan for what you're going to do and stick to it (e.g. first 5 minutes read whole paper, allocate time to each question). This will help you feel in control.

- Have a plan for dealing with problems, such as not remembering names and dates.

- Be very well prepared, to give you confidence (e.g. check out the venue).

- Avoid a late night before the exam (or even worse, doing the exam with a hangover).

- Don't stay up late revising the night before; it's too late to take in information and it's more important to be fresh when you do the exam.

- Look at Chapter 15 'Handling time and pressure'. Try some of the relaxation exercises during the exam (e.g. breathing exercises) and to help you sleep the night before.

- If you panic – stop. Spend a few minutes working out what to do.

- After the exam, limit the time you spend thinking about it: enough time to identify what to do differently next time (see Section C7) but not so much as to beat yourself up.

- Try to move on quickly if you have another exam soon afterwards.

How could you get more ideas for coping with the exam/test you have to do?

You could:

- look at other books/on-line guidance on study skills;

- ask your tutors/metors/managers/colleagues;

- ask other students (either at the same stage as you, or from higher levels);

- seek help from student services or from academic guidance in your university/college.

What will you try?

Which suggestions from this section will you try?	What actions do you need to take to use the suggestions?

C5 Revising

The techniques you use will vary with the type of exam/test. This is why this section comes after the section on doing the exam/test.

It may be that your revision should:

- be about having practice at the exam/test (e.g. if you're going to be observed; if you have to apply knowledge to a particular case);

- focus on making good notes to take in with you;

- focus on learning material for the exam/test.

What sort of exam/test am I about to do and what's required for it?	What does that imply for what and how I need to revise or prepare?

If you need to practise or to make notes, see Section C4. This C5 Section considers how to learn material for an exam.

Identifying what to revise

See Section C3 for suggestions about working out what will come up in the exam/test. That's an essential first step. Here are possibilities for what you could revise.

What could you revise?	✓	What would this be for this exam/test?
Everything.		
Everything to some extent but concentrate on some things.		

What could you revise?	✓	What would this be for this exam/test?
The most important/key issues/theories for the topic.		
Things we've spent a lot of time on in class.		
Things that usually come up.		
Something my gut feeling says might come up.		
Things the tutor/mentor has hinted will come up.		
Things that are my best topics and where I know I'll do well.		
Things that are my worst topics and where I need to most improve.		
What else?		

You then need a list of items to revise. It might help to have these in smallish 'chunks' so you can see what you've done and keep a check on progress.

Do you need to revise items in a particular order; e.g. do some items depend on earlier ones? You may want to look at the most difficult topics first or the easiest ones. You could put your list of items to revise in the order in which you need to work on them.

Planning

You need to develop a plan early enough to cover all the material. For help, see Chapters 14 'Action planning: identifying actions, making recommendations' and 15 'Handling time and pressure'.

Do you have all the material to revise from? If this includes borrowing books or other resources, you may need to do this early, to ensure you can get them. You may need to check you understand your own notes. If you can't, get help as soon as possible (e.g. from a tutor; learning centre/library staff; books; other students; colleagues).

As part of your plan, you need to identify:

- resources you'll need to use to revise (e.g. books; notes; computer; files; pencils; pens);

- support you'll need from others (e.g. tutors/mentors; other students/ colleagues);

- how you'll get feedback on your progress. This might include testing yourself (e.g. by: summarising material and then checking the original to see if your summary was accurate; asking others to test you; using quizzes or phase tests).

Chapter 15 'Handling time and pressure' looks at how to monitor and adapt plans. This is very important when you're revising, so do look at that chapter now. You may need to prioritise your actions and adapt what you do to meet any new demands on your time, deal with any difficulties and allow for a change in circumstances.

C6 Revision techniques

What have you done in the past to revise?	What's worked well about this?	What hasn't worked very well about this?

How could you get ideas of other ways to revise?

You could:

- look at other books/on-line guidance on study skills;

- ask your tutors/mentors/managers;

- ask other students/colleagues (either at the same stage as you, or from higher levels);

- seek help from student services or from academic guidance in your university/college.

Possible revision techniques

Revision needs to be active; you're unlikely to learn and remember just by reading. The 'constructivist' view of learning suggests that in order to learn, you must make something your own (Biggs 2003).

- Make notes on what you read, either to use later or to help you focus (e.g. read a page then summarise it in note form).

- Re-write your notes: put the contents in an order than makes more sense; pick out key points; add information you missed; clarify what you don't understand.

- Tape yourself reading/talking about the material (e.g. dates; key points; formulae) and listen to it wherever possible.

- Watch a video of particular techniques and practices.

- Discuss the material with others (e.g. students/colleagues). Could you form a revision group?

- Explain the material to others (e.g. to a friend who knows nothing about it).

- Ask someone to test you, by asking you questions (you give them the answers in advance; the authors learned foreign language vocabulary like this).

- Make diagrams that show key points (e.g. flow diagrams showing cause and effect; time-lines showing what happened in what order).

- Make mind maps to show key ideas, concepts or facts and how they're connected.

- Create reminders, such as mnemonics (e.g. use the first letter of a list of facts to make a word).

- Use pictures. They may be important to your subject matter (e.g. in design subjects). If you tend to think visually, sketches might help you make sense of/remember information.

- Would doing something practical (or physical) help? Making models? Walking while listening to a tape or going over ideas in your head?

- Think about where you revise best. Is home distracting?

What will you try?

Which of the suggestions in this section will you try?	What actions will you take?

C7 How effective were you? Improving for the future

As soon after the event as possible, it helps to think about what you did and what you could repeat or do differently in future. You can really learn to improve revision and exam skills.

What sort of exam or test was it?			
What did you do to *revise* (techniques used)?	What worked well and why?	What didn't work and why?	What will you do next time? For which sorts of exams/tests?
What did you do *in the exam/test* (techniques used)?	What worked well and why?	What didn't work and why?	What will you do next time? For which sorts of exams/tests?

ENHANCED SKILLS

E1 Identifying what you want to achieve

What do you want for the future and how do exams fit against this?

Possible aims or concerns	Implications	Your notes
I never want to do another exam.	This may rule out professions that require them (e.g. accountancy; law). Check which professions need exams.	
I'm good at exams and want to make use of this.	Many postgraduate courses don't have exams. Check in advance. Some professions rely on you doing more exams.	
I need a good degree to get into the job I want.	If your degree result depends on exams, you need to make good use of this chapter.	
I know what profession I want to work in.	Check: if it has a professional body that has exams for membership; if jobs you're interested in have tests as part of the selection process.	
I already work and want to know how to get further in my profession.	As above.	
What sorts of tests are there in selection processes for jobs?	Ask at your university/college careers service. Check with your subject's professional body. Many employers use mathematical and reasoning tests. Others may put you in a work situation, to see how you react. They focus on skills and reasoning rather than on what you know about the company.	

E2 What exam and revision techniques would best suit me?

What aspects of your personal situation might affect you in doing the exam or test?

Possible aspect	Implications	What actions could you take?
What other demands are there on your time (e.g. work; other modules; domestic)?	See Chapter 15 'Handling time and pressure' for help. What could you drop or change until the exam is over?	
My constraints (e.g. lack of resources such as home computer; lack of money).	Can you work around the constraint? Can you do something to allow for it, if it's unavoidable?	
My attitude towards exams/tests.	See the end of Section C4.	
My attitude towards trying new things.	See Chapter 18 'Personal Development Planning ('PDP'). Limit the risks of trying new things if the exam is very important. Could you try limited things?	
My own needs.	What are they and what are the most important ones? Do you need: encouragement; support; distraction?	
The support available to me.	Could family members take on more responsibility for a time? Could others help (e.g. student services; friends; mentors)?	
My skills (strong or weak points) (e.g. using time; communication; analysis; numeracy; ICT).	What are you good at and could build on in preparing for and doing exams? What do you need to improve? See Section E3.	
My knowledge of the topic.	See Sections C5 and C6 on revision and Chapter 7 'Finding, using and analysing information and evidence'. See Section E3.	
My preferred way of studying.	See Section C. Which ideas fit how you like to study? Could you try something new?	

Possible aspect	Implications	What actions could you take?
My preferred way of being assessed.	See Section E1. If you don't like exams but have to do them, make good use of Section C.	
My short term motivations.	How important are these in relation to the outcome of the exam and what that outcome will lead to?	
My long term motivations.	See Section E1 and Chapter 18 'Personal Development Planning ('PDP)'.	
What else?		

E3 Developing your exam and revision techniques

Trying new techniques or strategies

How important is the exam/test facing you? Will the outcome determine your degree/ professional membership result? How important is the mark/grade (some jobs want applicants to have 2:1s; for postgraduate study you may need high grades)?

Some suggestions in Section C carry more risks than others (e.g. doing breathing exercises in an exam for a couple of minutes to calm you down is not a big deal; changing how you format notes you take into an exam might be risky if you've never tried it before).

Look back at the last exercises in Sections C4 and C6 that asked you to identify techniques/strategies to use. How risky is each one, where 1 = low risk, 2 = medium risk, 3 = high risk?

If it's risky, what could you do?

- Ask yourself how risky it is compared with what you were doing before. If that didn't work well, it may be better to risk something new.

- Practise the technique beforehand. How? Using the example of producing notes to take into an exam, you could: make the notes, leave them for a week, then try to answer a question using them (to see how easy they are to use); try making notes in this format for other purposes (e.g. for seminars; coursework); try them in a mock exam.

What if the unexpected happens?

What if you're ill at the last minute? Or there's a family problem? What if something happens that may affect your chances of doing as well as you want?

Firstly, even if you don't think this will happen, find out in advance what the rules are. There'll be a procedure whereby, providing you can give evidence, examiners will make allowances. The regulations should cover both the revision period and the exam/test itself.

There are some elements of 'good practice' to use in any case but that will really help if the unexpected hits.

- Don't leave anything till the last minute. If 'the unexpected' is your computer or the university network breaking at the last minute, you won't get much sympathy ('you should have done it earlier'). Building in leeway is a good way of anticipating problems.

- Being well organised (e.g. having well-organised notes; see Chapter 9 'Making notes).

- If you have a problem, you may need to amend your plans. You could prioritise topics which are most important to revise, or use revision strategies that take up the least amount of time.

Look at Chapters 15 'Handling time and pressure' and 16 'Solving problems and making decisions'.

Using methods to improve what you do

Section C covered techniques you could use. How could you use these to maximum effect?

Is your revision plan SMART? In other words, are the actions Specific, Measurable (can you see when you've done them?), Achievable (do you have the skills/resources?), Realistic (can you do them in the time?), Time-bound (have you set time limits?).

Chart your revision progress. You should have a list of items to revise and a plan (see Section C). How could you monitor this? Would any visual methods help? Possibilities are:

- using a spreadsheet on a computer;

- computer based planning tools; a chart on the wall;

- a time-line with the exam at the end and points along the way when you need to have covered certain topics;

- a 'critical path analysis' (i.e. noting what's crucial if you are to succeed).

In the exam itself, you might stop (e.g. each half an hour) and ask yourself if you are doing what you intended to do and are following the strategy you decided upon (e.g. dividing up your time; using methods to calm yourself: see Section C).

E4 Evaluating what you do and improving it

Although it's always helpful to evaluate what you do at the end of an activity, to see what to do next time, this exam could be the last big one you'll take. So you also need to evaluate what you're doing as you go through.

Topics/items I've decided to revise	What's working well about this?	What isn't working well?	What I'll do now

Revision techniques I am using	What's working well about this?	What isn't working well?	What I'll do now

Once you have considered the above:

Issue	Your notes
What support and resources do you need to help you?	
Do you need any more information on anything?	
What has affected what you have done so far?	
What might affect what you do from now on?	

If you get used to thinking about what's working well, what isn't and what to do next, it'll become second nature. This is important as you could also do this in the exam, where you won't have the above formats to help. During the exam you could stop at a certain point and ask:

- what am I doing here that's working well?

- what am I doing here that isn't working well?

- now what am I going to do?

What do you most need to improve in the future in revising and doing exams? In the column headed 'actions I need to take' you could put support, resources (e.g. software) and information you need (e.g. more ideas on exam techniques).

This is what I'm doing well	This is what I'm not doing well	This is what I need to improve	Actions I need to take

REFERENCES

Biggs, J., (2003, 2nd edn), *Teaching for quality learning at university*, Buckingham: OU Press.

Marton, F. and Saljo, R., (1984), 'Approaches to learning', in Marton, F., Hounsell, D. and Entwistle, N., (1984), *The experience of learning*, Edinburgh: Scottish Academic Press.

7
FINDING, USING AND ANALYSING INFORMATION AND EVIDENCE

HOW THIS CHAPTER CAN HELP YOU

The 'crucial skills' part of this chapter aims to help you:

- identify search techniques to find a range of information sources and select relevant items;
- identify the aspects of each item that will be useful and relevant to your purpose;
- record information and evidence in a useful form for your purpose;
- evaluate the information, recognising appropriate evidence and identifying opinion, bias and any distortions;
- interpret the information and evidence and bring it together coherently, including comparing information from different sources to identify similarities and differences;
- review what you did to identify improved search strategies for the future.

The 'enhanced skills' part of this chapter is shorter; it helps you operate to a higher level. As well as the 'crucial' skills outcomes, you'll be able to:

- plan an information search over an extended period (e.g. for a long project, dissertation or thesis);
- identify and explore particularly efficient search techniques;
- use primary resources where appropriate;
- critically analyse information and evidence, question assumptions and identify any uncertainties, ambiguities or limits of the information;
- synthesise information and evidence;
- critically review what you did to improve what you do in the future.

CRUCIAL SKILLS

C1 Why is this chapter so important and how can it help you?

Locating and using information and evidence is an essential skill in higher education (HE).

A dictionary definition of 'information' is 'items of knowledge' (Thompson, 1996). 'Information' usually refers to knowledge gathered from sources such as publications, organisations, the media and on-line. It may include facts, theories, policies or descriptions and may be written, visual or oral. Most HE and work tasks are based on information gathered.

What do we mean by 'evidence'? One definition is 'the available facts, circumstances etc. indicating whether or not a thing is true or valid' (Thompson, 1996). In HE and at work, judgements and decisions need to be based on evidence. You can't just make claims without substantiating them. You may need to do a project that depends on gathering evidence about the topic; one assessment method, the portfolio (see Chapter 3), is about presenting evidence of work; evidence is important in Personal Development Planning (PDP) and Continuing Professional Development (CPD) schemes (see Chapter 18).

This chapter is concerned with how you use and analyse evidence provided by others about their own context or to support their research and/or their claims.

You can use this chapter to help with a specific task that involves finding and using information and evidence. Then use it again the next time you have a task to do. After that, you could refer to it as a reminder.

An important starting point is to be clear about the purpose of your information gathering or use of evidence. This might affect what you do.

Possible purpose	✓	What would affect the result (e.g. grade, mark)?
To develop your own knowledge (rather than others just telling you).		You might need to find key information for a topic and for it to be full and accurate.
To see what others know about a topic before you start work on it.		If you don't do this before starting your own work, you might waste a lot of time.
To help you think about a topic from different perspectives.		You may need to look at a range of very different items or authors.
To give you ideas (e.g. for creative work).		You might look at a wide range of items before finding what you need (or you may be lucky and find 'it' straight away).
To develop information skills.		How you carried out your search might be more important than what you found.

Possible purpose	✓	What would affect the result (e.g. grade, mark)?
To prove you can do academic work.		This is implied in any HE task. You must correctly reference everything you use (see Chapter 8 'Plagiarism and referencing').
To find examples (e.g. of how theory relates to practice).		You may need to find relevant, up-to-date items from a range of different sources.
To see how others present complex information and ideas.		Presentation methods influence an audience/ reader's understanding of something, so seeing how others do it is very helpful.
To prove what you claim.		You'll need to back up claims with good evidence.

C2 Other chapters you need to use together with this one

All chapters in this book are concerned with using or presenting information and evidence; see Section C11 for the full list of chapters that look at how to **present** the information or evidence you've found. It's particularly important to look at the following chapters alongside this one, when finding and using information.

Chapter	Title	How it relates to this chapter	Page
8	Plagiarism and referencing.	This is very important; look at it to see which details about your sources of information you need to record.	173
9	Making notes.	You need to make notes about information used and notes might be used as evidence.	187
15	Handling time and pressure.	You need to plan your time well when gathering information.	327
17	Reflecting on your learning and experience (including feedback).	Section C4 looks at how to use and interpret personal evidence about your skills, knowledge, ability and achievements (see Section C4.2 in particular).	379
5	Doing a project.	This looks at methods of collecting evidence (see Section C7 in particular).	97

C3 Getting started

What's the task that you're using this chapter to help with?

Task	Purpose(s)	Deadline

This checklist gives you things to think about before you start looking for information.

Do you know...	✓
clearly what the task is?	
the standard required (e.g. what will pass; get a good mark; meet the criteria)?	
how you will use the information or evidence?	
how you will present it (e.g. a report; poster; presentation; in a debate; create an artefact; give a performance; in a portfolio)?	
the boundaries/limits of the task (e.g. how much information/evidence is needed)?	

If you're unsure about any of the above you could:

- look at the assignment brief or any guidelines;

- ask your tutor, mentor or manager;

- talk to others (e.g. students; colleagues);

- find examples that others have done (including published reports or journal papers).

To help you focus on the task, make notes on what's needed and refer to these while finding and using information and evidence. You could store the information/evidence in a hard (paper) file or electronically (see Chapter 9 'Making notes'); whichever you use, having a section or file on 'requirements of the task' is a very good idea.

Task (putting this in your own words can make the focus clear)	What's needed/requirements (e.g. standard needed/assessment criteria; presentation method; boundaries/limits)

C4 Planning to meet your deadline

Here are some principles you could to bear in mind.

- Others may want the same physical resource (e.g. book), so it may be unavailable.

- Computers and computer systems break down.

- University/college computers and printers are in heavy use as assessment deadlines get closer, so you need to allow more time.

- You probably need to allow as much time to write it up as to collect the information.

- Given the above, an information search might take twice as long as you think it will.

You need to have a plan to allow for this.

- Start work early. Aim to have found and used the information or evidence well before the deadline for doing this (e.g. a week before).

- Identify resources you need early and book them out. If everybody in a group needs the same resource, work out how to share it.

- Allow for things going wrong (e.g. avoid leaving work till the last minute when a computer problem could be disastrous).

- Being organised saves time (it takes much longer to chase resources at the last minute) and means you'll produce better work (a better mark or grade). It is even more important if you have several tasks to do at once, all with a similar deadline.

Your plan will depend on how much information or evidence you need to find and from where, so we suggest you develop and amend the plan as you work through the rest of this chapter (see Chapters 14 'Action planning: identifying actions and recommendations' and 15 'Handling time and pressure' for fuller guidance on planning).

In your plan, you need to work backwards from the deadline to identify interim deadlines. Here's an example for writing a report (the principle applies to any size/type of task).

Example

1. *Deadline 20 January.*

2. *Finish final draft 15 January to allow time for checking.*

3. *Start to write final draft 1 January.*

4. *Start to write first draft 1 December, allow time to collect more information.*

5. *Start to look at information on 1 November, make notes, complete by end Nov.*

6.   *Start to identify information needed 1 October; find the information by end Oct.*

You'll need to amend your plan as things rarely go exactly as you think: build in leeway. Here's a format you could use.

Example of a plan

Actions	Interim deadline	Progress

C5 Plagiarism and avoiding it; referencing

Plagiarism means using someone else's work without acknowledging whose it is and where it came from.

Most people don't mean to cheat but may do so without realising; it's is a real 'sin' in HE. If you do it deliberately it's cheating and could have very serious consequences. Universities, colleges and professional bodies have clear penalties. Check the rules where you're studying/working!

It's **now very** important to look at Chapter 8 'Plagiarism and referencing', for more detailed guidance, before looking at the rest of this one. It helps you see what details to note about any source of information.

Basically, if you mention anything that somebody else has written or produced, or who's influenced your thinking, you **must** acknowledge them. If you don't, you're plagiarising (i.e. stealing somebody else's work). This applies to anything somebody else has produced (e.g. text; films; photos; designs), including items that may not be published (e.g. internal reports) and novels, films, programmes, musical recordings – anything!

One way to avoid plagiarism is to 'cite' anything you use and have a list of references at the end of your work, with details so the reader/user could find each item. 'Cite' means that, in your work, when you mention something somebody else has produced, you give brief details that allow the reader/user to find the full details in the list of references. There are set ways of doing this and Chapter 8 explains them.

C6 Recording your information or evidence

At the start, it's worth considering how you'll record your information/evidence. You need to avoid finding that you didn't record a crucial bit of information and so have to look for it again. For example, you need to record the details for referencing, any direct quotes (or images etc) and the page number/location in the original where it appeared. How will you record evidence? You don't want to find you haven't kept key evidence you need.

How will you use the information/evidence? This may affect what you record and how. The following gives some starting points; add your own for your task. See Chapter 9 'Making notes' for much more on recording, organising and storing notes and evidence.

What/how will you record?	The implications are:
A complete article/journal/book/ webpage/visual/artefact.	Find a way of storing it so you can find and use it easily (box files; ring binders; folder on your computer).
Just need a summary of key points or aspects.	Make separate notes on each item in case you need to use them again separately. Store them, e.g. by name of author or topic (whether physical or electronic storage, label them clearly). See Chapter 9 for more ideas.
Going to use it electronically (e.g. using software for creating presentations).	Store it electronically so you can cut and paste (but don't forget to reference it!).
A core text for your subject, so you may need the information again.	Store it where you can find it easily and in a format you can use for different sorts of tasks.
Need a summary of lots of similar items.	Make a standard format and use it for each item (see example overleaf).
Your notes on what/how you'll record.	*Your notes on implications for what you do.*

Example of a standard format

Author(s)	Date	Title	Location of publisher or url of web site	Name of publisher or date accessed for web site

Notes

Here are a few more principles.

- Having information in random piles on the floor makes your life hard.

- Having a filing system (paper or computer) that doesn't make it clear where you've stored things makes your life hard.

- Not recording information or not recording evidence and having to try to find it again, or not recording or storing it in a way you need, makes your life really hard.

See Chapter 9 'Making notes'.

C7 Locating sources of information

Information Communication Technology (ICT) has given us access to a wealth of information but it can be difficult to sort through it all to find what you need.

You don't just need information: you need good information. What makes a good source for your task and purpose? This will vary according to what you need to do but sources used in HE (and for tasks at work) generally have to be 'reputable'.

The source of the information influences how credible it is and how you might criticise it; for example, if you heard that aliens were about to invade the earth, would you react differently if you heard it from:

- a tabloid newspaper;

- a sci-fi magazine;

- National Aeronautics and Space Administration (NASA);

- a special broadcast by the Prime Minister?

How do you know if a source is reputable? Below are some general principles.

- Any item in a 'refereed' academic journal will have been approved by at least two specialists in the subject before it was accepted. This means it's a reputable source.

- A book will have gone through a publisher's approval and editing process.

- A government report will have been approved by a government department.

- Internal documents produced centrally by an organisation will have been approved by somebody. Internal documents produced by an individual may not have been approved by anybody and could just be that person's own opinions.

- Magazines and newspapers have varying reputations for being 'serious'.

- Anybody can put anything on the web, so you'll find everything from complete rubbish to highly reputable information.

How can you tell if something on the web is from a reputable source?

The following gives some thoughts, but also ask advice from lecturers or managers or information specialists in university/college libraries or learning centres.

* In the following, 'Depends*' means it depends on the nature of the information. For example, if the source is a large company, its annual report giving legal/formal information would be OK: its claims for its products might be treated with caution. A small company may have few resources to produce high quality information and may cover a limited field, but they may be experts in something.

Source	Examples	Is it OK to use?
A government (national or local) web site.	Department for Work and Pensions; Sheffield City Council.	Yes
A professional, regulatory or statutory body.	British Medical Association; Qualifications and Curriculum Development Agency.	Yes
A large company or organisation.	Marks and Spencer.	Depends*, probably yes.
A small company.		Depends*, but possibly no.
A university or college.	University of Bath.	Yes
An on-line journal.	Dermatology On-line.	Yes
A blog	Rosie's blog of her trip to New Zealand.	No (unless it's a record of what you did that's needed as evidence).
A personal web site		As above.
A wiki	Wikipedia	Depends*, probably not (anybody can add to Wikipedia); OK as a starting point for ideas.
What else? Add your own as you come across them...		

How can you locate sources of information?

Dewey number

Look along the shelves in a library/learning centre. They use a classification system (the Dewey system) that gives numbers to items according to the subject matter. You could find out the classification number for your subject and browse the relevant shelves (e.g. 'Drew, S., and Bingham R. (2001) *The Student Skills Guide, 2nd edition.* Aldershot, Gower' has the number 378.015 in one university). The number may vary between institutions, as information specialists interpret subjects differently.

On-line catalogues

However, looking at shelves isn't a very efficient way to find items. University/college libraries/learning centres have on-line catalogues that allow you to search by:

- keyword (i.e. a word that is likely to appear in the title or in an abstract);

- name(s) of author;

- title of item;

- subject heading;

- subject number (e.g. our example above has the subject number 378);

- International Standard Book Number (ISBN) (for each published book).

Databases

You can also use library/learning centre databases. There are many ways to search a database and the starting point is similar to the above list.

To find whatever there is on a topic, use key words (e.g. 'assessment' might be a key word in an education database). However, only using that will give you thousands of hits. You can narrow it down by using 'and' with another key word/phrase (e.g. 'assessment and civil engineering' for items on assessment in civil engineering). To widen a search, use 'or' instead of 'and' (e.g. 'assessment or civil engineering' will give everything on assessment and on civil engineering). You can use more than one 'and' and more than one 'or' (e.g. 'assessment and civil engineering and Italy).

What if you use a mix of keywords but still have too many items to look at? You could.

- look at items published in a particular timescale (e.g. last 5 years);

- look for well-known authors;

- look at the actual titles;

- ask others (e.g. information advisers in library/learning centres; tutor; mentor; colleagues).

Databases often allow you to save what you find and return to the search later.

Other ways to find information

- You could follow up items in the list of references in a piece of work you have looked at (e.g. a book or journal article).

- A web site may direct you to or have links to other web sites.

- You could contact somebody knowledgeable about the topic and ask for advice.

- You could get a list of organisations with the information you need.

- Ask others (students; colleagues; tutors) what they do.

Being imaginative

It's likely that you won't find information on exactly your topic and you may have to look at related ones. You need to think imaginatively about this.

For example: if you want to consider whether having women's-only building courses in further education improves women's achievement and you can't find relevant information, you could look at information on the achievement of girls in girls-only schools in other traditionally male-dominated subjects (e.g. science).

If there seems to be little on a topic, is it the key words you've used? Try different words with similar meaning or find words commonly used in the subject.

What sort of sources should you include and how many?

The answer to this is ...it depends: on your task, the purpose, the assignment instructions, the length of the piece of work and your assessment criteria. Check with your tutor/manager; look at examples. However, here are some thoughts.

Question	Your answer
How many sources will give you enough information to show what you need to show?	
Do you need a wide range of different types of sources or a narrower range of similar types of sources?	
If you only use one type of source (e.g. books), will you limit what you find out?	
If you only use one type of source (e.g. internet), will you seem lazy?	
What sort of sources will impress the reader/ user (e.g. the assessor)?	
If you only use the sources of information given by your lecturer, what will their attitude be?	

C8 Finding and identifying evidence

You need to provide evidence for what you claim (e.g. you can't claim that school meals are unhealthy unless you define the features of 'unhealthy' meals and give evidence that school meals have those features).

Be wary of making statements (claims) that seem self-evident without giving evidence for them. It's easy to make mistakes here as you can do this without thinking (e.g. you can't say it's dangerous for children to walk to school today without any evidence).

What might constitute evidence and how might you find it?

Type of evidence	Examples of items	How to find it
Information from reputable sources, including theoretical work; information can be evidence.	Books; journals; websites	See Section C7.
Information about you.	Feedback sheets; grades/ marks; certificates; formal letters/records. Examples of work produced.	Keep copies and examples (see Chapter 9 'Making notes' for ideas on storage).
Information about others.	Biographical data (gender, age, ethnicity etc); educational achievements; health statistics.	Note: need to be aware of data protection; information likely to be anonymised. Sources: census data; administration sections of organisations; web sites (e.g. 'Cancer Research UK').
Statements from others about your performance.	Feedback sheets; references about you; statements about what you did; letters/ emails thanking you.	See above. Also asking others (e.g. in a work team) to provide statements.
Physical items or visual work.	Art work; designs; prototypes.	Publications (e.g. art books); exhibitions and catalogues; permission from owner/originator to copy originals.
Written work.	Letters; reports; court files; opinion polls; memoranda; diaries; autobiography; novels; newspapers; speeches; testimonies. (Dobson and Ziemann 2009)	See Section C7 for published items; obtain from those producing or owning items (e.g. organisations; private individuals); use the web.
The results of research.	Statistics; data; findings from interviews or from observations; results of experiments; etc.	See Section C7 re published items. Libraries/learning centres have copies of PhDs from their university. From organisations with an interest in the topic.
Records of what happened.	Diaries; journals; logs; blogs; minutes of meetings; film; video; photographs; sound.	See Section C7 re published items and Chapter 3 'Producing portfolios and journals (including diaries, blogs, etc.)'. See archives (e.g. TV/radio/web; film).

Evidence may be primary or secondary. Primary evidence is direct from the original source (e.g. questionnaire data). Secondary evidence is from a source that's used the primary evidence (e.g. a journal article that refers to other research).

Just as information has to be 'good', evidence also has to be good.

What makes evidence 'good'?

Here are some useful criteria against which to judge evidence.

- Valid and relevant for the claim (does it prove what you say it proves?);
- Sufficient (is there enough to show something?);
- Authentic (does it really relate to what you're claiming?);
- Current (was it gathered at the time?).

Examples

Evidence	Claims to show...	Comments
Report written by a group.	effective group work.	Not valid. It's evidence for an investigation and for writing skills, not for group work (could have been written by one group member). Only valid if you had other evidence for how the group contributed.
Minutes of a group meeting.	effective group work.	Valid as an element of evidence; authentic if agreed by the group; current if written shortly after each meeting; but one set of minutes may not be sufficient.
Several sets of minutes.	effective group work.	As above, but better meets the 'sufficient' criterion.
Statements by group members about each other's contributions.	effective group work.	Valid as an element of evidence; authentic if signed by members; current if produced at the time. If members disagree about one person's contributions the evidence may not be sufficient and other evidence may be needed.

See Chapter 17 'Reflecting on your learning and experience (including feedback)' for more on this.

Look in detail at a piece of work you've recently produced and consider the following.

Question	✓
Has every claim you make got evidence for it?	
Can you get evidence for the claims? How? Where from?	
Do you need to remove any claims where you can't find evidence?	
Does the evidence show what you say it shows?	

C9 Extracting the information you need

Having found sources of information, how will you find what you need? You can use some simple techniques that avoid you having to plough through the whole of each item.

Which of the following have you tried?

Techniques	✓
Look at the contents list or menu.	
If it has an abstract, read that.	
If it's a report, read the executive summary.	
Read/view the introduction.	
Read/view the concluding part.	
Read the first and last paragraph of each chapter of a book or of each section.	
Skim read/scan titles; contents page; headings; images; charts and diagrams. Don't read every word/look at everything, but pick up the gist of the information.	
Look at any reviews or descriptions of it (e.g. of images; other visual items)	
What else have you or your friends/colleagues tried?	

Having found a useful item, look at it in more detail and note what's relevant to your task (see Chapter 9 'Making notes').

It's essential to keep on task. The reader/user/assessor won't be impressed by irrelevant information that may confuse or irritate them. If information isn't directly relevant to your task, don't use it. Your reader/user/assessor is looking for quality not quantity.

It might help to make a note of key concepts or ideas and then record information that supports those concepts or ideas.

Example

Key concept/idea	
Global warming is increasing.	
Supporting information	**Details**
Icecaps melting, glaciers retreating.	Include any data on the extent of the problem.
Weather events more extreme, sea levels rising.	Include any theories as to why and the possible effects.

You need to work out how much detail you need to record. Consider the following checklist, for a piece of work you are doing now.

Question	✓
From the information, have you summarised key ideas relevant to your topic?	
Have you noted enough detail to explain each idea?	
Are any sequences or processes important, where you need to be clear about each stage? If so, have you noted enough detail about the stages?	
What's essential (if you note too much detail, you might get bogged down)?	
Will you be able to follow your notes about the information in a few weeks time?	
Have you noted all the information you need so you won't have to revisit the source?	

C10 Analysing and evaluating information

Analysing information is about breaking it down into its component parts. What are the main points it covers?

Example

The original	Main points
'Employers want to know that you will be able to use your knowledge or your intelligence at work. They are keen to recruit people who can write and talk effectively, who can work well with others, who can solve unforeseen problems and learn new things quickly.' (Drew and Bingham, 2001, p. 2)	Employers want to recruit people who can use what they know and have a range of skills.

Evaluating information is about making judgements. How useful, believable and valid is the information?

These might be questions you would ask about the original statement above.

Example

The original	Questions to ask
'Employers want to know that you will be able to use your knowledge or your intelligence at work. They are keen to recruit people who can write and talk effectively, who can work well with others, who can solve unforeseen problems and learn new things quickly.' (Drew and Bingham, 2001, p. 2)	Who says that is what employers want? What's the evidence? Do all employers want the same thing? Isn't what is 'effective' writing and talking dependent on the situation?

Recognising appropriate evidence and identifying opinion, bias and distortion

Without any evidence to back it up, Drew and Bingham's claim above is just an opinion. In this case, there's a lot of evidence of what employers say they want (e.g. survey results; analyses of employers' recruitment literature). You need to give appropriate (valid, authentic, sufficient, current) evidence for your own claims and to evaluate any information provided by others, to make sure it's based on evidence (e.g. for a journal article reporting on research, what was the researcher's evidence and how was it collected; if you're reading about a theory, what evidence is it based on?).

What sort of issues should you consider about the information you use?

You need to ask questions about validity, sufficiency, authenticity and currency of evidence so you can judge how trustworthy information is (see Section C8).

You could to consider when information was produced (there might be new evidence or information since then).

Might the person (or organisation) producing the information be biased or have a reason for making something look better, or worse, than it is (i.e. a 'vested interest')? For example, it's in the interests of the government in power to make their actions look effective, while it's in the interests of opposition parties to make it look less effective. This is another issue in considering if a source is reputable or trustworthy.

One way that bias might emerge is if information is missed out, distorted or exaggerated. We could tell you that 50 per cent of authors don't like chocolate. Really? Once you know that this is based on the sample of the two authors of this book, one of whom likes chocolate and the other doesn't, it changes things a lot (note: you shouldn't use percentages with very small samples).

You may need to interpret evidence to see what it 'means'. Let's imagine a group with five people, where each person provides a statement about the effectiveness of each of the other four. If for one person none of the four statements agree, what might that 'mean'? Possibilities are: personal likes or dislikes between people; each has worked with the individual in different ways; the individual behaved in different ways with different people. You need more evidence to find out what it does 'mean'. See Section C6 in Chapter 17 'Reflecting on your learning and experience (including feedback)' for more on this.

Here are some questions you might ask when looking at information

Questions to ask when critiquing information	✓
Are there opinions/claims with no evidence?	
What evidence is the information based on?	
Is there any reason why the source of information might be biased?	
Is there any missing information or distortions?	
Is the source of information reputable?	
When was the information produced?	
Is the evidence that the information is based on valid, authentic, current and sufficient (see Section C8)?	
What else do you need to ask, in your subject area or for your task?	

Comparing information

You often need to look at the same information from different sources and compare what they say. For an information task you need to do now, consider the following.

Possible questions	Notes
Do the different items say the same thing? What is it?	
Do they say different or contradictory things? What?	
Where does the weight of opinion lie? What do most items agree on?	

Possible questions	Notes
Do any items suggest asking further questions of an original item (e.g. what evidence it was based on)?	
Which items seem the most trustworthy (e.g. based on evidence; reputable source)?	
Is there any difference over time (e.g. did people do something 5 years ago, but now do something else)?	
In what other ways can you compare the items for your subject and task?	

C11 Using your information

For more help, look at the chapters on presenting information in this book.

- Chapter 1 'Writing essays and dissertations.

- Chapter 2 'Writing reports'.

- Chapter 3 'Producing portfolios and journals (including diaries, blogs, etc.)'.

- Chapter 4 'Giving a presentation, viva or being observed'.

- Chapter 10 'Presenting your work; making it look good'.

Whatever you're producing, you need to pull it together in a way that makes sense to the reader/user/assessor. This means sorting information into themes and making it clear how all that information relates to that theme.

You may be asked to do a literature review. This isn't a book review, which looks at one book, describing its contents, appearance and so on. A literature review is a formal piece of work pulling together ideas/information from various sources, usually organised by theme (e.g. for a literature review on global warming, you might have paragraphs on: who's said what about its causes; effects on sea levels and who said that; on changing weather patterns and who said that). All work mentioned needs a reference (see Chapter 8 'Plagiarism and referencing').

You may be asked to do an annotated bibliography. Here you give the details about each item as you would in a list of references (see Chapter 8) but beneath each item you give notes indicating what it's about.

Here are some **ways of confusing people**. Try to **avoid** them!

- Have an introduction or a literature review that is about one thing and the rest of the work is about something else.

- Have information from lots of different items and don't put it into themes.

- Have information that's contradictory without commenting on the contradictions.

C12 Review: improving things for next time

Every time you seek out and use information or evidence you learn how to do it better. What will you do the same or differently next time?

Activity	This is what I'll repeat/do the same in future	This is what I'll do differently
Clarifying the task and what is needed.		
Planning my information search.		
Finding enough of the right sources of information/evidence.		
Analysing and evaluating information/evidence.		
Recording information/ evidence.		
Presenting information/ evidence.		
Referencing.		

ENHANCED SKILLS

E1 Planning an extended information search

Towards their end, undergraduate courses often have a major project or dissertation taking a semester or a year. Postgraduate courses have even more emphasis on this type of work and full-time PhD studies have at least 3 years of it (many more if it's part-time). All have something in common; it's 'self-directed' and it depends on information/evidence. You decide what to find out and how. You may end up knowing more about your topic than the lecturers, even at undergraduate level.

Many jobs involve large scale projects, often involving team work, that depend on using information/evidence. At work, if you lead a project, you'll also need to direct it and may become more expert in the topic than your managers.

A key reason why extended studies are part of courses is to help students show their learning and understanding and develop skills in locating and using information/ evidence, with limited direction from tutors. You'll continue to seek their advice and guidance, but it's much more up to you. This is also a preparation for work.

For extended pieces of work, in HE or at work, you must plan ahead really well; look back at Section C4 that considers planning. The principles it covers apply no matter what level you're operating at. Here are additional aspects to consider and build in.

Consideration	Implications
Identify your topic and focus as early as possible.	If you spend too long on this you may not leave enough time for the work. It might be better to have a less than ideal topic than have an ideal one with no time left to do it justice.
Choose a topic where you'll be able to find information.	As soon as you've an idea for a topic, do an initial search to see what existing information there is. If it's going to be too difficult to find, it may be better to have a different topic.
As you find more information/ evidence you may want to change your focus.	This is normal. One reason for looking for information is to help refine your ideas. Allow time for a change of direction.
You need very good recording systems.	You'll handle much more information for this sort of study, so make sure your recording systems can handle it. In 6 months time, how easy will it be to find your notes on an item?
Writing up or designing your final presentation will take a long time.	Think of a length of time and double it. Then add time on again for proof reading and checking. Finish your information search in time to allow for this.
What else? Ask tutors/ mentors/managers for advice.	

E2 Being efficient

There's a lot of work to do in any extended study. It'll really pay off to be as organised as possible and to make your search as efficient as possible.

You'll have already worked out ways of doing things that seem effective for you. It might help to note them down. What else can you consider? Here are some thoughts.

Effective strategies	Ideas/thoughts
Learn early on how to use search engines and databases.	Ask for guidance (e.g. from your library/learning centre). Make notes on how to use search engines/databases in case you forget.
Find out who can give good guidance and advice...	... and then ask them (but don't overburden them; you'll need their goodwill); see Chapter 13 'Dealing with other people'.
Develop a useable record system with an easy way of finding items.	Simple is good; computers can save time (e.g. cut and paste references). See Chapter 9 'Making notes'.
Don't be afraid to discard what you don't need.	... even if it took ages to find.
Only look at an item once.	Make notes of all the information you need so you won't need to go back to the item; see Chapter 9 'Making notes'.
Store notes on each item separately...	... you may need to use an item for more than one purpose.
What else?	

E3 Using primary sources

A **primary source** is the original evidence. A **secondary source** is something that is based on original evidence.

Examples

Secondary	*Primary*
A book about land ownership in medieval England.	*Parish records.*
A report on student satisfaction with their courses.	*Questionnaires from students.*
A journal article that discusses different findings about a topic.	*Each piece of research discussed.*

You'll probably need to use primary sources (e.g. from interviews; observations; experiments; surveys). One issue is making sure you can access information/evidence. Who's the 'keeper' of it? Will they let you have it and why might they be worried about that? How easy is it going to be to get it? For example, in the field of education, it's easier to get data from current students than past ones; for vocational education, it may be easier to contact students than employers.

Confidentiality may be an issue. You may need to assure the anonymity of the source (e.g. if you interview people or use questionnaires, you'll need to ensure individuals aren't identifiable). You may need permission from people to use information and they may want to check how you have used it.

There can be ethical issues in collecting primary information, and some subjects (e.g. health) have an ethics committee that gives approval to gather it. Check this with your tutor/manager/mentor. The bottom line is that in gathering information or evidence from people, it mustn't damage them and you need their informed consent (i.e. they know why you need the information and how you'll use it).

So with primary data/sources:

- can you have access to it?

- do you need somebody else to give you some of their time and if so, will they?

- who needs to approve it?

- are there any confidentiality/anonymity issues?

- are there any ethical issues?

Section C7 in Chapter 5 'Doing a project' gives some methods of enquiry for collecting information/evidence but you'll find lots of books on research and evaluation methods (e.g. questionnaires), some related to specific subjects (e.g. in education, Cohen and Manion, 2007).

Most books on research or evaluation methods cover analysis as well as collection methods and some look only at how to analyse it (e.g. using primary sources in history, Dobson and Ziemann 2009). If you can't find something within your own subject area, books on other subjects might help (e.g. Dobson and Ziemann look at analysing diaries from a historical viewpoint, but some aspects may be relevant to other disciplines too).

E4 Critical analysis

Review Section C10. You must make sure you ask those sorts of questions of any information, but at a higher level you need to be even more critical. By now, you should be more aware of key things to look out for in your subject area.

At higher levels you also...	What to consider	*Examples*
question assumptions.	What's the basic assumption that lies behind the information? It can be difficult to identify assumptions because of their nature, e.g. an assumption is something that isn't usually questioned.	*Theories of adult learning assume adults learn differently from children.* *Theories of learning assume that it's possible to generalise about how people learn.*
identify uncertainties or ambiguities.	Are there any uncertainties? Is there any missing information that might change the interpretation? Is there anything that we can't possibly know? Could something be interpreted in differently? What other views could there be?	*Health risks that seem related to diet really may be related to socio-economic factors.* *Physicists theorise about 'dark matter' but to date it hasn't been identified.*
identify the limits of the information.	What does and doesn't it tell you? Does it tell you how something is but not why?	*An opinion poll that tells you current voting preferences may not indicate reasons for them.*
avoid making assumptions.	It's easy, and dangerous, to assume something without evidence.	*If questionnaire respondents say a numeracy course does not meet their expectations, you might assume that's bad. But what if they had bad expectations and it's a good course? You'd need to also ask what their expectations were.*

E5 Synthesising information

Synthesising information is about seeing the absolute essentials and the key ideas that underpin them. It's the process of combining different ideas/influences/objects into a new whole. You pull together two or more different items of information/ideas, to create a new view/idea. It isn't just a summary of the information.

For example

Analysing cakes would involve identifying all the ingredients used in them.

Evaluating them would involve judging them in some way (e.g. by taste; texture; visual appeal).

Synthesising them would involve taking the ingredients from two or more cakes and combining them to make a new and different cake.

Once you've presented information you've collected, it can be very helpful for the audience/reader if you then synthesise it and show how it relates to your topic.

E6 Review: improving things for next time

Each time you seek and use information you learn to do it better. What will you do the same or differently next time?

Activity	This is what I'll repeat/do the same in future	This is what I'll do differently
Planning an extended information search.		
Being efficient.		
Using primary sources.		
Critical analysis.		
Synthesis.		
What else?		

REFERENCES

Cohen, L., Manion, L. and Morrison, K., (2000), *Research methods in education*, 5th edn, London: Routledge Falmer.

Dobson, M., Ziemann, B., (2009), *Reading primary sources: the interpretation of texts from nineteenth- and twentieth-century history*, Abingdon: Routledge.

Thompson, D. (Editor), (1996), *The Oxford compact English dictionary*, Oxford: Oxford University Press.

8
PLAGIARISM AND REFERENCING

HOW THIS CHAPTER CAN HELP YOU

The 'crucial skills' part of this chapter aims to help you to:

- identify what's meant by plagiarism;
- avoid plagiarism;
- identify the essential elements of referencing materials produced by others;
- correctly use referencing conventions.

There is no 'enhanced skills' part of this chapter.

CRUCIAL SKILLS

C1 Why is this chapter important?

Plagiarism means using somebody else's work without acknowledging it.

Plagiarism is a real 'sin' in academic settings (it might be compared to somebody who works with other people's money stealing it!). If you do it deliberately, it's called cheating because you're representing someone else's work as your own. It can have very serious results. Universities/colleges/other examining bodies (e.g. professional ones) have clear rules about this and about what happens to those caught out. Check the rules where you're studying.

Most people don't mean to cheat but may do so without realising it; not everybody understands what is, and what isn't, plagiarism.

A key way of avoiding plagiarism is to correctly 'reference' everything you mention that's the work of somebody else, or whose work has influenced your thinking. There are standard ways of doing this and you just need to follow the format; it's quite easy. In fact it's so easy that it can irritate the reader (e.g. an assessor) if you don't do it correctly.

Avoiding plagiarism and acknowledging the work of others is also important in any tasks in employment where you use information or do investigations or research and present the results to others (e.g. market research; reports on projects or investigations).

Why should you give citations and references? They help:

- show you've read/viewed a range of work and ideas to inform your own work;

- provide evidence for your thinking and ideas;

- give credit to those whose work you've used.

This chapter explains what counts as plagiarism, looks at how to avoid it and explains what's important in referencing others' work and gives guidance on how to do it.

C2 Other chapters you need to use together with this one

This chapter is important for any others that refer to producing work, e.g. essays/dissertations, reports, journals/diaries/portfolios/blogs, giving presentations and so on. It's particularly important to look at the following chapters.

Chapter	Title	How it relates to this chapter	Page
7	Finding, using and analysing information and evidence.	You must reference any information/ideas created by others (including films, art works etc) you use in your work.	147
9	Making notes.	You need to note all details required for references when making notes on anybody else's material.	187
10	Presenting your work: making it look good.	There are standard ways of providing the details for references that you must follow.	205

C3 What is plagiarism and how to avoid it

Some key issues

If you mention anything that others have written, produced or created, or which has influenced your work, you **must** acknowledge them. If you don't, you're plagiarising (i.e. stealing somebody else's work).

There are current concerns about this in higher education (HE) and among other examining bodies, as the web has made it easier for people to cheat by deliberately copying other people's work. We're assuming that this is not the case for you. Most people plagiarise because they don't realise what it means or that they're doing it.

Some assessors are so concerned about plagiarism (cheating) that they use special software to identify it. There's an increasing focus on assessment methods that make it difficult to plagiarise (e.g. exams; each student producing a piece that's individual to them rather than having one set topic/question for a whole group).

In HE you must use the work of others. Chapter 7 'Finding, using and analysing information and evidence' is pivotal for this book because the starting point for any academic work (or a project/investigation in employment) is to find out what's already been done. You generally base your thinking and ideas on what's gone before (excluding some sorts of creative work).

You therefore must use existing material but you don't just repeat it. You analyse and interpret (make sense of) it in relation to your topic (this applies to images as well as information). At the minimum, you paraphrase it (put it in your own words), to show you understand it. You may summarise it (pick out the key points or aspects). At more sophisticated levels you need to critique (question) it.

What is plagiarism?

Plagiarism is usually pretty easy to spot. For example, in a written piece of work you may suddenly get a section written in a different style; you may suddenly get ideas expressed at a far more sophisticated level than in the rest of the work; you may (as a tutor) know the original; several students may separately have used the same item. Given the possible penalties (check with your university/college/professional body), avoid it at all costs.

It's plagiarism if:

- you repeat exactly what somebody else has written, said, produced or created, without saying whose work it is;

- you describe somebody else's work without saying whose work it is, even if you don't repeat it exactly;

- if you reword something slightly or produce a design or creative item that's almost the same as that produced by somebody else, without acknowledging the original;

- you don't acknowledge work that influenced you (see below).

A few years ago, one of the authors was surprised to be shown some resources that she'd developed for internal use in her own University, presented as if somebody in another University had developed them. Imagine her surprise!

What sort of 'work' do we mean?

Basically, you must acknowledge all ideas and words (spoken, written) and visuals. Some of the common types of items that must be acknowledged are:

books	brochures/leaflets	photos	radio/TV programmes
journals/magazines	maps	poster	music (live or recorded)
reports	presentations	website	audio/podcasts
lecture notes	diagrams	sculptures	CDs/DVDs
internal documents	designs	paintings	films/videos
conference papers	emails	installations	phone conversations
unpublished theses	letters	adverts	face-to-face conversations
poems/stories	texts		Acts of parliament

It doesn't include things that are 'common knowledge' (e.g. 1066, the Battle of Hastings).

The only safe thing to do, if you've used anybody else's work at all, for any purpose, is to acknowledge it by giving it a correct reference.

This is what you do to avoid plagiarism

- If you use somebody's exact words you must put the words in quotation marks and give a 'citation' after the quote (see Section C4 for an explanation).

- If you use an image or design, or anything that exactly reproduces what somebody else has created, you must give a 'citation' at the point where you present it (see Section C4 for an explanation).

- If you refer to somebody's words, ideas, image or work without reproducing it exactly you must give a 'citation' at the point where you refer to it.

- If you use most of somebody else's words, ideas, image or work, changing it slightly, you must give a 'citation' at the point you do so. You don't need to use quotation marks unless you exactly use their words. However, changing slightly what somebody else did is not good practice and it's safer to either reproduce it exactly or to paraphrase or describe it. Whatever you do, you must still give a 'citation'.

- At the end of your piece of work (e.g. written; visual; portfolio; report; presentation) you give a list of all the references you've cited. This tells the user where to find the originals.

- Don't 'cut and paste' from any other sources and use it as if it's yours.

Next, we refer to the 'text' you've written, but the same principles apply to all types of work.

Checking your work

Have you got a citation and reference for...	✓
every name that appears in your work, where that 'name' has produced something?	
every item produced by somebody else mentioned in your work (see our list of items above)?	
any sources of statistics or numerical or factual information (you can't just give this without saying where it came from)?	
any quotations (even famous ones)?	

C4 What's a 'citation' and what's a 'reference'?

At the end of any piece of your work, you must give a list of **references** to the work of others that you've mentioned or used. You give enough details to enable the reader/observer/user to find the originals.

In your own text/work, at the point where you refer to somebody else's work, you give brief information to enable the reader (or user) to find the item in the list of references at the end: this is a '**citation**'.

For example, this is a **reference**:

> Drew, S. and Bingham R., (2001), *The Student Skills Guide*, 2nd edition, Aldershot: Gower.

This is an example of a **citation** for the above item.

> One skills guide is at two levels, a level for those new to higher education and one for those further into their courses (Drew and Bingham, 2001)

In a list of references organised using the Harvard system (see Section C5), a citation giving the surname of the author and date of publication is enough to find the item in the list of references.

Further examples are in Section C5.

C5 How to make a list of references

There are two main ways of making a list of references:

- the Harvard system;
- the Numeric system.

You use one or the other, not both together. Whoever you're producing the work for will specify which is needed. Harvard is very common (although there are different versions of it, so you need to check which you should use; the following guidance gives a brief overview of the most commonly used one). There are many books/on line resources with more details.

Harvard referencing (overview)

Here, the order of the items in the list of references is:

- alphabetical order by last name/family name;
- then, alphabetical order by initial in the name;
- then, date of publication/production.

This applies to all items regardless of their nature (e.g. journals; web addresses; Acts of Parliament; sculptures). They all go in the list of references in alphabetical order by author (or creator).

So, if there are four items by authors, D. Brown, G. Brown and two called E. Green, where one item by E. Green was published in 2000 and one in 2005, the order would be:

Brown, D. (it would appear here regardless of date of publication)

Brown, G. (likewise)

Green, E. (2000)

Green, E. (2005)

If an item has more than one author, it goes by order of the first author listed on the item (i.e. Drew, S. and Bingham, R: this would go in a list of references at the point for 'D').

If you refer to more than one item by an author published in the same year, then in the list of references you give each item a letter to differentiate between them. For example:

Bingham, R. (2000a)

Bingham, R. (2000b)

Bingham, R. (2000c)

In the Harvard system, each citation gives the author's last name and the year of production (e.g. Drew and Bingham, 2001), no matter what type of item (e.g. including on-line). The reader/user will then be able to find the full details in the list of references.

So, all you need in the citation is the surname and date of publication, unless:

- there are two authors in the list of references with the same surname (only where there's more than one author with the same surname, does the initial go in the citation).

- one author has more than one publication in the same year, in which case you also put in the citation the letter you've given it in the list of references, e.g. Bingham, R. (2000b).

Numeric referencing (overview)

In this system, the items in the list of references go in the order in which you mention them in your own text/work and you give each item a number. So the first item you mention is 1, the second is 2 and so forth.

If, later on in your work, you refer again to the same item, you don't renumber it. If it was item 1 and you cite it right at the end of your work again, it's still 1. From that number, your user can find details of the item.

For the citation, at the point in your text where you mention the item, you give the number of the item, usually in brackets. So if you had given Drew and Bingham's book the number 4 in the list of references you would put (4) at the point where you mention it. Some use 'superscript', that is little numbers (e.g. 'in their skills book, Drew and Bingham[4] state that...' or 'in one skills book[4], guidance is at two levels').

C6 The format for citations and for each item in a list of references

Items in a list of references follow a set format. You must find out what the format is for the type of item you're using (e.g. a film; a report; a poem; an Act of parliament).

Check before you start looking for information what referencing details you need for the type of item you're using, so you can accurately record them as you find them. It's a real pain to have to go back to an item later to find the details.

Your university/college library/learning centre should have a guide to referencing. You could look at the format used in journals in your subject. There may be slightly different interpretations of a system (e.g. Harvard), so find out any particular requirements for your subject, your tutor or professional body or a journal where you want to publish something.

The bottom line is you need enough information to find an item. Some examples are shown in the next paragraphs.

For a **book reference**, you need (it will be all on the first page of the book):

- Author(s) or editor(s).
- Year of publication.

- Title, in italics (to show it is the title).

- Edition, if relevant (e.g. 3rd edn; revised edn).

- Location of publisher.

- Name of publisher.

> Drew, S. and Bingham, R., (2001), *The Student Skills Guide*, 2nd edition, Aldershot: Gower.

For a **journal article reference**, you need:

- Author(s) or editor(s).

- Title of article, in inverted commas.

- Title of journal, in italics.

- Volume of journal.

- Number.

- Date of publication.

- Page numbers of article (e.g. 123–147).

> Drew, S., Thorpe, L., Bannister, P., 'Key Skills Computerised Assessments: guiding principles', in *Assessment and Evaluation in Higher Education*, vol. 27, no. 2, 2002, 175–186.

For an **on-line** item, you need:

- Author (this may be the organisation owning the website).

- Date (date of the actual item; sometimes it might be the date the site was last updated).

- Title of the item, in italics.

- URL.

- Date when accessed (because websites change rapidly, it's important to know this).

> QAA (2008) Framework for higher education qualifications in England, Wales and Northern Ireland, on-line at http://www.qaa.ac.uk, last accessed 27.9.08.

We've given below some of the more common items you'll need to cite and reference, with examples. You must find out the details of the referencing requirement in your subject area, as space here limits the information we can give.

The following *examples* use the Harvard method of giving citations

Item	Citation: example	Reference	Notes
Book/journal article; an item with two authors.	Drew and Bingham (2001) developed skills guides at two levels, including a level for those new to higher education.	Drew, S., Bingham, R., (2001), *The Student Skills Guide*, 2nd edition, Aldershot: Gower.	If the author's name is a naturally occurring part of the sentence, it isn't in brackets but the date is.
Book/journal article; an item with more than two authors.	Diagnostic tests should lead to the provision of support (Drew et al, 2002).	Drew, S., Thorpe, L., Bannister, P., 'Key Skills Computerised Assessments: guiding principles', in *Assessment and Evaluation in Higher Education*, vol. 27, no. 2, 2002, 175–186.	If the citation isn't a natural part of the sentence, it goes in brackets at the end of it. Give the name of the first author followed by 'et al'. In the list of references give the full list of authors.
On-line; with a named author.	Drew et al (2007) produced a website giving the results of research into electronic portfolios.	Drew, S., Stevens, A., Haughton, P., (2007), *Electronic PDPs for Art, Design and Media. Project website.* Centre for Research and Evaluation, Sheffield Hallam University, on-line at http://www.shu.ac.uk/research/cre/epdphome, last accessed 24.09.08.	You include the title of the item in your list of reference, not just the URL. The URL isn't given in the citation but it is in the reference. You have to give the date when you accessed it.
Electronic source, where the 'author' is an organisation hosting the website.	QAA (2008) has a framework for higher education qualifications.	QAA (2008) *Framework for higher education qualifications in England, Wales and Northern Ireland*, on-line at http://www.qaa.ac.uk, last accessed 27.9.08.	As above. You need the title of the item in the reference to be able to find it in a large website.
A direct quote (or image).	'Ideally, lecturers and tutors will tell students what they will be looking for …' (Drew and Bingham, 2001, p2).	Drew, S., Bingham, R., (2001), *The Student Skills Guide*, 2nd edition, Aldershot: Gower.	Give the page number where it can be found in the original in the citation. The page number does not go in the list of references.
On-line; direct quote, but no page number.	'The project aimed to inform colleagues about models of visual, electronic PDPs in order to stimulate practice and debate.' (Drew et al, 2007, on-line).	Drew, S, Stevens, A, Haughton, P., (2007), *Electronic PDPs for Art, Design and Media. Project website.* Centre for Research and Evaluation, Sheffield Hallam University, on-line at http://www.shu.ac.uk/research/cre/epdphome, last accessed 24.09.08.	For a website without page numbers, put 'on-line' instead of a page number. A pdf probably will have page numbers.

Our best advice is to find out what the format is for whatever sort of item you're using and follow it exactly! Keep examples of them so you can follow them in future.

Presenting referencing details

In your referenced items have you...	✓
checked that you know the correct format for the type of item?	
followed this correct format exactly?	
included any essential information needed by the user to find the item?	

Checking your work

In your citations have you...	✓
used only surname (or organisation) and date (unless there is more than one author with the same surname)?	
avoided using URLs?	
given page numbers where direct quotes (or images) originally appeared?	
used brackets correctly?	
used the same format consistently?	

C7 What's the difference between a list of references and a bibliography?

A list of references just has the items you mentioned in your text/work. A bibliography also has other items that are relevant to the topic but which you do not mention in your text/work. It would include items that have influenced your thinking.

An 'annotated bibliography' is one where you include notes about each item. In this case you need to check what's required. A normal bibliography that appears at the end of a piece of work would not have notes about the items, but would just list them.

A webliography is the digital equivalent of a bibliography. It would include all the links to items you'd either referred to, or which had influenced your work. This would be if you **only** have on-line items. If you have a mix of types of item (e.g. paper based/on-line/media; books; journals; films) then you usually have a bibliography that includes them all (if using Harvard, organised by author).

C8 Common difficulties and mistakes

Common difficulties

- An on-line item may not have an author but may be part of an organisation's website. In this case the 'author' is the organisation hosting the website.

- An on-line item may not have a date. There may (at the bottom of the website) be a date when the site was last updated. If so, use that.

- If an item (on-line or otherwise) has no date, then put 'undated' where the date should go in the reference.

- Government reports are often known by the name of the chairperson of the group producing them, but that person may not be the author. For example, for the 'Dearing report' into HE the author is not Dearing but The National Committee of Enquiry into Higher Education (1996). You need to check the original to see who the author is.

Common errors in citations using the Harvard system

You need to **avoid these**.

- Giving the author's initial as well as the surname (unless there are two authors with the same surname).

- Giving more details as well as the surname and date of publications (they aren't needed).

- Giving a URL for an on-line item (you only need the name and date of publication).

- Not giving citations to some sorts of items (e.g. Acts of parliament; novels; internal documents): everything you mention must have a citation.

Common errors in lists of references

You need to **avoid these**.

- Giving a URL without any other information, so that the reader/user doesn't know which item you want them to look at or when it was produced or when you saw it; e.g:

  http://www.qaa.ac.uk

- For an on-line item, not giving the date when you accessed it (if it was long ago, it may no longer be there).

- Putting a list of URLs at the end of the list of references, rather than putting each item in its naturally occurring place (i.e. in alphabetical order by 'author' for Harvard or in order of appearance in your work for Numeric).

- Not giving references for some sorts of items (e.g. Acts of parliament; novels; internal documents): everything you mention must have a reference.

- Having inconsistent information between references (e.g. having place of publication in some items but not in others).

- Not following the normal presentation format (e.g. if you don't either put in italics or underline the title of an item, it can be hard to see it).

Suggestion. If you see a format for an item in a publication (e.g. in a journal), save it and use it as the basis for similar items that you may want to reference. You could end up with a list of the common formats you need for your subject area.

C9 Improving what you do

What actions do you need to take to improve your referencing and remove risks of plagiarism?

Issue	Notes: actions needed
Checking out the regulations on plagiarism in my university, college, examining/professional body.	
Finding out what referencing conventions are needed in my subject/course.	
Finding examples of how to reference the sorts of items I need to use.	
Finding out what's needed if I have to make an annotated bibliography.	

Issue	Notes: actions needed
Checking any work I produce, of any type, to make sure I have cited and referenced everything mentioned.	
Checking any work I produce, of any type, to ensure I've used the correct citing and referencing formats.	

9
MAKING NOTES

HOW THIS CHAPTER CAN HELP YOU

The 'crucial skills' part of this chapter aims to help you to:

- make notes in a range of situations (e.g. from: books; web; lectures; images; recordings; meetings), including those that might be assessed;
- identify the purpose of your notes;
- and so choose appropriate methods for taking them;
- choose and use a style that suits you, the purpose and subject;
- organise and store your notes;
- select and record information;
- check and proof-read your notes so you (and others) can understand and use them;
- identify how to improve your note taking.

The 'enhanced skills' part of this chapter is shorter: it helps you operate to a higher level. As well as all the 'crucial skills' outcomes, you'll be able to:

- identify the best possible result you want from the notes;
- choose and adapt your note taking to allow for this;
- ensure you (and others) can understand and use your notes over an extended period (e.g. for a dissertation or project);
- note information that particularly shows your grasp of the topic and helps you question it;
- note ways of illustrating points (e.g. examples; ideas; connections);
- critically review what you did to improve what you do in the future.

CRUCIAL SKILLS

C1 Why is this chapter so important?

Virtually any work you do in higher education (HE) or the workplace will involve taking notes. This may seem a basic skill but that doesn't mean it's easy. It's well worth reviewing what you do.

What sort of notes might you need to make?

	✓		✓
Lecture notes.		Lab notes.	
Notes on information you read.		Notes on ideas you have.	
Notes on what you did/how you did it.		Notes on actions you need to take.	
Notes on what you agreed with others.		Notes on what others agree to do.	
Field notes.		Minutes of meetings.	
Notes of images.		Notes of performances.	
Revision notes.		Feedback from others.	
Notes of a legal/formal nature (e.g. hand-in slips for work; marks/grades; for appeals/extensions).		*What else?*	

Taking good notes makes your work better and it saves a lot of time (you can waste hours looking again at things you didn't make good notes about). Inaccurate notes may mean you get something wrong or misunderstand it. You also may need to store notes that others have made (Section C3 has examples, such as medical notes).

Here are some principles:

- it's better to spend time now noting something than to need it later and not have it;
- it saves time if you have a system that helps you find notes quickly;
- you may need to make sense of notes a long time after you made them.

If this chapter mentions ways of doing things on a computer that aren't familiar to you, your university/college should have ICT support where you can get advice and in a workplace colleagues may help, especially those in technical roles.

C2 Other chapters you need to use together with this one

It will help to use this chapter with **every** other chapter in this book.

Chapter	Title	How it relates to this chapter	Page
7	Finding, using and analysing information and evidence.	Taking notes of information is essential.	147
12	Working in a group or team.	You need minutes/notes of meetings and what was agreed.	253

Chapter	Title	How it relates to this chapter	Page
3	Producing portfolios and journals (including diaries, blogs, etc.).	Notes may form an essential part of the evidence for a portfolio.	49
	All other chapters.	You need to note what you plan to do, what you've done, achievements, etc.	

C3 What's the purpose of your notes?

This is a really important question as it determines what you need to make a note of and how. Here are some idea starters.

Possible purpose	Possible types of notes	Why it's important
To have records of what happened in relation to formal requirements.	Hand-in slips for assignments. Marks, grades, modules studied. Other qualifications/courses. Feedback received. Sick notes or evidence of any personal difficulties.	In case things go astray. For CVs. For Personal/Professional Development Plans (PDP) or Continuing Professional Development (CPD). To monitor actions needed. For procedures needed if you can't submit (or attend) work.
To be able to find a source of information.	Citations; a list of references; a bibliography (e.g. author; date of publication; title). Check what is needed to cite or give a reference for the items you're using.	So you aren't accused of plagiarism. So you follow academic conventions (and don't irritate tutors). So you and anybody else can find sources again.
To record the content of a source of information.	Key ideas/concepts; quotes; images; factual information. For use in an essay; dissertation; report; presentation; project; creative/ design piece.	As evidence. To see what others think/ know. To get different perspectives/ new ideas. To gather factual information.
To help me make sense of information.	Summaries; paraphrasing in your own words.	To check if you understand it. To avoid plagiarism.
For revision/to help me remember.	Summaries; key words; highlights; underlines; cue cards.	To help you learn it. To remind you of key points.
To record what happened in meetings.	Minutes of meetings (e.g. for a group activity or project).	So everybody: has the same information about what was said; knows the action points. To trace how plans developed through meetings.

Possible purpose	Possible types of notes	Why it's important
For assessment (e.g. log/diary; portfolio).	Summaries of your key learning points during an event/activity.	To help you think about what you learned and how.
To take into an exam (e.g. 'open book'; 'seen exam')	Summaries; key points; quotes; images; diagrams. Bullet lists; highlights; underlines.	So you can use your notes effectively. So you have essential information easily accessible.
What else?		

What are the purposes of notes you currently need to keep?

Purpose	Types of notes	Why it's important

Clarification of some terms used in this section

summarise	Briefly give the main points.
paraphrase	Put in your own words.
plagiarise	Pass off somebody's work as your own.
citation	Brief details about the source of information, given in your own text.
list of references	Details helping the reader find a source of information you have mentioned in your work, in a list at the end of your work.
bibliography	Details helping the reader find a source you've used, but which you haven't mentioned in your work: usually in a list at the end of your work.
cue card	Card with a few words that remind you of something.

C4 What do you need to note?

This depends on your purpose. It's also closely linked to the format you'll use (see Section C5).

For something you need to do no, have you taken notes in the past for a similar purpose?

What was good about your notes in the past?	What was not very helpful?	What will you do this time?

Here are some questions to help you think about the information you need to record and some thoughts about the implications.

Question	Implications
What's needed for the assignment?	See Chapter 7 'Finding, using and analysing information and evidence'.
Do you need concepts/ideas/ principles?	You may need to summarise or paraphrase key points.
Do you need factual information?	Your notes will need to be accurate.
Are you likely to need the notes again for another piece of work?	Your recording system needs to make it easy to find the notes again.
Do you need evidence?	Keep notes on aspects that demonstrate something (e.g. a direct quote; an image; statistics).
Will you need to look at the notes after a time lapse?	Avoid abbreviations or 'shorthand' that you may not be able to interpret later. It needs to be legible.
Does anybody else need to use the notes?	Avoid personal abbreviations or 'shorthand' others won't understand. It needs to be legible.
How will you present the results of your work?	You may need to use direct quotes or reproduce images (with the page number where they appear).

Question	Implications
Do you need the original (rather than your own notes)?	You may need to just record how to find it (e.g. the link to something on-line, the Dewey number).
Will you just quickly glance at the notes (e.g. for a presentation)?	The layout will be important to help you quickly spot things. Use highlights; different fonts; colours.
What is it about the notes that could really mess up your work?	Possibilities are: inaccuracy; irrelevancies; having to search for information again; losing notes.
How can you avoid plagiarism?	See Chapter 8 'Plagiarism and referencing'.

Using computers can really help in note taking, particularly if you want to cut and paste quotes or images into your work (acknowledged of course! See Chapter 8 'Plagiarism and referencing'). It'll also help you to use or find notes again; for example, the authors of this book keep using key texts for different pieces of work and have the references in a well-organised computer folder.

C5 Organising your notes

The critical question is: how will you want to search for the notes? What will best help you find them again? This will depend on your purpose and what's important to you.

Possibilities are:

- by name of author;
- by type of notes (e.g. minutes);
- by subject (e.g. psychology);
- by topic (e.g. child development);
- by concept (e.g. global warming);
- by date;
- by assignment title;
- by module title.

You could record an item under more than one heading (easy with a computer, by saving it with a new file name or cutting and pasting into an existing file).

You may store some items physically and keep others on a computer

If you store items physically you might consider how bulky they are, but possibilities are as follows:

- shelves for books;

- box files;

- ring binders with coloured dividers;

- an individual note book per topic;

- note books with sections;

- note books in date order;

- concertina files;

- cards in a card box.

Whatever you store on a computer, make sure you back it all up. Possibilities for organising how you store them are:

- in a folder with overarching folders and sub folders;

- using different applications to store different types of items (e.g. word processing package; database; desktop publishing/photo manipulation software);

- making a template to use for similar items, to save you time;

- keeping an ongoing list of references you continually update;

- putting links from your list of references to the notes on the item (if your computer skills are up to it).

Keep an index so you know what sorts of things you've put where.

Whatever you do, be consistent. If you aren't, you'll get mixed up

For example, if you record alphabetically by author you need to always put the surname first. If you don't, you could end up looking in the wrong place: if you sometimes record the work of Rosie Bingham by her surname and sometimes by her first name or initial, you could be looking under R or B.

If you use a computer, it's a good idea to give an item a filename that will mean something to you at a later date; for example 'DB1' won't mean as much to you as 'Drew Bingham Skills Book 2001'.

'Version control' is a very good idea, giving successive drafts a name that tells you which version it is; for example file names on a computer might be:

'minutesOct15thmeetingdraft1', 'minutesOct15thmeetingdraft2'.

C6 The format of your notes

This will depend on your purpose, the situation in which you take notes and your personal preferences for what you find helpful.

C6.1 Taking notes whilst something is happening

Examples of such situations include lectures, seminars, fieldnotes (e.g. notes of observations), meetings, labs or workshops.

You'll need to react quickly and to have materials that are easy to use. If you need to know exactly what was said (e.g. in an interview), you could use a tape/video recorder (but ask the person's permission first). Usually it's key in such situations to note what's important and to miss out the rest. This means you need to know what's important and what isn't. How can you work this out?

This is something you get better at, as you become familiar with the topic. You could:

- read about it in advance so you have some idea of what to expect;
- swap notes with somebody to see what they've noted (but not if this puts you in danger of being accused of cheating);
- check with the person leading a session what they're going to cover;
- ask a speaker to explain something you didn't catch or understand;
- agree with others (e.g. people in a meeting) what sort of things to note;
- look at your notes afterwards to make sure you understand them;
- ask others to check your notes; for example formal meetings begin by 'agreeing the minutes' of the previous meeting (all present say whether or not the minutes are accurate).

What sorts of materials are easily used in such situations? Clip boards can provide a firm surface, as can hard backed note books or ring binders. Ring bound note books are small and easy to use. If others involved don't mind, you could use a lap top (but ask permission).

Will you use the notes as they are or will they be a basis for more permanent notes? Whatever the use, they need to be in a form that means you can store them.

C6.2 Agenda and Minutes of meetings

These have a common format.

Agenda (the list of what's going to be covered in the meeting)

- title (e.g. name of committee/group/project);

- date of meeting;

- numbered list of points to be discussed;

- any other business (AOB); this is always at the end of an agenda as a 'catch all';

- date of next meeting.

Minutes (i.e. the record of the meeting)

- title (e.g. name of committee/group/project);

- date of meeting;

- attendees (list of those attending, usually in alphabetical order);

- apologies (list of those apologising for not attending);

- numbered items with notes on what was discussed (given in the same order as in the agenda); each item usually ends with 'actions' to record who's doing what;

- AOB (notes on what was talked about under this heading);

- date of next meeting.

Example

Meeting to plan the skills book

Date of meeting: *18.10.08*

Attendees:
   Rosie Bingham
   Sue Drew

Apologies:
   None

Minutes:
1. *There was discussion about how to draft the learning outcomes for the chapters. Action: RB to draft by 25.10.08 and SD to review by 30.10.08* (Note: often initials are used in minutes)
2. *Further discussion about Note taking chapter. Action: SD to write at 2 levels.*

AOB:
   Gower Publishing suggested a meeting. Action: SD to contact.

Date of next meeting: *2.11.08*

You should record minutes accurately, with no personal observations or emotive language. If you're not sure about what to include, ask someone to check them. Sometimes you may be asked 'not to minute that', particularly if there are arguments or something confidential is discussed. This is fine.

C6.3 What if you need to use notes 'on the spot'?

You may need to refer to notes while doing a presentation or in a viva (Chapter 4 'Giving a presentation, viva or being observed'), when you are being interviewed or in the sort of exam where it is permitted to use notes (Chapter 6 'Succeeding with exams (or tests').

In such cases you need to have notes you can just glance at.

- It might help to have key words that remind you of something (e.g. on a cue card).

- Electronic presentations, overhead project slides or other visual aids can double up as your notes (see Chapter 10 'Presenting your work; making it look good').

- Have a layout for notes that's easy to follow (e.g. two columns, the left for key words and the right for more information that you could refer to if need be).

- Use colour to pick out key ideas and information.

- Have your notes in the right order (you may get flustered if you can't find something).

C6.4 Possible formats for notes

Here are some examples. It might also help to ask others how they structure notes. You may be used to doing it in one way but a different way might be much more helpful.

You may need to consider a number of issues in deciding on a format to use. What do you prefer?

- Do you like visuals? If so, you may want to note things in diagrams (see example below) or sketches. You could use colour to pick out different types of items or issues. Can you photocopy complex visuals? What about taking photos?

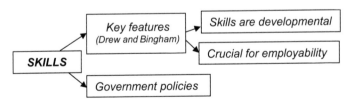

- Do you like sound? Could you record your notes? Some people like listening to revision tapes, for example while driving.

- Do you like things in a logical order? You could have structured notes using a common structure.

Example

Source	Key points
Drew and Bingham, 2009.	Skills are developmental. Crucial for employability.
Government.	Skill development crucial for workforce/international competition. White/green papers from 1980s onwards.

- Do you like variety? You could use different ways of noting the same thing, to help you see if from different angles.

- Are your own thoughts about something important? You could have a margin in which you put your own thoughts. An example is given below.

Example

Notes	My thoughts
Drew and Bingham (2009) say skills are crucial for employability.	Who else says this? Check Government policy.

What's needed for the topic or for the purpose? How might that affect your format?

Topic	Purpose of the notes	Format that's appropriate for topic/purpose	Format that I personally like to use	Format that I will use

C7 Selecting and noting information

You need to go back to your purpose and the instructions or guidance for a task. The key thing is to note what's relevant. It's easy to get interested in what you're looking at and go off at a tangent. This might be OK, for example, if the purpose of note taking is to gather ideas for creative work, but often it'll waste time and lead to producing unfocussed work.

Some questions you might ask yourself concerning material (written/visual/audio) you're making notes about are suggested below.

- What are the key ideas in this material that relate to my task/topic/purpose?

- What evidence is there in the material for those key ideas (e.g. facts; statistics; quotes; visuals)?

- Is there a sequence I need to note (e.g. order in which an experiment is carried out; stages in solving a problem; date order)?

- If I miss out a stage in the sequence, will it mean I won't understand it later on?

- How much detail do I need?

- How many sources of information do I need?

- Will anybody else see my notes? Why, and what effect will it have on what I note?

- Is everything I've noted related to the task/topic/purpose?

Things to beware of (especially for project work) include the following.

- Is any information confidential?

- Do you need permission to use it?

- If you've referred to someone in your notes, would you be happy for them to read it?

- If the information is sensitive, are you storing it somewhere safe?

C8 Checking and proof-reading notes

What sort of things might lead you to say 'I wonder what I meant by that? '

Possible things to make clear in your notes include the meaning of:

- abbreviations or acronyms;

- shortened forms of words (in your notes, does 'con' mean contradictions, contrasts or conservative?);

- specialist terms;

- who named individuals are (e.g. authors; key theorists; researchers).

Try to look at your notes soon after you make them. The following checklist might help you make sure they're as useable as possible.

	✓		✓
Do you understand the ideas/ concepts in your notes?		Have you recorded all the details needed to give a reference?	
Have you missed out any steps in a sequence?		Which items do you need to record as an original?	
Have you recorded details to help you find items again?		Have you missed out any important information?	
Have you recorded direct quotes correctly?		If somebody else is going to use the notes, will they understand them?	
Is the language understandable?		If the notes are going to be assessed, what will get a good mark/grade?	
Are the notes legible?			

C9 Review: improving things for next time

How can you improve your note taking next time round?

Activity	This is what I'll repeat/do the same in future	This is what I'll do differently
Being clear about my purpose.		
Being clear about what I need to note.		
Organising my notes.		

Activity	This is what I'll repeat/do the same in future	This is what I'll do differently
Having useful formats for my notes.		
Selecting and noting information.		
Checking and proof reading my notes.		

ENHANCED SKILLS

E1 What do you really want from the notes?

What current tasks or situations do you have where you need to make notes, what do you want from these tasks or situations and therefore what do your notes need to do?

For example

Task	What would get a good mark/ grade?	Implications for my note taking
Dissertation based on literature.	Range of sources used. How important the information is for the topic. Grasp/in depth understanding of the topic. Accuracy of the information. Most recent information/ideas. Showing how information links together. My opinions and critique of information/ideas.	Need a regularly updated list of references following Harvard format. Need to mark/highlight really key information. Paraphrasing/summarising ideas/ concepts. Need my own comments/ views on these. Quotes need to be correct with page numbers, factual information/ diagrams and charts needs to be accurate. Record my thoughts/critique in margins of my notes.

Task	What would get a good mark/ grade?	Implications for my note taking
Project involving interviewing people.	Recording what I asked and what they said. Proving they did say that. Showing how I analysed what was said. Relating my findings to other findings/theories/practice.	Need: my list of questions; notes on what they said; to anonymise notes so person/setting not identifiable. Example of notes on an interview to go in an appendix. Notes about how I analysed the interviews with an example. Notes on others' work so I can make connections with my work.

What about the tasks you currently have to do?

Task	What would get a good mark/grade?	Implications for my note taking

E2 Producing notes to meet your needs

Section C5 identified possible formats for your notes. Which would particularly suit the tasks you identified above? Could using a technique you haven't tried before be useful?

New techniques I could try

E3 Note taking for an extended piece of work

You may have a piece of work that's extended in size, scale and the time in which you must complete it (e.g. at the end of an undergraduate course there's often a large piece of work taking a whole semester; on postgraduate courses it can take a year and work projects can be long term).

The suggestions offered in the 'crucial skills' section also apply to an extended task but are even more important and for an extended piece of work the following are critical.

- You should note everything you'll need from an item to avoid having to go back to it. It may be better to note more information than you need than to need to return to it.

- Accept that you won't make use of everything you note; it's part of the process of working out what's needed (everybody makes notes on things they find they don't need). Be prepared to discard things.

- You must have all the details for referencing using the correct format (e.g. the correct referencing format for: an act of parliament; a radio programme).

- For a project or investigation, you may need an 'audit trail'; that is, you may need to prove you've done the work you say you have. This proof is often in the form of notes.

- You must be sure your notes will be understandable in 3 months', 6 months' or a year's time. By then you'll probably have forgotten what you read/saw/heard and all you'll have to go on will be your notes.

- Adopt a very good 'retrieval system' so you can find notes easily. Piles on the floor won't do it!

- You need a plan. The plan for note taking ties in with the plan for finding and using information, so it may be useful to work through this chapter and Chapter 7 'Finding, using and analysing information and evidence' together.

E4 Showing a grasp of your topic

What shows your understanding of a topic or subject? Do you know? If not, ask a tutor/mentor/manager. It'll vary from subject to subject and possibly between courses in the same subject (e.g. some history courses have a stronger emphasis on knowledge and others on using historical skills). Knowing this will help you see what to note.

Possibilities for showing your grasp of a topic are:

- knowing who the important writers/artists/researchers are in a subject/topic;
- knowing the key concepts;
- knowing about current issues or current ways of thinking about the subject/topic;
- being aware of different views and perceptions about something;
- knowing what is contentious, ambiguous, uncertain;
- knowing what questions to ask about something.

How could these sorts of issues affect your note taking? You could:

- highlight the most important individuals (e.g. authors) in the subject;
- organise notes by key concepts, noting who said what about it;
- keep up to date; for example, bookmark important websites and look at them weekly; collect/store exhibition notes; keep newspaper cuttings;
- store different ideas and perceptions about something in the same place;
- have a margin where you can write in any questions/thoughts you have.

E5 Illustrating points

It's very important to have evidence for what you claim. If you have notes on important issues, you can look out for things to illustrate claims you make about them and keep examples in your notes. An obvious example is making a note of useful quotations, but what about diagrams, charts, statistics, facts, images, news items?

Assessors will be asking questions like the following.

- How do you know that?

- What's that view based on?

- Where's the proof for that?

- Who said that?

- How many individuals were in the sample?

- What's the evidence that this artist used that technique?

- How do you know that was when the technique was first used?

E6 Review: improving things for next time

What could make your future note taking even better?

Activity	This is what I'll repeat/do the same in future	This is what I'll do differently
Knowing what I really want from the notes.		
Producing notes to meet my needs.		
Note taking for an extended piece of work.		
Note taking to show my grasp of the topic.		
Illustrating points.		
What else?		

10
PRESENTING YOUR WORK; MAKING IT LOOK GOOD

HOW THIS CHAPTER CAN HELP YOU

The 'crucial' skills part of this chapter aims to help you:

- be clear about the requirements for your work and the appropriate format (e.g. essays; reports; poster; video/audio; on-line; etc.);
- structure and organise your work to make it clear for the audience;
- match your style, approach and language to the subject, purpose and audience;
- use appropriate methods to illustrate points and engage your audience;
- use accepted conventions (e.g. for labelling and referencing);
- identify factors that may affect the outcomes of your work;
- check your work, proof read and edit it;
- plan to improve.

The 'enhanced' skills part of this chapter is shorter: it helps you operate to a higher level. As well as the 'crucial' skills' outcomes, you'll be able to:

- identify what you want to achieve from your work;
- adapt what you do to achieve what you want;
- use language/visuals to convey particular effects, anticipating the effect on your audience;
- illustrate uncertain or ambiguous or complex points effectively;
- evaluate your effectiveness by getting feedback and making judgements about the choices you made;
- identify how you can further develop your skills in presenting work.

CRUCIAL SKILLS

C1 Why is this chapter important and how can it help you?

What your work looks like is very important, for two reasons.

1. How information, ideas or images are presented strongly affects how they're understood. Simple errors in presentation can make it hard to follow work and if your assessor, or other user, can't follow it, it won't get a good mark/grade, or be seen positively.

2. We're all influenced by appearances, assessors included. If your work looks good, your audience is well disposed to it from the start (the content, of course, must still be good!).

ICT is both a blessing and a curse here. It helps make work look professional, but because we're bombarded by well-presented information and images in the media, we're used to things looking good and expect high standards.

Unless you're on a course, or working, where presentation is a skill in its own right (e.g. media; design; architecture), you won't want to spend too much time on the presentation of your work, time that could be spent on the subject matter. This chapter aims to help you find quick and simple ways of making work look good. If there are any mentions of ICT techniques you're unfamiliar with, you could seek help from your university/college ICT support or from colleagues.

C2 What sort of presentation aspects does this chapter consider?

This chapter is concerned with ways of presenting work in higher education (HE) or at work:

- on paper, in text form (e.g. essay/dissertation; report; portfolio; journal; brochures);

- in images (e.g. in posters; presentations; portfolios; electronically on the inter/intranet);

- in sound (e.g. viva; tapes; sound files; podcasts);

- as visual aids for presentations (e.g. PowerPoint; overhead projector slides; slides);

- on the intranet (e.g. your e-learning environment) or internet.

This chapter covers aspects of presentation common to all the above i.e. use of language; structure; conventions. It's mainly about physical appearance and the presentation of ideas, information and images.

If you want to consider more sophisticated presentation techniques you'll need to seek additional help (e.g. from: your college/university; colleagues).

C3 Other chapters you need to use together with this one

There are several other chapters that look at presenting information. These mainly focus on content and structure, whereas this chapter focuses on presentation and appearance.

Chapter	Title	How it relates to this chapter	Page
1	Writing essays and dissertations.	Layout of text and references; following conventions is important to make your meaning clear.	7
2	Writing reports.	As above.	31
3	Producing portfolios and journals (including diaries, blogs, etc.).	You may be able to choose how you present and that can be both an opportunity and a difficulty (no set format to follow). How you present work is very important in making meaning clear.	49
4	Giving a presentation, viva or being observed.	There are different and important issues in presenting information in 'time-bound' situations (i.e. where the audience has to grasp your meaning on the spot).	69
8	Plagiarism and referencing.	You need to use the correct format for references.	173

C4 Your starting point: which format and what's needed for it?

You may be given a format for your piece of work (e.g. report structure). If so, the first information you need is about the requirements for that format. Ask your tutor, mentor or manager and look at examples. Later in this section we consider how you can decide on a format if you haven't been given one.

Some possible formats

Essay	Portfolio (physical)	Log or journal
Report	Portfolio (electronic)	Poster
Flip chart	PowerPoint	Overhead projector slides
Handouts	Slides	Photographs
Diagrams/charts	CD/DVD	Exhibition/performance
Blog	Website	Computer conference posting

Here are some issues to consider in identifying what's required, for any format.

Issue	Comments
How long/big should it be?	For a written document, be guided by any word limit (so you don't do too little or ramble in an unfocused way); if assessed, some tutors refuse to mark more than the given word count. For a poster, it'll be indicated by its dimensions (e.g. A1 size). For a presentation, it'll be indicated by the time allocated (e.g. 15 minutes): you need to decide how many visual aids you can show in that time. Sometimes there may be no indication of size or amount (e.g. a portfolio): if it's assessed, you may get an idea by how many credits it's worth. For a website or other electronic media, you may be given a specified number of pages or file size (e.g. 5 MB).
Are there any specified presentation requirements?	Commonly in HE, you'll be asked to submit word-processed work. Check if handwritten is acceptable. At work, it'll always be word-processed. You may be required to use specified software or specific materials. For on-line work you might be asked to put in hyperlinks.
Does the format limit you in any way?	For example: if you present work via an e-learning environment/internet, does that limit how you can present it; is there a size limit for files you can attach; for a poster, is there a limit to its size, and hence to what you can include?
Conventions.	The likelihood is that you must follow conventions, academic or professional. This usually means correctly referencing, labelling and using accepted abbreviations. In this book we use some casual language, like 'don't'. This is not generally acceptable in a formal written work.
Assessment criteria.	If work is assessed, first check the assessment criteria carefully.

What if you can choose the format for your work?

This may be the case if you have to do a project, produce a portfolio, or provide evidence of your learning. It's up to you to decide on the evidence and how to present it. Here are some issues to consider in deciding which format to use.

Issue	Comments/thoughts
Who'll look at it?	Apart from an assessor, who else? What format might appeal to them (e.g. web-based)? Will anybody outside HE look at it (e.g. employers if it's a portfolio of work)?
How/when will they look at it?	If it's on a wall (e.g. a poster; a projection) make it big enough to see. Will they take it away to look at/read or will they have limited time? If so, make it short and snappy (e.g. bullet points). If you're giving a presentation you need to consider visual aids. In a presentation, will appropriate equipment be available? Will the audience see it from a distance? Will this affect the sort of visual aids you use? If your audience needs to download your work, can this be done easily? Images can download slowly. Will they have specialist software needed?

Issue	Comments/thoughts
What does your subject matter lend itself to?	If it's mainly text, a written format may be best. An essay allows you to explore ideas freely and to develop and discuss an argument. A report is more structured. If it's mainly images, then use a format that can display them well. If it's very detailed, the audience will need time to look at it. Do you need to show connections between things? Use hyperlinks; diagrams; arrows.
What are your own skills and preferences?	What are you good at? If speaking is a strength, you might choose an audio/video clip or podcast. Would you like to try out or practice using other media?

What's needed or required for the format you think you'll use?

From here on, this chapter will assume you have a particular format in mind.

Which format do you think you will use?

What are the requirements you have to work within?

C5 Structure

The first thing that affects how well somebody understands your work is how it's structured. Identifying which ideas/information to put in what order is covered by other chapters in this book. This chapter is concerned with what it 'looks like' or 'sounds like'; rather than content.

C5.1 Signposts

You need to provide 'signposts' telling the audience what's coming (or what's already gone). Here are some ways of doing that.

Signpost	Text	Sound	Images
A contents list.	List of section headings with section numbers, if used, and page numbers.	Tell the audience what will be covered in what order.	List titles of all images in the order in which they appear; give any page numbers; for artworks give materials/size.
Page numbers or equivalent.	Any text you produce (essay, report, portfolio, journal etc.) must have page numbers.	Separate audio files need numbering to indicate sequence.	All images must be numbered and placed in order, matching the contents list.
Section headings.	Essays may not have section headings. Nearly everything else does. It helps the reader see where they are.	Say when one sub topic has ended and you are about to embark on another sub-topic.	Exhibitions can be organised into areas or themes (e.g. there's text explaining the theme of a particular section).
Section numbers.	Where the reader needs to find sections easily, they're numbered. They must match the contents list.	This will probably not be relevant to a sound presentation.	If areas or themes are large, they can be further sub-divided.
Titles and labels.	Any tables, diagrams or images need a title and labels that explain them (see Section C7.1).	This may not apply to sound presentations.	All images need a title and details that explain them (e.g. size; materials made of) (see Section C7.1).
Map/plan/ diagram.	Pictorial representation can make the structure easier to grasp.	This may not apply to sound presentations.	A visual plan will help your audience find their way round your work.

Note: For a presentation (e.g. for visual aids), the above notes on sound, text and images may all be relevant.

Structure for internet/intranet/electronic items

Anything web-based allows you go to town on signposting. Well-designed websites enable the user to go immediately to a particular topic/item and to direct you to what the site owners want you to see. Visit a website you have to pay for and try finding out how to cancel your subscription (it's usually much harder to find than information on how to subscribe!).

Websites often differ in how you navigate them i.e. how you're directed to items. What makes something hard or easy to find? This should help you avoid making such errors on your own website.

For ideas on how to present an electronic portfolio, look at the many examples on the web. Make notes on: their different structures; images (still; moving); colours; fonts, folders and links. What makes them confusing, over-whelming, boring, too busy? Avoid those things!

C5.2 Layout

In addition to signposting, layout also helps the audience follow your structure. Some simple things can really help.

Layout in text

Make it clear where paragraphs start and end. If you're handwriting, indent paragraphs; that is, the first line of a paragraph starts further in from the left hand edge. If word-processing, leave a line between paragraphs. A common mistake is for students not to do this. To make it worse, sentences often don't 'run on' (i.e. there's a line break after every sentence). Below is what it looks like when you do this:

Example of what not to do!

Make it clear where paragraphs start and end.
If handwriting, indent paragraphs, that is, the first line of a paragraph starts a bit in from the left hand edge of your writing.
If word-processing, leave a line break between paragraphs.
A common mistake not to do this.
To make it even worse, sentences often don't run on i.e. a line break is inserted after every sentence.

Why does this matter? A paragraph is a grouping of ideas about one thing. If you don't know where it begins or ends, the work can be difficult to read and can change the meaning.

Example of how layout can obscure or change meaning

Original statement

Action needs to be taken to improve the course. Negatives about the course included inadequate support for students and more help needed to develop some subject knowledge. There is commitment from the course team...

Comment

The reader of the above real example skimmed through it quickly and thought that as the paragraph was about negatives it meant the course team needed more commitment. It was revised as follows to show what it really meant.

Revised statement

Action needs to be taken to improve the course. Negatives about the course included inadequate support for students and more help needed to develop some subject knowledge.

There is commitment from the course team...

Text in visual aids

If you're using text in a visual aid the audience will only see it briefly (even if you give them copies of the slides, they'll usually look at them after, not during, the event).

The visual aid backs-up what you're saying, so doesn't need to include everything you say. Use few words and a clear layout (e.g. bold headings; bullets). Look at these two examples. Which looks best as a visual aid?

Example 1

> *The visual aid is a back-up to what you are saying and does not need to include everything you say. You need very few words and for the layout to be very clear, e.g. very clear what the headings are and clear where each point starts and ends ('bullets' are good here). Look at these two examples. Which one looks best as a visual aid?*

Example 2

> - *The visual aid backs-up what you say.*
> - *You need few words.*
> - *You need clear layout.*
> - *Look at these two examples. Which one looks best as a visual aid?*

Layout for visuals

Will your audience have time to look at your visuals or must they make an immediate impact? The way they're displayed will impact on how the audience understands or appreciates it.

Here are some thoughts.

Issue	Comments/thoughts
What can only be presented visually?	Many items are difficult, if not impossible to describe and can only be appreciated if shown (e.g. photographs; films; paintings; sculptures; maps; plans).
What will have more impact if presented visually?	Numerical information has more impact if presented in charts, graphs or diagrams. Diagrams can show connections between ideas/information.
Is order important?	Which images do you want to have the greatest impact? In which order would they most have that impact?
How much should you include?	Less is often good. It's hard to follow text that's too detailed; in a visual it's even harder. What's essential?
How will you connect ideas visually?	Possibilities are: • hierarchies of things (top to bottom or vice-versa) • flow charts showing connections between stages • arrows showing connections and the direction of those connections • spirals or circles can convey the idea that things are repeated. • Venn diagrams show inter-connections.

Examples

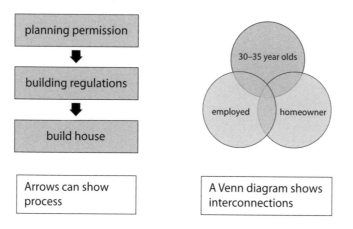

Visual aids for presentations

Visual aids tend to be text-based, but may include diagrams, photographs or slides.

There are two considerations here: preparing the visual aids and using them during the presentation. These should be considered together.

It's important to check the room, its equipment and resources. If in doubt, take equipment/resources with you. You don't want to spend ages making an electronic presentation to find there's no computer or digital projector. It may be better to take it on a memory stick than to rely on internet access. Allow time to set up. Be prepared to be flexible and for things to go wrong. Chapter 4 'Giving a presentation, viva or being observed' considers such issues.

See the guidance in Section 5.2 about layout using text or visuals.

Numerical information

There are two important principles when presenting numerical information:

1. the meaning of the information needs to be clear to the user/audience;

2. the presentation of information should not be misleading.

One way of ensuring this is by following conventions in presenting numerical information (see Section C7) (e.g. labelling tables, charts and graphs correctly).

Layout is equally important. How you show tables, charts and graphs has a big impact on how well the user understands the information. A useful (but older) book by Huff (1992) gives examples of how you can mislead your audience when presenting numerical information (e.g. by using scales that distort the information).

When you present tables it helps if you:

- don't have too many rows and columns, as it's harder for the user to follow;

- use lines and space to divide up rows and columns, to help the user's eye follow them;

- give percentages in the table with the actual (base) number clear at the top of the column. (Giving both numbers and percentages in a table can mean too much to take in; but see Section C6.2 about percentages).

A table can give two dimensions of information (e.g. age and gender of individuals). If you want to give three dimensions (e.g. age, gender and nationality of individuals) you may need more than one table or to use a graph or chart instead. Visual representations of numerical data can be very effective (e.g. pie chart; bar chart; cluster diagram; scatter graph).

Different sorts of graphs and charts are used for different purposes, so check which meet your purpose. For ideas, look in your subject text books, relevant websites or journals. What do they use for what purpose?

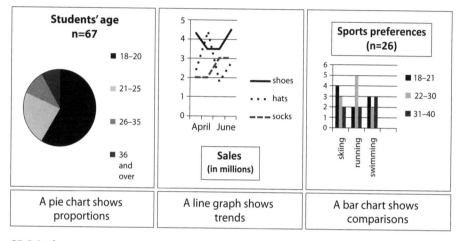

C5.3 Style

We use the word 'style' here in the technical way used in word-processing, to mean the size and font used for letters. This applies to hand-produced work too.

You can signal different sorts of items by having a different 'style' for them, e.g. different styles for main headings and sub headings. In many computer applications you can set styles for what you want to call 'heading 1', 'heading 2', 'heading 3', and so on. A similar approach can also be used in handwriting.

FOR EXAMPLE this is heading 1

For example this is heading 2

For example this is heading 3

You must be consistent or you'll confuse your audience (e.g. use 'heading 1' for the title of the whole work; 'heading 2' for the main section headings; 'heading 3' for sub-headings). If you're handwriting, you could use capitals for one type of heading and underline another.

This doesn't just apply to headings. You might decide to use *italics* to always show similar things (e.g. for examples; to show emphasis). Be consistent. If you start using italics to indicate examples, the reader will expect all italics to be examples, and if not they'll be confused. If you're word processing you can use **bold** to highlight important things (e.g. headings). If handwriting, you could <u>underline</u>. **Be consistent**.

Using styles effectively is particularly important for visual presentations (e.g. posters) as they need to make an immediate impact.

Some **typefaces** are harder to read than others (especially by people with dyslexia or sight difficulties). You need to be aware of the impression created by some typefaces (e.g. some are associated with children or with jokey items: is that what you want?).

The size of typeface or writing is important. If you want to really antagonise a busy, overworked assessor, handwrite a piece of work in tiny, spidery lettering that they'll need very strong glasses to see.

Warning

Don't use too many different styles. Probably, you want one style for the main text, perhaps three different types of headings and italics and bold. More than that could look a mess.

Look at the following example. It uses three different typefaces, bold, underlining and italics. Your eyes are drawn to groups of words and it's hard to even see the other words. Compare it with the paragraph above, which uses only one typeface.

Example of what not to do!

Do **not** use too many <u>different styles</u> or **it will look messy**. Probably you want <u>one style</u> for your main text, perhaps <u>3 different types of headings</u> and *to use italics and bold*. More than that could be **a mess**.

Style in visuals

Here are some brief thoughts (we're using 'style' here to mean how you present).

Issue	Comments
Is scale important?	In a photograph, you might include a person to indicate scale. For maps or plans, you need to show scale (see Section C7). The time span of the life of the earth is often presented as a clock, where humans appear in the last couple of minutes. How could you indicate scale?
How can colour help?	It can be used to pick out sections or ideas or headings. What works together? Pale yellow text on white background is hard to see. Too many different colours can look too busy and confuse.

Issue	Comments
Photographs.	What do you want your audience to focus on and does the photo show that? Can you see the required detail? Is the light good enough to make the photo clear? If you enlarge it, is the quality still good enough for your purposes?
Video.	What sort of moving image will be best for your work (e.g. live motion; computer animation)?
Paper, bindings, etc.	This can cost a lot and the audience may be much more impressed by simple clear layout than by fancy paper. Decide which is important.
Self-publicity.	If you're an artist/designer, what about a postcard with images of your work on one side and your contact details on the other? Check the cost.

C6 Language and numerical information

C6.1 Language

Other chapters (see Section C3) look at the appropriateness of the language you use. However, a summary of the advice is:

- use words appropriate for your audience and purpose (e.g. formal/ informal; specialist or not; technical or not);

- sentence length should be appropriate for the audience and purpose (e.g. short and snappy; long and discursive);

- you must use words correctly;

- you must spell and punctuate correctly.

The last two points are important. You can create a really bad impression by getting them wrong. A slide with a wrongly spelt word or an apostrophe in the wrong place draws people's eye and may discredit your message or detract from its meaning.

C6.2 Numerical information

There are different functions you can use to describe numerical information and you need to identify which you need. For example, there are different ways of describing the middle point of the data (averages).

- **Mean**: the sum of the data divided by the number of items of data (what people commonly intend when they use the word 'average').

- **Median**: the middle value in the range.

- **Mode**: the most frequently occurring value.

These functions have different uses and you need to choose the most appropriate for your data (e.g. use the mode for representing average shoe sizes, rather than the mean – there's no shoe size '5.67').

You need to select the best way of making your data meaningful to your audience (note: 'data' is plural, so you need to say 'the data are' not 'the data is'). For example:

- the range is the difference between the lowest and highest values (e.g. age 42–22 = 20 years);

- percentages allow you to make comparisons between sets of data with different numbers of items of data. However, they're misleading if used on small sets of data (e.g. if you only have two items, saying one out of two gives a different impression from 50 per cent; here it's best to use numbers instead). If you give percentages you must **always** give the base number.

Presenting numerical data can be specialised; check in your subject area for examples.

C7 Using conventions

C7.1 Labelling

Without accurate and complete labelling, your audience can be very confused.

Images, tables, charts, diagrams

Each item needs a title and number (e.g. 'Table 1' would be followed by a title indicating what's in it, then 'Table 2' and so on. Diagrams and charts are usually called 'Figure', so you'd have 'Figure 1' followed by its title. 'Plate' is generally used for images (e.g. photos; prints; pictures).

You may need to give the numbers and titles of all tables/figures/plates in a list after the main contents list, so that the audience can identify which they want to refer to.

Numerical information

If you include numerical information, charts or graphs there are some essential things you must do to help your audience interpret the data. For example, you need to give the total number of items (base number) that the table/chart/graph refers to, normally by having n= followed by the base number. In a table give the total for each column and row.

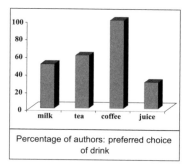

This bar chart suggests 50 per cent of all authors like milk. It's misleading as n=6.

Percentage of authors: preferred choice of drink

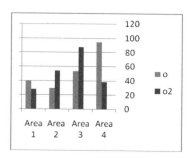

This chart is very confusing and could be misinterpreted. Some key information is missing so it's hard to understand.

In your work, clearly label axes and scales and give titles (e.g. number and gender of university students studying maths, by geographical area).

Image/visual taken from somewhere else

This must have the reference to its source so your audience can find it. If it's a diagram from a book, the page number where it appeared should be included in the citation (see Chapter 8 'Plagiarism and referencing'). If it's art work you may need to indicate the owner or person giving permission for it to be included.

Images of your work

These need titles and any information important for the user. You need to be consistent (e.g. in a portfolio with photographs of your art work, if size and materials are important, you must include this information on every item, not on some. Inconsistency looks sloppy and may be confusing.

C7.2 Academic conventions

In text

You must use commonly accepted academic conventions. Space is too limited here to cover every possibility, so check this out in your subject. Common ones are:

- eg is correctly written e.g. and ie is correctly written i.e.

- If you use an acronym (i.e. a word made up of the first letters of other words) you must give it in full the first time you use it, with the acronym in brackets after it. Thereafter, you can just use the acronym (e.g. 'The Department for Innovation, Universities and Skills (DIUS) was created from the former Department for Education and Skills (DfES). DIUS now deals with...').

- Citations and references have to be presented consistently, to make an item clear, e.g. according to the Harvard system (see Chapter 8 'Plagiarism and referencing'),

This example is correct.

Bingham, R., Drew, S., (1997), 'Student Skill Packs', in Hudson, R., Mason-Prothero, S., Oates, L., (1997), *Flexible Learning in Action. Case Studies in Higher Education*, London: Kogan Page.

This is incorrect, because it's not clear (it's hard to pick out the titles).

Bingham, R., Drew, S. (1997) Student Skill Packs in Hudson, R., Mason-Prothero, S., Oates L. (1997) Flexible Learning in Action. Case Studies in Higher Education. London. Kogan Page

In numerical, scientific or musical notation

There are also other conventions to be followed so that everybody understands 'shorthand' information e.g.:

- numerical notation (e.g. > represents 'greater than'; < represents 'less than')

- scientific notation (e.g. $E=MC^2$, where E means energy, M means mass, C means the speed of light)

- musical notation (e.g. different note values, e.g. ♪ represents a quaver and is equivalent to half a beat).

Space is too limited here to go into further detail so check what the conventions are in your subject area.

C8 What might affect how you present your work?

Section C4 suggests you identify any requirements for a format or in assignment instructions. Section C5 referred to the limitations that may be imposed on you by facilities or resources. What else might affect how you present work?

If you haven't much experience of the type of work you're producing, try to find examples as idea starters. Look on the internet, at journals, ask tutors/managers, other students or colleagues.

What about your own skills? What are your strengths? Do you need to learn new skills or further develop ones you have? The previous sections might help you identify this (e.g. your use of language; your ICT skills; your photography skills). Could somebody help you (but check this is not likely to lead to accusations of cheating) or train you in the skills?

What about equipment or software? If you don't have access to certain equipment it may mean that you can't create certain effects. The good news is that you can probably do much with relatively simple equipment or software.

Notes. Actions I need to take

C9 Proof-reading

It's essential to check your work for errors. Ask your tutor about how important presentation is to your mark, so you do it well enough but don't waste time on something less important.

Have you checked the following?

	✓		✓
Spelling.		Numbers are calculated correctly.	
Punctuation.		Academic conventions are used correctly.	
Consistent heading styles and typeface.		References are correctly laid out.	
Paragraph breaks.		Copyright permission obtained, if needed.	
Tables/figures/images are numbered.		It's within time or size limits.	
All tables/figures/images are labelled.		It's not visually confusing/too busy.	
Labels, titles, etc., are consistent.		Hyperlinks work, documents and audio/video clips work.	
Scale is indicated (where relevant).			

C10 Reviewing and improving what you do

How can you improve your skills in making your work look good next time round?

Activity	This is what I'll repeat/do the same in future	This is what I'll do differently
Identifying an appropriate format.		
Being clear about what is required for that format.		
Targeting what you do at the audience.		
Signposting.		
Using layout and style.		
Labelling and following conventions.		
Identifying and allowing for factors affecting what I do.		
Proof-reading.		

ENHANCED SKILLS

E1 What do you most want to achieve from your work?

You might want to consider the following in relation to a piece of work you're doing now.

Issue	Your notes (what this means you need to do)
How much will your audience/mark/grade be influenced by your presentation of this work? What are the implications for the time you'll spend on making it look good?	
What will influence your audience/mark/grade? • How understandable it is? • How easy it is to follow? • The impact it creates. • *What else?*	
Do you want to use this work for more than one purpose (e.g. for assessment; to show an employer)? If so, are there any implications for how you present it?	
Do you want to develop any presentation skills? Would this work allow you to do that (e.g. skills you'll need in future)?	

E2 Creating particular effects

The 'crucial skills' section of this chapter covered aspects of presenting information that are the 'baseline' of what good presentation needs. However, it may be that you want to create particular effects.

Here's an example based on the authors' development of this chapter.

Example

Question	Our notes
What effect do we want to create?	*For readers to see how presentation can affect meaning and how the audience is reacting.*
Why?	*It may mean the difference between passing and failing or between a poor impact on the audience.*
What will our audience need or respond to?	*They'll want familiar examples that relate to their own experience as students/in the workplace.*
How can we do this?	*Have examples of good and bad practice, so they can see the difference.* *Illustrate points.* *Make sure the chapter follows its own advice, so it acts as a role model.*

Your own notes

Question	Your notes
What effect do you want to create?	
Why?	
What will your audience need or respond to?	
How can you do this?	

Here are some suggestions of presentation features that can create different impressions:

Feature	Different aspects
Language.	Formal/informal; first/third person (I/one); short/long words; short/long sentences; objective/emotive words.
Structure.	Formal/informal; changing order may create different effects.
Images.	Photographs; cartoons (beware, may have the effect of 'dumbing down' or being too 'jokey'); sketches; photographs; video/film; tables; graphs/ charts; maps; diagrams.
Variety.	Too much variety may confuse, too little may be boring; could introduce at certain points to create particular effect.
Style.	Bullet points or discursive; typeface/style of writing; headings/no headings; use of colour or monochrome; white space (space around the text/image); consistency and breaking from it to create a special effect.
Presentation format.	Quality of paper/folder; type of software; backgrounds; 2D or 3D; shape; size; sound quality; display resolution; size of documents, video clips, podcasts, photographs.

E3 Illustrating points

Some points are difficult to get across to an audience. Your first task is to identify which ones and why (so you can avoid patronising your audience by thinking they can't understand your simpler points).

Some possibilities are points that:

- are complex;

- have no one answer;

- are uncertain or ambiguous;

- are far from the audience's experience;

- need some prior knowledge the audience doesn't have.

Your second task is to put yourself in your audience's shoes and work out what they might find difficult about the point and what might help them understand it. Use friends/colleagues to help.

Your third task is to come up with a way of getting the point over. Look at lots of examples. Reading a lot, looking at the media or browsing the internet, will give ideas of how others get points across. For example, some films are mainly black and white but suddenly introduce colour; some animations cut to real film footage; films use different types of soundtrack. Documentaries may repeat key ideas in different ways; there may be a mix of inputs (e.g. interviews; film snippets). Books may include photos or diagrams to illustrate things.

We're not suggesting you'll be producing a film or a documentary or writing a book, but we are suggesting that you become aware of how points are explained.

E4 Review: improving things for next time

What feedback have you had about how you present work?
Which aspects of this are important in helping you present work better and what are you going to do about it?

What could improve your skills here?

Activity	This is what I'll repeat/do the same in future	This is what I'll do differently
Being clear about the impact of how I present work.		
Knowing what I want from this.		
Knowing what effects I want to create.		
Having ideas about how to create those effects.		
Having the skills to create those effects.		
Identifying which points might be difficult to get over		

Activity	This is what I'll repeat/do the same in future	This is what I'll do differently
Identifying what would help the audience understand the points.		
Being aware of how others present difficult points.		
Presenting difficult points so the audience can understand.		

REFERENCES

Huff, D., (1991), *How to lie with statistics*, London: Penguin.

11
DISCUSSIONS: FACE-TO-FACE AND ON-LINE (IN SEMINARS, GROUPS, ETC.)

HOW THIS CHAPTER CAN HELP YOU

The 'crucial' skills part of this chapter aims to help you:

- be clear about the purpose of the discussion and what you and others want from it;
- identify what may affect the outcomes of your discussions;
- use an approach that's appropriate for the purpose and those involved;
- contribute points and ideas in a way that's appropriate for the purpose and people involved;
- protect your own rights and those of others;
- be a resource for others and use them as a resource;
- encourage others to contribute;
- give constructive feedback and receive feedback positively;
- maintain co-operation and handle conflict;
- plan to improve how you work in, and learn from, discussions.

The 'enhanced' skills part of this chapter is shorter: it helps you operate to a higher level. As well as the 'crucial' skills' outcomes, you'll be able to:

- identify the outcomes you want from discussions;
- choose methods and adapt what you do to get these outcomes;
- engage in ongoing or repeated discussions with people;
- take a lead role and manage discussions where there may be complexity, uncertainty or ambiguity;
- negotiate with others, responding perceptively to their contributions and being aware of how your discussion style may affect others;
- evaluate your effectiveness by getting feedback and making judgements about what you did;
- identify how to develop your skills in discussing.

CRUCIAL SKILLS

C1 Why is this chapter important and how can it help you?

This chapter deals with discussions that have a specific purpose (rather than more casual conversations) and where there may be debate, the examination of an argument or consideration of issues leading to actions.

Many courses include discussions because they're seen as so important for learning. By hearing others' views and trying out yours on them, you can come to new understandings.

Discussions are also essential in the world of work: think of meetings, talking to clients and negotiating. How effective you are at this could have a big impact on your career.

In higher education (HE), you may be assessed on your ability to engage in discussion (e.g. via on-line discussions; computer conferences; seminars). Even if discussions aren't assessed, they're important to the impression you create. People (in HE or at work) will make assumptions (even though they may be incorrect) about engagement in discussions. Those who don't contribute may be seen as uninterested. Those who over-contribute or fool around may be seen as a nuisance (not only by tutors, most students get pretty fed up with this).

You could use this chapter:

- if you're concerned about a particular discussion, to help you prepare for it;
- to think about all discussions in which you're involved (say over the coming week). You could keep notes and review them at the end of the week, then use the chapter again to think about discussions for the following week, and so on;
- to review how effective you are in general in discussions.

C2 What sort of discussions does this chapter consider?

Although this guidance applies to any discussions (face-to-face or on-line), it primarily considers those in:

- large groups (e.g. whole class discussions; conferences);
- small groups (e.g. as part of class activities);
- seminars (i.e. one person presents a topic then participants discuss it);
- tutorials or supervision (in a group or 1:1);

- meetings;

- computer conferences or discussion boards;

- email.

C3 Other chapters you need to use together with this one

A discussion may be one aspect of a situation requiring other skills too. Some other chapters in this book are particularly related to discussions.

Chapter	Title	How it relates to this chapter	Page
12	Working in a group or team.	Discussions are a key part of group work.	253
13	Dealing with other people.	Discussions are key in dealing with others.	275
4	Giving a presentation, viva or being observed.	You may need to invite questions, comments or encourage discussion.	69
5	Doing a project.	Your project may involve discussing plans with others.	97
17	Reflecting on your learning and experience (including feedback).	Getting and using feedback on how you take part in discussions will be very useful.	379

C4 Your starting point: what's the discussion for and what's wanted by those involved?

For a discussion you are about to take part in, what might its purpose be?

Possible purpose	✓	Implication
To reinforce understanding of a topic.		You need to have done preliminary work, so you know something about the topic.
To come to an agreement about something.		You may need to negotiate (see Chapter 13 'Dealing with other people').
To exchange ideas and views on a topic.		You need to prepare and make sure you know about the topic.
To show what participants know about something.		You need to be willing to offer contributions and to listen to others.
To provide mutual support.		You need to be willing to offer contributions and to listen to others.
To talk about how something can be applied to a situation.		You need to be willing to contribute to the discussion and to compromise.

Possible purpose	✓	Implication
To decide what to do and plan actions.		As above; you may need to negotiate (see Chapter 13 'Dealing with other people').
For a discussion you are about to have, what will be the purpose?		**What are the implications for this upcoming discussion?**

What do you want from your discussion? What might others want?

What you might want	✓	What others might want	What the tutor/ discussion leader might want	Implications
For others to think you have something worthwhile to say.		To learn something (e.g. to help them pass or get a good grade); for their views to be seen as worthwhile.	To see how much participants understand the topic and where there is confusion.	If you contribute you can get feedback on your views; if not, you won't. Everybody needs to avoid putting others down.
Other students to think you are entertaining.		To learn from the discussions; to enjoy the discussion.	For participants to learn from the discussion.	Being 'funny' is OK for a short time. It's a pain if it goes on too long.
The tutor/ manager to be impressed by your work.		The tutor/manager to be impressed by their work.	For all to engage in the discussion and show what they know.	The point of a discussion is not to be a platform for individuals but to get interaction.
To have your views treated with respect.		To have their views treated with respect.	To ensure people are treated with respect.	Each participant should treat others with respect.
To overcome a fear of speaking in groups.		To overcome a fear of speaking in groups.	For all to engage with the discussion.	Each participant needs to help the others take part.
To get others to agree with me.		To see what others think; to get others to agree with them	For all to engage in/learn from each other.	It isn't helpful for any one person to dominate.
To learn from what others say.		To learn from what others say.	For all to learn from the discussion.	The more everybody listens and contributes, the more all will learn.
To try out what I think on others.		To try out what they think on others.	To encourage debate and sharing ideas.	Everybody needs to both listen and contribute.

For a discussion you are about to have...	For a discussion you are about to have...	For a discussion you are about to have...	For a discussion you are about to have...
... what do you want?	... what might others want?	... what might the leader want?	... the implications are...

C5 Some conventions and two basic skills in discussions

C5.1 Conventions

Formal discussions

In formal discussions, or where there are many participants, somebody acts as chairperson. This role is to make sure the agenda items are covered and discussed fairly, with nobody dominating.

Here, it's normal for people to 'go through the chair'. When you want to speak, you attract the attention of the chairperson and they ask you to speak. This ensures everybody who wants to speak can do so. The chairperson also keeps order (e.g. the speaker of the House of Commons shouts 'Order!'); s/he ensures only one person speaks at once and that 'good manners' (see Section C7) are followed.

Seminars (or other class discussions or group tutorials)

Here, there's usually a discussion leader (e.g. a tutor or a student) who presents something and then leads a discussion on it (see Section E3 in this chapter for more guidance). You often have to attract the attention of the leader in order to speak.

Informal discussions with no leader or chairperson

See Section C7 for good practice here.

On-line discussions and email

There's usually an 'administrator' (e.g. a tutor) who encourages the discussion and makes sure that there are no inappropriate postings. Universities/colleges and workplaces have rules about what can or cannot be posted on intranets and e-learning environments, with penalties for breaking them. Check the rules in your institution. Basically, you should use these facilities for the purpose intended (i.e. for course work).

What are the main differences between face-to-face and on-line discussion?

Face-to-face	On-line
Something may not be heard or remembered or be lost in general chatter.	In print for all to see.
Takes place in 'real time'; people may not remember what was said.	Tends to be 'up' for some time, may be archived forever, people can go back to check what was said (ongoing record).
People can hear your tone of voice and see your expressions.	People can't see you and may interpret it in ways you did not intend.
What's funny face-to-face may not be on-line.	What's funny on-line may not be face-to-face.
What other differences can you think of?	

Most of us have sent emails or posted discussion items that we've later regretted; you only do it once before learning to read things carefully before sending (the authors of this book often ask a colleague to check something before it's posted).

Email users should follow 'netiquette' (i.e. conventions that ensure the communication is clear and nobody is offended). ICT support at your university/college/workplace may offer advice on this, Section C7 gives some ideas about what might offend (e.g. the use of bold and capitals for emphasis can be interpreted as 'shouting'; inadvertently forwarding something to somebody who shouldn't see it), and see Section E3 in Chapter 13 'Dealing with other people'. Basically, in on-line or email discussions you need to be twice as clear and twice as polite as you would normally be.

C5.2 Agendas and minutes

In formal meetings there will be an agenda (list) of items to discuss and minutes will be taken. Minutes are the record of what was said and what actions were agreed. For help on this, see Section C5 in Chapter 9 'Making notes'.

C5.3 Two basic skills

Listening

'Active listening' means not just being able to repeat what another person said (though that's a start) but understanding it (and that might involve listening to their tone of voice or choice of words). It's an essential skill in discussion. If you spend your time working out what you're going to say next, you may not hear what others are saying. If you find this hard, you could jot down notes, as people speak, of their main points.

Getting heard

A basic skill is to be able to get into the discussion and make a contribution.

- If there's a chairperson/leader, catch their eye (e.g. by raising your hand).

- If there's no chairperson, listen carefully to what's being said and as soon as the previous person has stopped talking, jump in and speak. This takes a bit of nerve but is worth trying. The worst that can happen is you'll be ignored or be asked to wait while somebody else speaks. If it doesn't work, just do it again until it does.

- Eye contact and making your presence known are important. Look at the person who's speaking (or in the chair) and make it obvious you want to speak (sit forward, look alert).

- Speak loudly enough to be heard.

- If you have a disability that makes the above suggestions difficult, then you need to agree strategies with the others involved in advance.

C6 What might affect the discussion?

Some things that might affect a discussion are:

- your feelings and needs, and your role;
- others' feelings and needs, and their roles;
- what's at stake;
- the format of the discussion or the situation in which it happens;
- what you can control and what you can't.

You can use the following to help you think about a discussion you'll take part in soon.

Firstly, what about you?

Item	Your notes for an upcoming discussion
How do you feel about this discussion (e.g. worried, excited, not bothered)?	
How do you want others to treat you? What do you need from them?	
Do you have any beliefs or feelings about the topic?	
What sort of relationship do you have with the others involved?	
What's your role in the discussion?	

What about the others?

Item	Your notes for an upcoming discussion
Who's taking part in this discussion?	
What characteristics do they have (e.g. gender; age; ethnicity)?	
Does anybody have a disability whereby they need help to participate?	
What might the participants' beliefs or feelings be about the topic? What might offend them?	
What could they offer to the discussion? What will interest or be attractive to them?	
Who has which roles in this discussion (e.g. is there a discussion leader/chairperson)?	

What's at stake?

Item	Your notes for an upcoming discussion
What effect might the others' reaction to you have on you (now or in the future)?	
What would happen if the discussion never happened or was a disaster?	
What might happen if the discussion is a great success?	
What might happen if you don't engage in the discussion?	
What might happen if you do engage in the discussion?	
What else is at stake (grades/marks; status; friendships)?	

In what setting or format will it take place?

Format or setting	✓	Implication
With a large group (e.g. whole class; conference), face-to-face.		There'll be a discussion leader. You'll need to attract their attention to 'get in'.
In a seminar group, face-to-face.		As above.
In a small group, face-to-face.		Less need for formality; less likely to be able to 'get away with' not speaking; need to avoid more than one person speaking at once.
In a room with seating facing the front.		You need to speak up so people behind you can hear, or to partially turn to face them.
In a room in a circle or round a table.		Easier to attract attention so you can contribute.
In a café, pub, canteen, and so on.		Surrounding distractions (e.g. noise) mean you need to keep focused.
Via email.		Need to be careful about how you word comments. Things to beware of include: humour; exclamations; emphases.
Via a computer conference or discussion board.		As above. Also, everybody will see what you put. Don't misuse it (e.g. to chat about other things).

What can and can't you control?

You **can** control your own behaviour and reactions.

If you're leading the discussion, set things up to encourage a good discussion (e.g. arrange seating where all can see each other; for on-line discussions, post clear and encouraging starting points).

You **can't** control what others say or do, but you **can** create an effect that encourages or discourages them to speak. The rest of this chapter is about how you do that.

However, before we turn to that, what happens if you're in a discussion with a tutor or colleague who isn't good at leading or controlling it? What if it's the tutor or discussion leader who puts people down (we hope not!)? What can you do? Here are some possibilities:

- engage in the discussion seriously;

- don't take part in disruptive behaviour or in making fun of or laughing at somebody;

- make a comment that supports somebody on the receiving end of unkind behaviour;

- get agreement from others in the group that you're all going to try to make it work;

- see the tutor or colleague privately and express your concerns; see the course/year/programme tutor or manager; ask the student representative to take the issue forward.

C7 Contributing appropriately: things that matter in all discussions

Some things are always important in any discussions. How well do you score on these, where 1= always, 2= mostly, 3= sometimes and 4= never.

Do you...	1	2	3	4
avoid gender stereotyping (e.g. say 'she or he' or 'they', other than when referring to actual people)?				
avoid racism?				
avoid racism stereotyping (e.g. don't assume all UK citizens are white)?				
avoid making fun of people's views?				
avoid making personal comments, rather than commenting on information or ideas?				
avoid making **judgemental** comments rather than reasoned ones (e.g. instead of 'that's rubbish', say 'I disagree with that because...')?				
avoiding interrupting?				
avoid losing your temper?				
avoid being aggressive?				
avoid swearing or obscenities?				
actively listen to others?				
treat people as you like to be treated?				
prepare the work needed for the discussion, so you don't waste other people's time?				

The best score here is a low one – that is, 13. If you got 52, you're in serious trouble (how have you survived so far?). What can you improve?

What about helping people with disabilities to take part in your discussions? You could:

- ask them what they need you to do;

- avoid singling them out and embarrassing them;

- if theirs is a mobility issue, ensure seating arrangements mean they can fully engage;

- if they have a hearing impairment: attract their attention before you speak; make sure they can see your mouth; remember that they can't look at visual aids and you at the same time; if they have an interpreter don't talk too fast;

- if they have a sight impairment make sure they can access any information that others can see.

Taking care of yourself

This is another important constant, in any discussion or situation: you have 'rights' as well as others. What do you normally do and what could you usefully amend?

Your right	How to encourage this	Suggestions for if your right isn't met	What I could do/try
To be listened to.	Be clear, be loud enough, identify what will gain the attention/ interest of others.	Say 'could I just finish what I was saying please', if interrupted.	
To express my views (in a way that does not infringe on others' rights).	Be clear, reasoned, avoid emotive expression that may upset or anger others.	Say 'I'd like to say something please' and if it has no effect say it again until it does.	
To be taken seriously.	Avoid 'messing about', do any preparatory work, make serious/useful contributions.	Review what you did/said to see if it caused the reaction. Politely repeat what you're trying to say.	

Your right	How to encourage this	Suggestions for if your right isn't met	What I could do/try
To learn.	Do any work needed for the discussions; listen to others; make useful contributions; note what you've learnt.	If others stop you learning (e.g. being disruptive), ask them to stop (others may support you). If repeated, involve the tutor/manager	
To make mistakes.	Identify what you learnt from the mistake and what to do next time. Use it positively.	Use others' feedback to help you learn for next time (rather than letting it damage your confidence).	
To be silent.	Choose when to do this. It may not be helpful (to you or others) to be silent all the time.	If you choose to be silent, just say 'I prefer not to comment' or 'I prefer to listen'.	

C8 Contributing appropriately to particular discussions

Your starting point here is 'appropriate for what?' (see Section C4). What's appropriate in a televised debate between politicians may not be so in a family discussion about where to go on holiday, or a work discussion about a project. Before you go into any discussion (no matter how informal), get into the habit of thinking:

- what do I want to get out of this?

- what will they need from this (getting in the way of what others need is not a good way to get them on your side)?

- how can I approach this?

Overleaf are suggestions for what you might do in a discussion. How helpful would they be in a discussion you're about to have and for the others involved in it?

Making points and expressing ideas

Suggestions	What might work for your upcoming discussion?
Use non-emotive language.	
Use language the others will understand and be used to, including relevant technical language.	
Make the point briefly, then expand on it.	
Give an example that they can relate to.	
Tell a story or describe a scenario.	
Use short, clear sentences, not rambling ones.	
Make eye contact.	
Use non-verbal actions for emphasis.	
Use similes (e.g. 'learning is like the growth of a plant') or metaphors (e.g. 'your learning may blossom').	

Being a resource for others and using them as a resource (e.g. for information; ideas; support)

Suggestions	What might work for your upcoming discussion?
Give others information relevant to the current point in the discussion.	
Ask for information.	
Thank others for information or ideas even if you disagree: they're more likely to offer more ideas (the next ones may be better).	
Make clear what you can offer (but avoid sounding big-headed).	
Make it clear you think others have something to offer/ask them what they can offer.	
Go prepared with information to share.	
Take notes for each other (e.g. you do 15 minutes then someone else takes over).	
Always do what you say you'll do (it may encourage others to do the same).	

Encouraging others to contribute. What would encourage you to contribute?

Suggestions	What might work for your upcoming discussion?
Be interested in what they say.	
Be positive about what they say.	
Ask them what they think.	
Ask who agrees or disagrees with you or with an issue.	
Remember what somebody said earlier in the discussion and come back to it later.	
Make eye contact.	
Ask others to explain what you don't understand.	
Ask others about their relevant experiences.	

Give constructive feedback and receive feedback positively

Suggestions	What might work for the purpose of your upcoming discussion, and for those involved?
When giving feedback: • avoid judgmental comments (e.g. 'that idea is rubbish' or 'that's great'); • make specific comments (e.g. 'I find your suggestion of xxx helpful'; 'I don't understand what you mean by xxx') to help them see what to do about it; • give feedback as soon after an event as possible. When receiving feedback: • thank the person for it; • ask for clarification if you don't understand; • ask for suggestions for what you might do; • reflect on the feedback. What's the evidence for it? Is it valid? If not you may decide to take no notice of it. See Section C4 in Chapter 17 'Reflecting on your learning and experience (including feedback)'.	

Maintaining cooperation and dealing with conflict

Suggestions	What might work for the purpose of my discussion and those involved?
Cooperation may be encouraged by: • identifying common ground or shared interests; • being cooperative yourself; • suggesting ways of cooperating to others. Avoid doing/saying things that may create conflict. If it occurs you could: • acknowledge the anger; • apologise if you've offended others; • take time out; • suggest you move on and return to the disputed issue later; • agree to differ and move on; • as what others think; • see if you can find common ground; • avoid inflaming the situation. See Section C7 in Chapter 13 'Dealing with other people'.	

C9 Reviewing and improving what you do

How can you improve how you take part in discussions next time round?

Activity	This is what I'll repeat/ do the same in future	This is what I'll do differently
Being clear about the purpose, the participants and their needs.		
Knowing the conventions of discussions (see Section C5).		

Activity	This is what I'll repeat/ do the same in future	This is what I'll do differently
Listening actively to others.		
Being heard by others.		
Being clear about what might affect the discussion.		
Treating people with respect in any discussion.		
Behaving in a way that's appropriate for a particular discussion.		

ENHANCED SKILLS

E1 What do you want to achieve?

Before any discussion, it helps if you work out what you want from it. Section C4 above looks at this, but here's another way.

For a discussion you have had in the last week...

Question	Your notes on a recent discussion
What did you get out of it?	
Was there anything you didn't get out of it that you wish you had?	
What helped you get what you did?	
What stopped you getting what you wanted?	

Think of a discussion you are going to have this week...

Question	Your notes on an upcoming discussion
What do you want from it in the short term (i.e. within the discussion)?	
What do you want from it in the medium term (i.e. in relation to the module/the year/the course or 3 or 6 or 12 months)?	
Is there anything you might want from it that's relevant to your future?	
Look at your notes in the above exercise about a discussion you've just had, what worked and you'll do again?	
Look at your notes in the above exercise about a discussion you've just had. What will you do differently?	

E2 Having more discussions with the same people

If you have a one-off discussion with somebody and it goes badly, the repercussions are not so great. However, if you need to have more discussions with them, they may be significant. How might it matter and which of these issues would concern you?

Possible people involved in a discussion	Implications for the future
Tutors.	They assess you. Our research (by the authors) has indicated that students who get on well with tutors get better support.
Other students.	They may peer-assess you. They are a major source of support. How well you get on with them may determine how happy you are.
Others at university/college who provide support (e.g. library or ICT staff).	Their help may be very important; they may be under pressure from others who also want help.
Employer/manager (e.g. placement; for work that is part-time, vacation, full time).	They can give references. They may assess you. They may promote you (or even sack you).
Friends.	Their support is important.
Family.	Their support is important.

Consider the following questions for discussions you are currently involved in...

Questions to consider	Your notes
With whom might you have ongoing discussions (or at least one) or ongoing contact?	
What will happen to ongoing discussions/contact if these discussions go well?	
What will happen to ongoing discussions/contact if they don't go well?	
What would encourage the others involved to want to continue to have discussions with you?	
What would encourage the others involved to want to avoid having discussions with you?	

For more on this, look at Chapter 13 'Dealing with other people'.

E3 Taking a lead role

You're likely to have views on what makes somebody good at leading discussions, as, by now, you'll have been in many such discussions. You may have been in ones where nobody spoke, one person did all the talking, the leader put people down or there were rows. We hope you've also been in ones where people contributed equally, interest was maintained and everybody got something out of it.

Here are some suggestions for how to generate a 'good' discussion, if you lead it:

- agree groundrules for how you'll all behave (e.g. everybody to listen while one person speaks; no making fun of people);

- encourage non-speakers by asking for their views, but don't try to force them;

- avoid putting people on the spot (e.g. asking everybody a question in turn);

- suggest people spend 2 minutes thinking alone first, to gather their thoughts;

- suggest people talk to a neighbour about the topic first for 2 minutes;

- your role is to get others to talk, not to talk yourself, so ask questions or make encouraging comments and then keep quiet;

- stick with the silence: if you fill every silence, nobody else will speak;

- give a clear question or issue to discuss;

- record key points on a board or flip chart where everybody can see it, to keep track of discussions;

- ask for clarification (e.g. 'Did you mean...?');

- every now and again (e.g. to move discussions on), summarise what's been said;

- start with a brainstorm to identify issues (i.e. you ask for items from the group and note them on a board/flip chart without initial discussion) and then discuss each one.

What if you're discussing something complex or with uncertainties or ambiguities? What would be most helpful?

- If you need to pool ideas, you may want an unstructured discussion, to see where it goes. After a while, you'll need to recap and summarise, to help reach conclusions.

- On the other hand, it may help to keep on track by agreeing an agenda first (i.e. a list of points to discuss) and then following it.

- Avoid cutting off discussion by saying (or letting others say) that something isn't true or is rubbish, or any of the other put downs that stop people in their tracks.

- It might help to ask participants how they want to manage the discussion (e.g. break into small groups; have an agenda; have a time limit on particular items).

Which of the above ideas could you try in a discussion you'll lead?

E4 Being an effective participant

Think of discussions you've been in recently. How do you think the others would have seen you (helpful; interested; stroppy; a know-all)? If you're unsure, you could ask. Is that how you want to be seen? If yes, do you know what you did to create that effect? If not, what do you want to be different? What about the others in the group? What did they do that was helpful or not? What ideas does this give you for what you might do?

Are you...	Your notes	Do you...	Your notes
aware of your body language and the impression it creates (bored; interested)?		acknowledge everything somebody else says (verbally or non-verbally)?	
aware of your tone of voice and the impression it creates?		offer supportive comments to others?	
aware of the sorts of words you use and the impression they create?		find a way of saying what you think that is acceptable to others?	
polite?		know when to stop speaking?	

E5 Improving what you do

Feedback from others is crucial here, as your success in discussion is so tied up with others perceptions of what you do or say.

What feedback have you had in recent discussions?

In relation to your contributions to discussions...	Your notes on recent discussions
What has the body language of others told you about their reaction to what you did/said?	
What do things others said suggest about their perceptions of what you did/said?	
What happened as a result of what you did/said? (Was it ignored? Did it change the tack of the discussion?)	
Who agreed/disagreed with you, why and how?	
Did anybody comment on how you behaved or what you said? (Have you asked them?). What did they think worked well or did not work well?	
If you'd been a fly on the wall, what would you have thought about what you did and said?	

What will you do in future discussions?

Activity	This is what I'll repeat/do the same	This is what I'll do differently
Being clear about what I want from the discussions.		
Having effective ongoing discussions with the same people.		

Activity	This is what I'll repeat/do the same	This is what I'll do differently
Leading discussions.		
Being an effective participant.		
Being aware of what I do/say in discussions and the effect it has.		
What else?		

12
WORKING IN A GROUP OR TEAM

Note: this chapter should be read together with Chapter 13 'Dealing with other people'.

HOW THIS CHAPTER CAN HELP YOU

The 'crucial' skills part of this chapter aims to help you:

- agree objectives for working together and what needs to be done to achieve them;
- agree roles, responsibilities and working arrangements;
- identify factors that might influence the outcome;
- meet your own responsibilities and complete agreed tasks;
- develop cooperation in the group/team;
- share information on progress, amending plans where necessary;
- present the outcomes of your group/team work;
- evaluate the extent to which with the group/team work has been successful and identify how to improve your work in groups/teams or in the future.

The 'enhanced' skills part of this chapter is shorter: it helps you operate to a higher level. As well as the 'crucial' skills' outcomes, you'll be able to:

- identify opportunities for group/team working, to get the outcomes you want;
- research information to help you get the most from the group/team work;
- efficiently plan work and arrangements with others, negotiating resources, timescales, actions and responsibilities;
- amend your strategies, given uncertainties, ambiguities and complex situations;
- take a leading role to help develop effective cooperation;
- evaluate the effectiveness of the group/team and of yourself within it in meetings is objectives and how it did so;
- identify ways of further improving your skills in working in a team or group.

CRUCIAL SKILLS

C1 Why is this chapter important and how can it help you?

In higher education (HE) many (most?) courses include activities where students work in groups or teams. This is for several reasons.

- Working in groups/teams is essential in virtually any employment situation; courses want to give students experience of doing it and of learning how to do it better.

- People learn from each other; evaluations show that students really value the support of other students (peers).

- It's a way of organising courses so that students aren't only operating in one large group; it widens out the sorts of learning activities that are possible.

Many group/team work activities are assessed but you might also be asked to work with others for mutual support and to share resources (if so, make sure that any work you produce is your own, to avoid being accused of cheating; see Chapter 8 'Plagiarism and referencing').

In the workplace, most people operate in teams at some stage (e.g. you might be in a pair or a larger group, working on a particular project).

Why do people work in such a way? A well-operating group/team can achieve more than an individual. Five people can do five times as much work in a given time as one person, and they may have five times the knowledge and skills (well, perhaps not five times but a lot more). In an effective group/team:

- work is divided up to make the best use of time;

- work is divided up to make the best use of individuals' skills and knowledge;

- individuals pull together.

Think of groups/teams you've been in. Is that how it works?

What's needed for good group/team working, in your experience?

Group/team work is often assessed because it adds value to the activity (students tend to take assessed activities more seriously). It also makes participants more aware of what's needed for effective group/team work and of how they, as individuals, operate.

Some people like working in this way whilst others prefer individual work. A common concern is fairness in group/team work: does everybody pull their weight; what do you do if they don't; does assessment really reflect what goes on?

Evaluations undertaken by the authors suggest that two things are very important to students:

1.   group/team members doing what they agree to do;

2.   group/team members doing their part of the work to a good standard (to get a good grade/mark).

However, that's not all that's important. Courses are often trying to develop 'interpersonal skills' when they set group/team activities, skills needed at work and in most situations.

C2 What sort of team or group work does this chapter consider?

This chapter is concerned with a particular sort of group/team work: a collaboration to produce something (e.g. an idea; a design; a report; a presentation; a poster). You're likely to be working on a joint project. This chapter looks specifically at how to achieve a group or team objective.

C3 Other chapters you need to use together with this one

Other chapters are relevant to group/team work and it's important that you look at them too, as the authors have tried to reduce repetition between chapters.

Chapter	Title	How it relates to this chapter	Page
13	Dealing with other people: **It's important to look at this chapter**.	This looks at how to deal with others in a range of contexts but it's very relevant to group/team working.	275
11	Discussions: face-to-face and on-line (in seminars, groups, etc.).	This considers how to take part in discussions and how to encourage others to do so.	229
5	Doing a project.	If your group/team is carrying out a project, this will be helpful (but you need to adapt the ideas to working in a group).	97
15	Handling time and pressure.	This is very important for group/team activities.	327

Chapters on presentation methods (2 'Writing Reports'; 3 'Producing portfolios and journals (including diaries, blogs etc)'; 4 'Giving a presentation, viva or being observed'; 10 'Presenting your work: making it look good') will help you present the outcomes of your group/team work.

Other chapters can help you with specific tasks (e.g. 7 'Finding, using and analysing information and evidence'; 17 'Reflecting on your learning and experience (including feedback)').

C4 Agreeing what you want to achieve

This is probably the most important stage of working in a group/team. It's particularly important to agree who will do what: not doing so might result in people not pulling their weight. If things are agreed and written down, it's much harder to claim you didn't know you had to do them. It may also avoid people taking on tasks that are unrealistic for them (one reason why people don't do what they are supposed to).

Look at the following for a group/team activity you need to do:

Question	Guidance	Your notes
What's the group/team aim? What's it trying to achieve? Is there a 'question' you need to address?	The more specific you can be the better. See Section C4 in Chapter 5 'Doing a project'.	
When is the deadline?	It's very important to be clear about this so you can plan.	
What has to be produced? What outcome is needed? Are there any special requirements for this?	Knowing what you need to end up with will affect how you do things (e.g. collect and record information).	
If assessed, what are the assessment criteria?	Find this out at the start (you might be assessed on the product or on how you work). If you aren't given any criteria, ask your tutor what is important.	

You may find that in your group/team there are different views on the above questions. If so, you need to find this out at the start and come to a shared view (see Section C5 in Chapter 13 'Dealing with other people'), or you'll all be going in different directions.

There's another issue you might discuss: the individual aims of the group/team members. If one person wants to do a really good job and others just to do 'enough', what effect will that have on the group and how can you allow for it? Not getting this out in the open can create problems later (it'll emerge eventually).

The table below gives possible individual motivations. You could each consider it separately and then discuss it. In it, what do we mean by 'implications for the group/ team'? What if your motivations differ? Perhaps you can persuade others to your views, or compromise. If one wants to learn new skills and others don't, perhaps that person can do the tasks requiring new skills. If most people just want to pass and one wants a high mark/grade, perhaps most can do the basic work needed and that one person can add what's needed for a good grade.

Look at the following for your group/team activity, individually and then together:

Motivation: want to…	✓	Implications for the group/team
get a high mark/grade.		
get a pass.		
do the best job possible.		
do the least work possible.		
enjoy it.		
get it over with quickly.		
learn new skills.		
practise existing skills.		
take risks, try out new things.		
be safe, stick with what is familiar.		
be very keen on the topic.		
not be interested in the topic.		
learn.		
just do what has to be done.		
What else?		

Once you've considered group/team and individual aims, you all need to decide how to divide the work into tasks and agree who'll do what (i.e. see Section C5 on planning). The basis on which you plan will depend on the topic, the tasks and the individuals, but here are some possibilities.

- Some tasks may need to be done before others.

- Some tasks may need different skills.

- Some tasks may be small or easy to complete.

- Some tasks may be large or difficult.

- Some tasks may be essential, and others may be nice to do if possible.

- Some tasks may need special resources you need to book or find.

You also need to consider your deadline. It's a good idea to set a deadline that's a few days before the real one, to allow for last minute work. Work back from your deadline to set interim deadlines for the tasks you must do to meet your objective. You also need to build in time for things going wrong. See Section C10 in Chapter 5 'Doing a project'.

Important: If you work in a group/team and an interim deadline isn't met, it affects the work of the rest of the group/team. This means interim deadlines need to be realistic.

C5 Planning

You now need a plan; see below for a possible one. To avoid difficulties later, it's a good idea to ensure everybody in the group/team agrees it and that they can do the tasks they're allocated. If they can't, it's better to know at the start so you can change your plan.

This sort of plan might be good evidence to show how you worked as a group/team.

Plan for a group/team activity you need to do

Group/team objective

Tasks	Interim deadline	To be done by (name of group/ team member/s)	Agreed by (signature of individual)	Notes on progress made

Is your plan realistic?

You could ask yourselves the following questions about each task you've identified.

- How long will it take to do the task?

- Have you added on at least half the time again, to allow for problems?

- What resources are needed for the task, how long will it take to get them and when can you therefore start work on the task?

- Does the person named to do the task have the skills and knowledge to do it?

- Are they the best person to do it?

- Will they need help from anybody else in the group/team?

- What will you do if they don't/can't do it, for some reason?

- How will you know if it's been done well enough?

- What will you do if it hasn't been done well enough?

What might affect your outcomes?

Looking at what might affect the outcomes of your group/team work helps you anticipate and make allowances.

In the following, you could give each item a 'risk assessment' 3 = high risk, 2 = medium risk, 1 = low risk. The bigger the risk, the more you need to plan for it; the higher the overall score, the riskier your activity.

Item	Risk (1–3)	Item	Risk (1–3)
Illness of group/team member.		Resources not available.	
Family problem for group/team member.		Computer breaks down.	
Work problem for group/team member.		Computer system breaks down.	
Tutor/manager not available.		Group/team members don't have knowledge needed.	
Extra unanticipated work given.		Group/team members don't have skills needed.	
Group/team members don't do work agreed.		Group/team members fall out or factions emerge.	
What else?			

You need to monitor your plan and amend it (it's unlikely all will go smoothly). How will you do this? Will you all meet to discuss progress and, if so, how often? Will one person check progress (how will you back them up if progress isn't made?) and will they check progress all the time or will you rotate this role?

If your plan is kept on a computer, you can amend it as you go along. Make sure everybody works to the same current plan using version numbers (e.g. Plan version 1, Plan version 2), or the date of amendment (e.g. Plan 5.1.09, Plan 8.1.09).

Your notes on how you'll monitor and amend plans

C6 Working arrangements

Section C5 considers one sort of 'working arrangement'; the creation and monitoring of a plan. What other sorts of working arrangements do you need? This may depend on the nature of your group/team activity but here are some thoughts.

Monitoring your plan

See Section C5.

Storing working material

By 'working material' we mean anything arising from the tasks you've identified.

Questions	Your notes
How will you store the results of work carried out (e.g. any information gathered)?	
How will you ensure it's accessible by all group/ team members who need it for their own tasks (if it's in somebody's house, 20 miles away, you may have a problem)?	
To make is easy for you all, will you have a standard format for notes (see Chapter 9 'Making notes')?	
How will you store material so that it's easy to put into your final product?	
Are there any special issues you need to consider when storing your working material (e.g. computer memory needed for images)?	
What else do you need to consider?	

Version control for the final product

Where more than one person is working on something, there's scope for mix-up over which document is the latest version, who has which information, and so on. It can take a long, frustrating time to sort out (you might spend hours correcting a version that wasn't the right one).

Example of version control

In writing this book we (the authors) are working as team (even though there are only two of us) and we've agreed the following (our working documents are on our separate computers).

- *Each chapter to have a file name indicating its title.*

- *In the file name, the title will be followed by a draft number (e.g. 'Writing a report draft 3').*

- *Every time a draft is changed, the draft number changes.*

- *Only one author works on a draft at a time, then passes it on and does no more on it until the draft returns.*

- *If either author is uncertain about any item in the draft, it's highlighted in yellow.*

- *Each author has a computer folder (e.g. 'book') with sub-folders (e.g. 'learning outcomes' and 'chapters').*

If you're not working on computers you still need a system. Perhaps one person could keep a file with the latest versions in it, carefully numbered (see Chapter 9 'Making notes').

Ground rules

In any group/team it can help to agree 'ground rules' for how people will behave (e.g. in a sports team, a referee oversees that all players adhere to the rules).

In your case, the whole group/team can act as the first 'referee' if somebody breaks the 'rules'. If you can't resolve the issue, then you have a second line 'referee' in the form of the person who's set the group/team activity (e.g. your tutor; manager).

The ground rules are up to you, but everybody needs to agree them (if one person imposes them, the others may ignore them). Possibilities for ground rules include:

- everybody turn up to meetings;

- everybody to do their best to do what's agreed;

- each person to say if they're behind with a task, can't meet a deadline or do the task;

- if things don't go well, members to avoid blaming each other and focus on what to do about it;

- if there are disagreements, focus on what must be done, not on the disagreement;

- avoid criticising people (as opposed to criticising work, which is essential);
- accept criticisms of your work without being angry or defensive.

C7 Meeting your responsibilities

The bottom line in a group/team is that you do what you agree by the time agreed. If you don't, it'll create difficulties for others.

However, life can throw unexpected things at us. Something may crop up that makes it hard for you to complete the task, it may be more difficult than anticipated or resources may be missing. If you can't do what you agreed, you need to alert the others as soon as possible, so you can all amend your plans.

This presupposes two things:

1.   the group/team members will be sympathetic to each other's problems;

2.   the group/team members will pull together to help each other.

Working together isn't about personal likes or dislikes. Most people in employment operate in groups/teams with those they wouldn't choose as friends, but within the limits of a work task, they allow for and help each other.

What if somebody just isn't doing the work? See Chapter 13 'Dealing with other people' for ideas. Recent research suggests that 'freeloaders' often know that they're not pulling their weight and feel bad about it (Pulman, 2008).

If the group/team can't sort out the situation, you may need to refer the matter to your tutor or manager. You have a responsibility to yourself as well as to the others and if your work or grade/mark might be damaged, it's important to deal with it.

C8 Developing cooperation

Group/team work is all about working together and helping each other. Chapter 13 'Dealing with other people' looks at this and we suggest that you make good use of it. Some of the issues it addresses are:

- encouraging others to contribute;
- resolving any conflict/difficulties;
- communicating;
- acting in a way that uses awareness of others feelings, beliefs, opinions.

What do you normally do in a group and what could you do differently? Are you cooperative yourself (willing to do things, to help others, to adapt)?

What I do	Usually ✓	Some times ✓	Do I want to keep doing this or do something different?
Take the lead.			
Follow others.			
Come up with ideas.			
Wait for others' ideas.			
Suggest what others should do.			
Do what others say.			
Take on more of the work than others.			
Take on less of the work than others.			
Take on the same work as others.			
Help others.			
Just do my own work.			
Smile.			
Frown.			
Encourage.			
Criticise.			
Be grumpy.			
Shout.			

C9 Presenting the outcomes of your work

We suggest you look at Chapter 10 'Presenting your work; making it look good', which is relevant to any type of product. There are also chapters on common products for group/team activities (e.g. reports; notes – including minutes of meetings).

In addition to a product, you may have to provide evidence of how you went about the task and worked together. If so, you need to keep on-going records of what you do, as this will become your evidence. These records could include:

- your original plan for the work, with subsequent amended plans (to show how you adjusted what you did);

- minutes or recordings of meetings (see Chapter 9 'Making notes');

- journals, blogs or diaries for each person, showing what they did;

- examples of work in progress (e.g. notes of information collected);

- an evaluation by each person of what they contributed: see Chapter 17 'Reflecting on your learning and experience (including feedback)'.

You may want to put this evidence into a portfolio: see Chapter 3 'Producing portfolios and journals, (including diaries, blogs, etc.)'.

You may be asked to assess each other's contributions (e.g. an evaluation of each group/team member; giving them a grade; dividing a mark between you according to how much each person contributed). This may be uncomfortable but it's done:

- so group/team members get feedback from their peers on how they operated (i.e. to help them learn for the future);

- as a way of encouraging all group/team members to contribute.

In evaluating somebody's performance, it's not helpful to make personal, judgemental, general comments that they can do nothing about (e.g. 'you were a lazy good-for-nothing' is not likely to achieve much, other than anger or upset). It's helpful to be specific and refer to what happened, with some ideas on what might have been more useful (e.g. 'when you didn't collect the information by the date agreed, we got behind and others had to do more work. It would have helped if you'd told us sooner that you couldn't do it').

Although it may be uncomfortable to give feedback and even a mark/grade, it will be more help to others if you're honest, not to pretend all was well. It's really important to tell people what they did well and to use the same principle. 'You were just great in this team' may be nice to hear but it isn't useful in knowing what to do in future; be specific (e.g. 'You were really helpful to other members in discussing problems they were facing').

C10 Reviewing and improving what you do

How can you improve your group/team skills? Firstly, how well do you think the group/team worked together?

Group/team activity	What worked well?	What could have been improved?
Agreeing our objective.		
Being clear about what we had to produce.		
Deciding on the tasks to be done.		
Agreeing who would do the tasks.		
Making a plan.		
Monitoring the plan.		
Amending the plan.		
Allowing for what might affect what we did.		
Carrying out the plan.		
Cooperating with each other.		
Presenting the outcomes of our work.		
Being aware of/evaluating what we did.		

Now, what do **you personally** need to do next time, to build on good things you noted above and to have an influence on the things that needed improving?

Activity: add your own items here	This is what I'll repeat/do the same in future	This is what I'll do differently

ENHANCED SKILLS

E1 What do you most want from group/team work?

The 'Crucial skills' section of this chapter considered group/team objectives and how they might be affected by individual motivations (Section C4). It might help to consider further what *you* want from current group/team activities.

For a group/team activity you are currently required to do...	Your notes
what do you personally want to achieve from it?	
what will you need to do/how will you need to behave in the group/team in order to achieve this?	
will you need to develop any new skills or learn any new ways of behaving?	
who or what could help you?	

Do you have an activity to do where working in a group/team might help? What opportunities are there for improving what you do by collaborating with others?

Activities where cooperating with others would help	Your notes
Do you share interests with others where you could cooperate (e.g. learning a new skill; finding data). **Important**: Any work for assessment must be your own.	
Could you cooperate with others in order to release more time for studies?	
If you work, could a work task and course task overlap? Could you and work colleagues help each other? **Important**: Any work for assessment must be your own.	
Could you engage in group/team activities that would impress a future employer or would help you develop skills for future employment (e.g. via the Students Union; volunteering)?	
What groups/teams do you already operate in (e.g. sports) and could you use them to develop skills you know you need?	

E2 Finding out more about group and team work

If you're using this 'Enhanced skills' section, you've probably already experienced group/team work and have ideas about things you'd like to improve. How could you find out more about them?

Areas to explore	Possible ways of doing so
Group dynamics, what makes groups operate effectively.	There's a massive literature on group work. The bibliography at the end of this chapter suggests a few, which will lead you to other items.
Planning.	There's literature on planning methods. You could ask others what they do. Do you know anybody who works in or is studying project management?
Negotiating skills.	See Section C5 in Chapter 13 'Dealing with other people'. There are many books on this topic, including 'pop psychology' ones you'll find in any bookshop.
What about any specific needs for your topic (e.g. ethical/health and safety/ equality issues)?	The internet is a useful starting point. There may be legislation on some of these things. Your university/college or workplace will also have guidelines and rules.
What else might you find out more about?	Ask your tutor/manager for guidance.

E3 Planning revisited

What can you do to make your planning more effective and efficient, to make the best use of time and people?

Planning for a current group/team activity

What have you learnt about what makes bad planning for group/team work?	What have you learned about what makes good planning for group/team work?
What are you accountable for/responsible for in this group/team activity?	**What are you not responsible for in this group/team activity?**
What does this suggest you need to do when you plan for a current group/team activity?	

At this level, you'll probably be dealing with a topic where there are complexities, uncertainties, ambiguities. What can you do to plan for these?

To improve your planning, you could:

- spend time early in a group/team activity making sure you have the resources needed;
- spend more time negotiating and agreeing how to do things efficiently, rather than plunging in and using trial and error;
- find out more about helpful techniques (e.g. for planning);
- agree which aspects of the work could be done quickly and which need more attention;

- agree which tasks could be done by one person and which are best shared;

- list the relevant skills and knowledge of group/team members; ensure you use them well;

- set aside a chunk of time for planning, when you can give your full attention to it (rather than snatching a few minutes here and there);

- build in time for things you don't anticipate;

- agree communication systems so when a member comes up against an uncertainty they have somebody to discuss it with;

- brainstorm all the aspects of a complex issue at the start;

- don't be afraid of uncertainty and ambiguity: they're normal at higher levels of learning (or at work). What matters is that you know what is uncertain or ambiguous and why.

Section C5 suggested a simple plan. Here's a slightly more sophisticated **example** you could use for a current group/team activity. A 'milestone' is something that shows how far you have got and it helps to identify them in advance.

Group/team objective						
Milestones (i.e. interim targets)	Dead-line	Actions needed to achieve this	Group/team member responsible	Resources or help needed	Possible risks or problems	Progress

E4 Taking more of a lead

At higher levels of operating in a group/team you may be expected to take more of a lead. This doesn't necessarily mean you're the 'leader', but that you accept more responsibility, for your own work and for ensuring the group/team works well together.

Chapter 13 'Dealing with other people' looks at how you operate with others in more detail and it'll help to refer to it. However, in the context of working with others to reach a shared objective or create a shared product, you might consider the following.

Against each item you could rate yourself, where 1 is very good, 2 is good, 3 is needs improvement.

Item	Rating 1–3	Notes for what I could do in future
Being aware of the effect I have on others (e.g. working style; behaviour).		
Encouraging a working environment based on mutual respect.		
Avoiding actions that may offend, harass, discriminate.		
Encouraging others to avoid such actions.		
Anticipating others' need for information and support.		
Helping ensure tasks are done on time, to the standard needed.		
Helping ensure that resources are used well.		
Structuring what I say, using appropriate vocabulary, tone, emphasis to make points.		
Responding perceptively to others.		
Giving and receiving constructive feedback to help progress.		
Agreeing ways of managing any conflict.		

E5 Review: improving things

There are two elements to this:

1. Whilst working in your group/team, you need to constantly review how well you're doing to make sure you're working effectively. This enables you to amend your plans.

2. You're very likely to find yourself working in groups/teams in the future and you need to consider your own behaviour and whether you need to build on it or change it.

It may be helpful to evaluate how the group/team operated before evaluating what **you** did, as what happened in general will have had an impact on you.

Evaluating the group/team

This can be used while the group is operating or afterwards. Against each item you could rate your group/team, where 1 is very good, 2 is good, 3 is needs improvement.

Item	Rating 1–3	Notes on what the team could do/could have done
How well does/did the team negotiate its objectives, and allow for those of the members, in order to develop a shared approach?		
How efficient is/was the plan?		
How well is/was the group/team able to respond to circumstances and amend the plan?		
How efficient and effective are/were the working arrangements (e.g. meetings; records; version control)?		
How cooperative is/was the group/team as a whole?		
How well is/did the group/team meeting/meet its objective? How good an outcome will it be/was it?		
How far would you like to repeat the experience in this group/team?		

Evaluating your own contribution and identifying improvements for the future

Against each item you could **rate yourself**, where 1 is very good, 2 is good, 3 is needs improvement.

Item	Rating 1–3	Notes on what I could do in future
Being clear about the group/team objectives.		
Being clear about my own personal objectives.		
Finding out more about aspects of group/team work to underpin what I do.		
Planning efficiently and effectively.		
Taking more of a lead.		
Constantly evaluating how well I'm doing in relation to the group/team objectives.		
Constantly evaluating how I'm doing in working helpfully with the others.		

REFERENCES

Pulman, M., (2008), '"Knowing yourself through others": peer assessment in popular music group work', (PhD Thesis), Sheffield: Sheffield Hallam University.

13
DEALING WITH OTHER PEOPLE

HOW THIS CHAPTER CAN HELP YOU

The 'crucial' skills part of this chapter aims to help you:

- be clear about what you and others need from your interactions;
- identify factors that affect your dealings with others;
- be aware of, and take account of, others' feelings, beliefs, opinions and avoid actions that may offend, harass or discriminate;
- being aware of the effect of your approach on others;
- be assertive;
- negotiate with others;
- develop effective co-operation between yourself and others;
- resolve any conflict/difficulties with others;
- plan to improve your dealings with others.

The 'enhanced' skills part of this chapter is shorter: it helps you operate to a higher level. As well as the 'crucial' skills' outcomes, you'll be able to:

- identify the outcomes you most want or need from your dealings with others;
- anticipate the wants and needs of others in a situation and allow for them;
- adapt what you do to achieve what you want/need, given uncertainties, ambiguities and complex situations;
- choose the more appropriate way of communicating and use it effectively
- respond perceptively to others;
- build relationships with people over time;
- evaluate your dealings with others;
- give and receive feedback constructively;
- agree with others ways of improving your dealings in the future;
- identify how you can further develop your skills.

CRUCIAL SKILLS

C1 Why is this chapter important and how can it help you?

In higher education (HE) you will deal with a wide range of people, in relation to:

- practical issues (e.g. porters; security staff; caterers; ticket inspectors; bank staff);

- your wellbeing (e.g. in a health centre; student services; personal tutors; sports staff);

- your domestic situation (e.g. partner; family; house mates);

- your social life (e.g. other students; students union; leisure industry staff; anybody you meet);

- your learning (e.g. other students; lecturers/tutors; technicians; library/learning centre staff; ICT support staff; mentor; colleagues).

How you deal with these people may have a big effect on your success on your course. For example, our research (Drew in Drew, Nankivell and Shoolbred, 1992) found that the support received from tutors seemed related to how well the students related to them.

In work settings, having good relationships with work colleagues (or clients, etc.), regardless of their role, is very important. If you need somebody to do a small task for you and they don't do it, it can hold you up for weeks. Being able to deal with others is seen as vitally important to anybody recruiting graduates.

Dealing effectively with others also has a big impact on your personal happiness and wellbeing.

Dealing with others is, however, difficult and we all get it wrong from time to time. This chapter aims to help you be more effective (and to forgive yourself if it doesn't work). Learning to deal with others is lifelong: you keep meeting new people and new situations.

C2 Other chapters you need to use together with this one

There are some other chapters you need to look at that relate to contexts where dealing with others is vital. This 'Dealing with other people' chapter underpins them.

Chapter	Title	How it relates to this chapter	Page
12	Working in a group or team.	You need good interpersonal skills to work in a group or team.	253
11	Discussions: face-to-face and on-line (in seminars, groups etc).	Interpersonal skills are important for the sorts of discussions you have on a course or at work.	229

For all chapters in this book, effectively dealing with others is important but it will be particularly helpful to look at this chapter in relation to the following ones.

Chapter	Title	How it relates to this chapter	Page
4	Giving a presentation, viva or being observed.	If you're giving a group presentation or you intend to involve your audience in the presentation, this chapter will help.	69
17	Reflecting on your learning and experience (including feedback).	This looks at the use of feedback to help you learn and this is very important in dealing with others.	379

C3 Why are you dealing with others? What's wanted from the situation?

Does referring to what you want or need from others make you feel uncomfortable, as if you're 'using' people? This chapter doesn't take an approach whereby you get what you want regardless of others. Its approach is to consider how you can behave so that everybody can get something positive out of a situation, not just you. This chapter concentrates on dealing with others in a particular context – that is, being successful on your course and at work. For this, you'll need help and cooperation from a lot of people.

A starting point is to work out for a particular situation what you want or need, what others want or need and what might affect what happens. The alternative is just to do what comes naturally to you without thinking about it. This may or may not work. Even if you're normally 'good with people', it can help to think through what's going on.

Dealing with others effectively largely depends on being able to see things from their point of view: some of us find this harder than others. It can help to think about it in a structured way.

Here's an example

Situation facing me			
Asking a member of library or learning-centre staff where to find information on a topic.			

What might affect this?			
How busy the centre is. How many others want the same information? Whether or not the information is available.			

What do I need/want?	What does the library/learning centre person need/want?	Where are the common interests?	What are the different interests (clashes/tensions)?
To find good information as easily as possible, with the least amount of effort on my part.	To understand what I need. To provide this. To feel they've done a good job. To take as little time as possible so they can get on to help the next person.	We both want to find good information.	We both want to spend as little time as possible on it (i.e I want the staff member to do it for me; they want me to do it myself).

What can I reasonably expect from them?
If they aren't busy they can spend more time with me, but if they are busy they won't. I can reasonably expect them to show me how to find things and to do so in willingly, but not to do it for me.

What can they reasonably expect from me?
Clarity about what I need; asking for everything at one go to avoid having to keep going back; politeness and thanks.

What are the implications for me?
I need to allow enough time to find the information in case they're busy or the information isn't immediately available. If I leave it 'til the last minute I may be stressed, less polite and less tolerant if they don't have time to do it for me.

You could now identify a situation currently facing you where you need to deal with somebody and follow the same process.

Situation facing me			
What might affect this?			
What do I need/ want?	**What does the library/ learning centre person need/want?**	**Where are the common interests?**	**What are the different interests (clashes/tensions)?**
What can I reasonably expect from them?			
What can they reasonably expect from me			
What are the implications for me?			

If you do this a few times, in this structured way, for different kinds of situations, you may start to do it naturally. You can use this structured approach when faced with any situation that makes you apprehensive.

C4 What sorts of things affect your dealings with others?

Your dealings with others may be affected by things in the environment, in other people or within yourself.

Things outside yourself	Implications
Practicalities (e.g. facilities or resources not being available).	Plan in advance to avoid this.
Having shared interests.	Focus on them rather than on differences.
Conflicting interests (wanting different things).	Negotiate (see Section C5).

Things outside yourself	Implications
Others being upset about something not related to you	Be aware of and allow for others (see Section C8).
Others being 'difficult' (e.g. aggressive; uncooperative).	See Section C6 on cooperation and Section C7 on dealing with conflict.
How trustworthy others are.	If you don't trust them, have a fall back position. Behave in a way that others can trust and hope they follow your example. See Sections C5 and C6.
What else seems to affect your dealings with others?	

Things within yourself	Implications
You not seeing others' points of view.	See Section C3. Ask others what they want.
You being busy or stressed.	See Chapter 15 'Handling time and pressure'. Being stressed isn't great in dealing with others (it may cause anger and irritation).
What you want is so important to you that you don't care how you get it.	If you don't think about the 'how' you may never get to the end point that's so important to you.
You being 'difficult' (uncooperative; aggressive).	See Sections C6 and C7. Ask yourself why you're doing this.
How much they trust or respect you.	Are you behaving in a way that others can trust or respect?
Your manner.	How would you/others describe your manner? What effect does it have? When is it appropriate?
How clear you are and your communication skills.	Could it be that others just don't understand what you want or need? Have you told them?
What else?	

Being aware of what you do is a major step in dealing effectively with others.

What do you do that works well in dealing with others?	What do you do that doesn't work well in dealing with others?	What would you like to change or improve?

C5 Being assertive and negotiating

C5.1 Being assertive

It's important to differentiate between being aggressive and being assertive. Being aggressive is getting what you want at the expense of another. Being assertive is getting what you want in a way that isn't at the expense of others and allows for what they want.

Assertiveness is about making it clear what you want in a way that allows others to agree or disagree. If you discover that you have different needs or views, you can then negotiate to find a point that's OK for both of you.

What is not assertive? Shouting at people isn't, or forcing them to do what you want or manipulating them. There are many ways people manipulate each other; for example, making somebody feel guilty or responsible for you, or behaving as if you need looking after.

What effect do anger and manipulation have on you?

Have you been on the receiving end of anger or bullying?	
How did it make you feel?	What would you have liked to happen instead?

Have you been on the receiving end of manipulation?	
How did it make you feel?	What would you have liked to happen instead?

If anger and manipulation have such effects on you, perhaps others feel the same if you're angry with or manipulate them.

Books on this subject often start by looking at your 'rights' and those of others. You need to believe you have a right to your views, opinions and needs, and that other people have a right to theirs. If you think others have rights but you don't, you'll have difficulties in getting what you need; if you think you have rights but others don't, you may antagonise them.

Here are some assertiveness techniques.

- Make clear what you'd like; ask others what they would like.

- Just say no. If you're asked to do something you can't or don't want to do, just say no without giving reasons, apologies or justifications. The other person will generally accept it. If they don't, then the negotiation starts.

- Don't offer reasons or long explanations (e.g. 'I'd like help with setting up a spreadsheet please' is enough). If you start giving reasons it can sound apologetic. (But if asked why then briefly give reasons).

- Acknowledge ownership. If you want, think or feel something, say 'I' (e.g. 'It isn't fair' might become 'I don't think it is fair').

- Be clear. If you go all around the houses before saying what you want, the other person might not be able to work out what it is.

- Use 'broken record' (what a useful technique!). This means repeating the same phrase (e.g., if you want to complain 'Please can I speak to the manager' *'Can you tell me your problem?'* 'I'd just like to speak to the manager' *'Perhaps I can help you?'* 'I'd just like to speak to the manager').

- Don't start from the ultimate position but work up to it if necessary.

Being assertive is important in negotiating. Keep practising. It gets easier!

C5.2 Negotiating

This is important in virtually any situation involving others. Where people don't want the same thing, somebody must give way or you have to negotiate.

Giving way may be a reasonable choice: the issue may not be very important to you; the other person's feelings may be more important to you than what you wanted. We often decide on the spot whether to accept a situation, give in or make a stand (we assume you agree that bullying or manipulating others isn't helpful).

Below is a process you could go through for a situation facing you where it may help to negotiate. It assumes that you're being assertive in saying what you need and want and are open to listening to what the other person needs and wants.

Question	Your notes on a current situation
What's the situation and what are the issues?	
What would you ideally like in this situation?	
Have you asked others what they'd like? What is it?	
What's the minimum you'd accept (your bottom line)?	
What common ground have you both got (where do you both want something similar)?	
Where do you differ?	
What might appeal to others' interests?	
Are there any solutions other than the ones you both first thought of?	
What could you give way on that might move things forward?	
What could they give way on that might move things forward?	
Is there one thing that's the key stumbling block?	
How important is this? What will the worst thing be if you give way?	
Who else might help resolve the matter (e.g. a tutor or colleague)?	
Would a cooling off period provide space/ time to think how to deal with it?	

How does the thought of having to negotiate make you feel? Excited? Worried? If you're anxious, can you identify why? Is it not getting what you want/need or is it more to do with having to face the other person? Are you afraid of being laughed at, feeling foolish, upsetting others or them not liking you? Look back at Section C5.1 on assertiveness. The fear of something may be worse than doing it.

C6 Cooperation

Cooperation means working with others in a helpful way to achieve something. What makes you want to cooperate with others?

Why did you cooperate in some recent situations?

Possible reasons for your cooperation	✓
The aim was important to me.	
I could see a good reason why I should cooperate.	
It was in my interests to cooperate.	
I wanted to be helpful.	
I felt responsible.	
I like the other person.	
I was appreciated, and this made me feel good.	
It was a way of making friends.	
I wanted others to like me.	
What else?	

What do you count as 'not cooperating'? Why don't you cooperate? Look back at the list above and mark the items where you wouldn't cooperate, if the statement was reversed (e.g. the aim isn't important to you).

If you don't cooperate with others in a situation you are currently facing.

What short term effect will it have?	What longer term effect will it have?	What would be the effect if you did cooperate?

How can you encourage others to cooperate with you (you may want to look again at the checklist above for ideas)? For example, how could you appeal to their interests or encourage them to feel responsible or to help you?

Example

Issue	Actions I could take
e.g. Encourage them to feel appreciated.	e.g. Thank them for what they do; say in what way it's helpful; ask if they can contribute in a way that makes use of their strengths.

Your issues	Actions you could take

C7 Dealing with conflict

Conflict is natural between people: people often just want different things or perceive things differently. It's likely that you'll encounter conflict, although you can try to avoid it. Being assertive and cooperative are good ways of avoiding conflict (the reverse may encourage it). However, regardless of what you do, conflict may still arise. What can you do about it?

What if you're the one who is angry?

This section incorporates ideas from a mix of books (Goleman 1996; Lerner 2005; Macaskill 2002).

Expressing anger may feel like a release but it's unlikely to have a good lasting effect. Giving vent to anger tends to make you even angrier. Going into a long, rational explanation about how the other person has offended you is also unlikely to work (they'll probably say you've gone over the top or are over-analysing). Sulking prolongs the problem without resolving it and if you're doing the sulking, you become the one in the wrong.

Many people find anger difficult. Getting angry with someone is likely to change the nature of your relationship, not necessarily for the better. This doesn't mean you don't feel angry. Everybody does. It's what you do with it that matters.

So what can you do with your anger? Here are suggestions:

- Tell the other person calmly and briefly they've upset you as soon as possible (one sentence only) and avoid long explanations, getting into discussion about it or defending your position. You could use 'broken record' (see Section C5) to avoid getting embroiled (e.g. 'I felt annoyed when you didn't do the work you said you'd do.' *'So what was I supposed to do when I was so busy?'* 'I just felt annoyed when you didn't do it.' *'Well, it's no concern of mine what you thought.'* 'Fine, I'm just telling you I felt annoyed.'). You can't control their reaction or make them sorry. All you can do is tell them and then leave it.

- Write down the thing you're annoyed about, why you're angry, why you're sad about it, what you're afraid of, what you regret about it and what positive feelings you have about the person. You might see it differently.

- Write down what the opposite way of looking at it would be; if you changed your beliefs about a situation, would it look different?

- Go away, thump a cushion and shout, on your own.

- Avoid making connections between different 'slights' against you. See each occasion as separate rather than as a long list of grievances.

- Avoid going over it again and again in your mind. If you find yourself doing this, force yourself to think of something else (count backwards from 500; talk to yourself about something completely different).

- Avoid letting it happen again (e.g. try not to be dependent on someone who let you down before). This doesn't mean avoiding them, just not being in their 'power'.

- Forgive them. Have you never done something wrong?

Suggestions for if others are angry

- Acknowledge it. It defuses it. The first thing customer-service staff do is to acknowledge your anger (e.g. 'I can quite appreciate you're annoyed').

- If you offend people without meaning to and are unsure what you did, try to get feedback on it. Could you ask the person or somebody else about it?

- Listen to the person who's annoyed: being ignored makes people angrier. Listen for a reasonable time, though, and only if they're rational. If they're abusive, you've the right not to listen (e.g. 'Please talk to me again when you feel more able to do so').

- Find out the key issue they're annoyed about.

- Focus on the solution. If you come up with a solution they'll calm down quickly and may even apologise for losing their temper.

- Take time out until everybody has calmed down.

- If the other person has just cause to be annoyed, apologise and offer to put it right.

- If others are angry with each other (not with you), acknowledge it, suggest they take time out and see if you can help them focus on positives. Support them in trying to sort it out with each other but if you try to sort it out for them, beware! If you try to resolve an argument between others, one or both of them may end up annoyed with you.

C8 People's feelings, beliefs and opinions

There are two sets of feelings, beliefs and opinions that matter here: yours and theirs. Where they coincide all is fine. Where they don't it may lead to somebody being offended or to misunderstandings. There are two main tasks here: not offending others; not allowing others to offend you.

What might offend others? Do you do any of the following? Are you on the receiving end of any of them? In either case, what can you do about it?

Possible offences	Examples of such offences	I do it ✓	Others do it to me ✓	Suggestions if you do it to others	Suggestions if others do it to you
Saying discriminatory things.	Racist, sexist, ageist, about disability.			Don't do it! Ask people how they like to be referred to.	Politely point it out and say 'I don't find it acceptable'. See Sections C5 and C7.
Using non-inclusive language.	'He' instead of 's/he' or 'they': assuming all are white or able bodied.			Check who you may have excluded by the language or examples you use.	Politely point it out.
Making fun of people.	Of their backgrounds, appearance. Imitating them (e.g. accents, mannerisms).			Just don't do it. It isn't funny. It's cruel.	Ask them not to do it (in private or at the time). Seek help from a tutor/ manager if done repeatedly.
Putting people down.	Personal insults, laughing at their ideas.			'Do to others as you'd like them to do to you'; you tend to get back what you give out.	See above
Bullying or harassing people.	Making people do what you want (by words or actions).			See Section C5. Be assertive instead. You can be excluded or sacked for it. Check your institution's policies.	See Section C5 Being assertive counteracts a bully. Bullying is an offence. Check your institution's policies. Get help.
Saying or implying others views are worthless.	Judgemental words (e.g. 'rubbish'), sighing, body language.			Comment on ideas; use reasoned arguments. Take their views seriously even if you disagree.	Ask the person what they disagree with and why (to move them from personalising it).
Patronising other people.	Using patronising language (e.g. 'dear').			You may do this without meaning to. Check what others find patronising.	Tell the person (e.g. in private) that you feel patronised and how.
Ignoring them.	Not looking at them; acting as if they aren't there.			You won't be able to deal with them at all if you do this.	See Section C5 Be assertive. Address people who ignore you.
Not listening to them.	Talking over them; interrupting.			You may miss something. You'll make them feel as if they don't matter.	Say 'Please could I just finish what I was saying?' (It works every time!).

C9 Reviewing and improving what you do

If something goes wrong in your dealings with other people, what's your likely reaction?

My reaction	✓	Suggestions
I don't usually notice if something's gone wrong.		You may need to improve your awareness of others. Ask for more feedback from others.
I see it as their problem, not mine.		It is unlikely that something is one person's 'fault'. How might you have contributed to the situation?
I shrug it off.		This may be quite healthy, provided you've first thought through what your responsibility was and what you could do differently in future.
I'm sad about it and try to see what I could do differently next time.		Feeling sad if things go wrong with others is normal. Looking to what you could do in future is vital.
I blame myself and feel bad about it for ages.		It's unlikely to be all your 'fault' and blame isn't helpful. What would you say to your best friend in a similar situation? Be your own best friend. Forgive yourself. We all get it wrong sometimes.

How can you improve your skills in dealing with others?

Activity	This is what I'll repeat/ do the same in future	This is what I'll do differently
Being clear about what I want/ need, what others want/need and what the situation requires.		
Being aware of what I do and the effect it has.		
Being assertive		

Activity	This is what I'll repeat/ do the same in future	This is what I'll do differently
Negotiating.		
Developing cooperation.		
Resolving conflict.		
Being aware of/taking into account others' feelings, beliefs, opinions.		
Avoiding actions that offend, harass or discriminate.		

ENHANCED SKILLS

E1 What do you most want to achieve?

What's important to you in dealing with others? What are the implications of this for how you behave? How important to you is each aspect below in situations you are currently facing on a scale where 3 is very important, 2 is of some importance and 1 is not important at all?

Aspect	Importance rating 1–3	What effect does this have on what you do?
Establishing friendships.		
Ensuring that others feel OK.		
Being liked by others.		
Being respected by others.		
Being trusted by others.		
Helping others.		
Getting good references.		
Having more responsibilities (or promotion).		
Leading others.		
Working in a team or group with others.		
Working mostly independently.		
Getting an end result.		

Are there any tensions here? What if you rate as 3 (very important) both 'being liked' and 'getting an end result'? Sometimes, if you're a leader, you may need to take actions that others don't like. What's more important to you? Could you achieve both?

E2 Anticipating what others want, need or may do and what might happen

People may not behave as expected; new situations may arise. Others may operate in many different situations, as you do (family, friends, tutors, students). They (and you) may have conflicting demands. How can you anticipate what might affect your dealings with others and how can you then adapt what you do?

Some ways of anticipating what might happen

You could ask them:

- what sort of issues they have that may affect their dealings with you;
- how they would like to operate (e.g. how you and your tutor could work together);
- what they want, what they're worried about or what they're looking forward to.

Using your previous experience of the people or of similar situations, you could estimate:

- how likely it is that they'll do something (e.g. turn up to an event; do what they say);
- what difficulties they may encounter;
- how they tend to react;
- the risk of things going wrong.

Try putting yourself in their place.

- How would you feel?
- What would you want?
- What might you do or how might you react?

Ways of dealing with the unexpected when dealing with others

These include:

- allow more time than you think any task should take and plan for this;
- be clear about what you want (See Section C3);
- be flexible and prepared to change your approach;
- behave in ways that are unlikely to cause offense (see Section C7);

- behave in ways that are likely to be effective in most situations (see Section C5);

- have a fall back position for if things go wrong.

In the following, use a rating scale where 3 = very likely, 2 = likely and 1 = unlikely

What might happen or how might others feel or react?	Likelihood 1–3	What could you do about this?

E3 Communicating effectively

Which method(s) might be good in a situation facing you now?

Method	Advantages	Disadvantages	Useful to me ✓
Email.	Can communicate quickly. Provides a record. Can contact several people at once. Can send documents.	Email overload means people may not read them. Need to be aware of 'netiquette' (see next section). Dangers: zapping off badly worded emails; forwarding things you shouldn't.	
Phone.	Immediate. Informal, personal. Allows for discussion. Can hear tone of voice. Can put right things that don't go well immediately. Familiar to most people.	No record of what was said. Can be intrusive if the person receiving the call is busy. Getting through can take hours. Things might be said that you regret or that hurt. Phone may be slammed down.	
Letter.	Good for formal situations where you need a record. Has 'the human touch'. Allows you to think through what to say. Can say things that may be hard face-to-face.	Time taken to arrive and for reply to be received. They may not reply. May seem distancing or formal.	
Fax.	Allows for sending of letters or other documents.	Getting outdated. People/organisations may not have fax machines now.	
Computer discussion.	Can share views/ideas/ information. Can get feedback on your ideas.	All participants can see it (so wording needs to be careful). People may not contribute: some 'lurk', that is, read but don't contribute.	
Meeting face-to-face.	Can see and hear people; can judge how they feel. Time to explain views. Able to correct/clarify misunderstandings. May save time in the long run.	No record (unless notes taken or it's taped). Can prepare but need to think/ react on the spot. You're open to bad reactions as well as good ones. Needs to be set up/organised. Can take longer than other methods.	

Netiquette

It's good practice with email to:

- reply to emails so the senders know they've been received;
- be as short/concise as possible;
- use headings that reflect contents;
- make it clear what's attached;
- make clear whom it's 'to' (i.e. those who need to respond) and those who just have a 'cc' ('carbon copy' for information);
- avoid sending heated messages and aggression (you'll regret zapping off a crabby email), sarcasm and 'shouting' by using capitals; be careful about being funny (senses of humour differ);
- check the contents of anything before you forward it;
- avoid forwarding bulk emails or spam (they may have viruses);
- respect other people's privacy.

Letters

Below is an example of a formal letter, with brief descriptions about its structure.

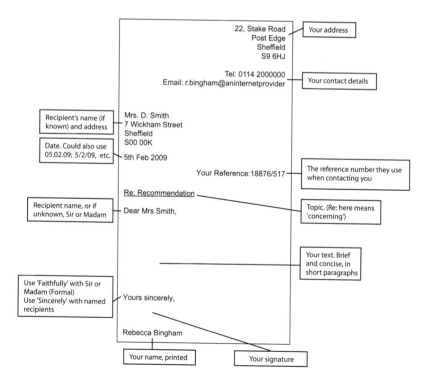

E4 Being perceptive about others

The more perceptive you are about others' feelings and thoughts the better you can deal with them. Here are some things that might help you:

- look at their body language. There are classic signs of distress or anxiety (e.g. biting nails; arms crossed over chest; feet jerking), boredom (e.g. fidgeting; yawning; looking away from you), involvement (sitting forward; looking at you; facial expressions) or sympathy/empathy (e.g. mirroring how each other is sitting);

- listen to how they say things as well as what they say. What sorts or words do they use (e.g. emotive; objective) and what's their tone of voice (e.g. annoyed; amused)?

- anticipate (see Section E2);

- ask them how they feel and what they think;

E5 Building relationships over time

If you're going to deal with somebody for any length of time you need to be careful in your communications. You might be able to get away with offending somebody you'll never see again, but not if it's somebody you work with everyday or who's supporting your learning. Section C should help.

As well as communicating well, you also need to establish some sort of relationship with them. How you do this may depend on your gender and background but, in general, relationships may be helped by:

- sharing interests and views;

- finding a topic to talk about that you can both relate to;

- taking time to chat about things not directly related to whatever brought you together;

- being open with each other;

- telling each other how you feel;

- being there when they need you, doing what you say, being trusted by them;

- giving them your time;

- making an effort (even if you're the one making all the effort, it usually pays off!).

It's always worth having smooth relationships with people even if you think you'll never see them again. You never can tell who'll turn up as your boss or a friend's partner.

E6 Feedback

Chapter 17 'Reflecting on your learning and experience (including feedback)' deals more fully with giving and receiving feedback, but here's a brief summary.

If you give feedback to others it needs to:

- be specific and refer to what they did or what happened (rather than judgemental comments about them as a person);

- be as soon after the event as possible;

- use language that indicates what they could do about it (as opposed to 'good' or 'bad' which tells them little).

If you receive feedback from others you need to:

- ask for feedback on specific things;

- accept it without being defensive or aggressive (or they won't give it you again);

- make judgements about the aspects you think are valid and need to act upon (other people aren't necessarily right): what's the evidence?

E7 Improving what you do

The first step in improving what you do is to evaluate your effectiveness in dealing with others.

Think about recent situations where you had to deal with others.

	What did you do well?	What did you need to do differently?
Being clear about what I wanted.		
Being clear about what others wanted.		

	What did you do well?	What did you need to do differently?
Anticipating what others might need or feel or how they might react.		
Planning to deal with what I anticipated.		
Choosing and using effective forms of communication.		
Being perceptive about others.		
Building relationships over time.		
Giving and receiving feedback.		

Where you'll continue dealing with the same people, could you agree with them how to improve things? Could you take turns in making decisions; could you agree 'ground rules'?

What can you agree with others for improving things?

What do you need to develop in dealing with others: how (e.g. who could help; books)?

This is what I need to improve	These are actions I need to take

REFERENCES

Drew, S., 'Student perceptions', in Drew, S., Nankivell, M.C., Shoolbred, M., (1992), *Personal skills – quality graduates: staff and student perceptions of personal skills development in higher education in the UK*, SCED Paper 69, Birmingham Standing Conference on Educational Development.

Several of the ideas in this chapter are based on ideas in the following books and we are very grateful to those authors.

Goleman, D., (1996), *Emotional intelligence: why it can matter more than IQ*, London: Bloomsbury.

Lerner, H., (1985, revised 2005), *The Dance of anger: a woman's guide to changing the pattern of intimate relationships*, New York: HarperCollins.

Macaskill, A., (2002), *Heal the hurt. How to forgive and move on*, London: Sheldon Press.

14
ACTION PLANNING: IDENTIFYING ACTIONS; MAKING RECOMMENDATIONS

HOW THIS CHAPTER CAN HELP YOU

The 'crucial' skills part of this chapter aims to help you:

- see how identifying actions is essential in planning and improving your learning;
- develop useful actions and recommendations;
- identify how actions/recommendations might be built into plans and what factors might affect them;
- identify short, medium and long term actions (academic/learning; personal; professional);
- use sources of information, resources and support to help identify actions or recommendations;
- check progress on and amend actions;
- present evidence for actions taken;
- identify how you can improve your identification of actions and recommendations.

The 'enhanced' skills part of this chapter is shorter: it helps you operate to a higher level. As well as the 'crucial' skills' outcomes, you'll be able to:

- work out what you most want to achieve, now and in the future;
- accept appropriate responsibility for and use initiative in identifying actions in a range of situations (including complex and unpredictable ones);
- develop actions for an individual plan that: take into account your personal preferences, motivation, needs and circumstances; try different ways to meet new demands, address difficulties and take advantage of the unexpected;
- identify actions or recommendations when you are leading or managing others;
- be tenacious in following through on actions;
- critically reflect on the effectiveness of your action planning;
- plan your further development.

CRUCIAL SKILLS

C1 Why is this chapter important and how can it help you?

Virtually every chapter in this book involves planning actions. Without a clear idea of what you need to do to achieve something, it'll be pretty hard to achieve it. 'Action planning' has a direct impact on your learning and success on courses in higher education (HE). It also has a direct impact on your ability to operate at work. Without it, you'll be dependent on others to tell you what to do and that will limit responsibilities you're given and how far you progress.

Action planning has two main elements: identifying actions; making plans to carry them out in the time needed. This chapter is about identifying useful actions. You need to use it together with Chapter 15 'Handling time and pressure' that looks at how to make plans to complete the actions.

What's an action and what's a recommendation?

An action is something specific that you or somebody else does or needs to do.

The term 'recommendation' is used in relation to the outcomes of an investigation; for example, a project report usually has 'recommendations' (actions that need to be taken to address the issues raised). Recommendations are courses of action.

Identifying actions or recommendations is not as straightforward as it sounds. If you ask students to identify actions or make recommendations, they often don't come up with actions or recommendations at all. This suggests a possible lack of understanding about the terms.

Basically, if you can't do it, it isn't an action or a recommendation. For example:

- *'the course will ensure equal opportunities for all students'* is not an action or a recommendation. It's more like an aim: in order to identify actions or recommendations you have to ask 'how?'

- *'I'll check that the language used in course documents is not discriminatory'* is an action. I can do it. *'The language used in course documents should be checked so it is not discriminatory'* is a recommendation. With an action or recommendation you'll know when it's been done (has the course documentation been checked or not?).

This chapter aims to help you identify actions or recommendations that'll be useful to yourself and others and that are a basis for making plans to achieve your aims.

In this chapter, the guidance and suggestions refer to both actions and recommendations.

C2 Actions, aims and targets. What's the difference?

Actions (or recommendations) are often linked to 'aims' and 'targets'. It's important to be aware of the differences between these terms, or you may produce something that isn't what's needed (by an assessor on a course or a manager or client at work).

- An **aim** indicates the direction in which you're heading. It's usually worded in such a way as to suggest a purpose. It's a fairly broad statement.

- A **target** is a specific point that you need to hit. It's worded in such a way that you'll know when it's been reached (i.e. it's measurable). A target may be an end point or an intermediate point on the way to achieving an aim.

- An **action** is something you do to get to a target or to achieve an aim. On its own, unrelated to an aim or a target, it may be unclear what its purpose is.

Example

Aim	*To understand different approaches to constructing a footbridge.*
Target	*Find 3 different constructions.*
Actions	*Use Learning Centre to identify different constructions of footbridges.* *Search web for images of different constructions.* *Identify relevant British Standards and their requirements.*

C3 Other chapters you need to use together with this one

There are several other chapters on topics where identifying actions/action planning is an essential part. You really do need to look at this chapter when you use them.

Chapter	Title	How it relates to this chapter	Page
15	Handling time and pressure.	Working out what actions are needed is the first step in planning to manage your time and handle pressure.	327
17	Reflecting on your learning and experience (including feedback).	A major reason for reflecting is to identify what you need to do in future, i.e. identifying and taking actions.	379
18	Personal/professional development planning (PDP).	Action planning is essential in implementing your personal/professional aims and needs.	401
16	Solving problems and making decisions.	Working out what actions/recommendations are needed is essential in solving problems.	357

For other chapters, being able to identify and plan actions is an important element. It's key for working out how to find information, what needs to happen in a team activity and what tasks are needed for a project. Many project reports need recommendations.

C4 Wording actions and recommendations

When identifying or wording actions, it's helpful to use the following acronym. This is usually used in relations to targets you set, but it also works with actions.

S – it needs to be **S**pecific

M – it needs to be **M**easurable

A – it needs to be **A**chievable

R – it needs to be **R**ealistic

T – it needs to be **T**ime-bound.

Here's an example of what this means in practice

	Example of an 'action' that's not at all SMART *'I'll make sure the course ensures equal opportunities for all students'.*	*Example of an action that is more SMART* *'I'll check that language used in course documents is not discriminatory'.*
Specific	*It doesn't say how.*	*It does indicate how.*
Measurable	*Doesn't indicate how you'd know when it's done. Could include for example rooms being accessible; resources being appropriate for everybody.*	*You'll know when it's been done. The documents will have been checked.*
Achievable	*There's no boundary round this. It's potentially huge.*	*You could certainly do it.*
Realistic	*There's no boundary round this. It's potentially huge. It'll depend on how long you have to do it and how many people are involved.*	*You'd need more information (e.g. the number of documents). You could amend it to say 'check course handbooks' or 'check learning resources'.*
Time-bound	*There's no indication of how long you have to complete it.*	*There's no indication of how long you have to complete it. You could amend the action to say 'by the end of April'.*

C5 Identifying actions

Whether or not you make the connections deliberately, you'll probably find that when you identify any action, you've already got an aim and a target in the back of your mind.

For example (working backwards)

Action	Target	Aim(s)
I'll cook my meal at 5.30pm.	Eat at 6pm.	Be able to watch TV news while eating.

If you have an aim, it helps if you identify targets to be met along the way: you can then identify actions needed to meet a target. You can break actions down into small parts, if it's helpful. For the above example, the author doesn't need much detail as experience suggests it'll take about 30 minutes. If this was a new task it might need breaking down more.

Here's an example of increasing levels of specificity

First level of specificity	2nd level of specificity	3rd level of specificity
I'll cook my meal at 5.30pm.	Put potatoes on at 5.35pm.	5.30pm, peel potatoes. 5.35pm, fill pan with cold water, add salt, put in potatoes, light gas. When it boils turn down to simmer.
	Put meat on to grill at 5.50pm.	etc.
	Put vegetables on at 5.50pm.	etc.

It's important to ensure your aim, targets and actions are linked to each other (or you'll lose focus). You could have several targets within one aim and several actions for one target.

Example format to use for a course or work activity facing you at the moment

Your aim		By when does it need to be met?	
Your target(s) along the way to this aim	By when (deadline)?	Actions needed to meet the target	By when (deadline)?

You need to look now at Chapter 15 'Handling time and pressure' as this has guidance on making plans and setting timescales. It also suggests you identify the resources and help you need; Section C6 looks at this too.

C6 Making sure your actions/recommendations are realistic and achievable

Have you identified all the actions needed?

For example

If an action is 'to find some information on the web', this implies that:

- *I have access to a computer;*
- *I have access to the internet;*
- *I know how to use a computer;*
- *I know what sort of key search words might lead to the thing I'm looking for;*
- *I can make judgements about how trustworthy the source of information is;*
- *I can record the information I find (this assumes I have note taking skills and/or a printer).*

What might, then, be needed for all those things above to happen?

- *I may need money to buy a computer and pay for internet access.*
- *I may need to find computer and internet access (e.g. internet café; library).*
- *I may need to find somebody who can help me to develop the skills I'll need.*

This then might lead me to identify further actions and to consider the order for them.

Consider the following for an action you need to take now

What will be needed before you can take the action?	What other actions does this mean you need to take? In what order should you do them?

There are two main reasons why things take longer than you expect:

1.   underestimating what's needed before you can take the action

2.   not building in leeway for unexpected things to happen.

See Chapters 15 'Handling time and pressure' and 16 'Solving problems and making decisions'.

Ensuring actions or recommendations are realistic and achievable

When considering how realistic an action is, you also need to think about how realistic it is:

- to find and use the resources/support needed for it;

- to develop knowledge and skills needed, in the time available.

Another thing that's important in considering if actions and recommendation are realistic or achievable is to look at what would have to happen next.

Using the example of checking course documents for discriminatory language, what if the documents are found to use discriminatory language? Who would revise them? How would their time be paid for? Must everything be reprinted? How long would this take and what would it cost? Without more recommendations about how to fund and staff the work, the original recommendation may look unrealistic.

You need to think through the implications of your actions/recommendations to see if they suggest a need for more actions/recommendations (e.g. if you apply for a job in a particular location, what actions would be needed if you got it?).

Putting this into practice

Identify 3 actions or recommendations you, or others, need to take	What's needed to implement it? If it's implemented, what would be needed then?	Do you need to revise the actions or recommendations? How?

C7 What about risk?

Might the actions you identify have any risks attached to them? Possible risks include:

- health and safety risks to yourself or others;

- offending or upsetting others;

- you being offended or upset yourself;

- things that might stop the action being taken (e.g. illness; unavailable resources);

- people not doing what they say they'll do;

- ethical issues.

When you identify an action it may help to also consider how risky it is. You could do a risk assessment for each action, giving 1 for low risk, 2 for medium risk and 3 for high risk.

Clearly, you may need to take risks. You may not, however, want all your actions to be very risky, and you may need ideas about what you'd do if things did go wrong.

C8 Identifying actions/recommendations for the short, medium and long term

Chapters 15 'Handling time and pressure' and 16 'Solving problems and making decisions' also look at some of the issues here and how to build them into plans.

There may be differences between identifying short, medium or long term actions/recommendations.

- There tends to be more uncertainty if planning is long term.

- The shorter the timescale, the more detailed may be the action/recommendation. For a long-term action, too many things might change to start with very specific actions.

- Long term actions/recommendations may be more related to what's valued and seen as important (see Section C3 in Chapter 18 'Personal/Professional Development Planning'). Very short term ones may be more practical.

Is there a connection between your short, medium and long term aims/targets/actions? What, for you, is 'long term' mean (a semester, a year, 5 years)? Therefore what does 'medium term' mean?

Think of a particular situation facing you now and identify the following

	Long term	Medium term	Short term
Aim			
Target(s)			
Action(s)			

Are your short term actions likely to help or distract from what you want to achieve in the medium or long term?

C9 Having valid actions or recommendations

Identifying actions or recommendations is likely to be the end point of a process involving gathering information about something, investigating something, evaluating or reflecting on something. There must be a logical connection between what's gone before and the actions or recommendations identified, so others can see the basis for them.

Connections	✓
Are all your recommendations/actions clearly linked to what you found out (e.g. from a report; project)?	
Have you got actions or recommendations for each key issue you've identified?	
Is it clear what the reason is for each action/recommendation?	
Do you have evidence that indicates why the action/recommendation is needed?	
Could others see how the actions/recommendations would address the main issues identified?	
Do you need to remove any actions or recommendations that don't have a basis?	

C10 Monitoring progress, amending actions and providing evidence of them

Monitoring

This means checking things are going to plan. It's important: it alerts you to difficulties, so you can change plans and actions (and it makes you feel good to see what you've achieved). Wording actions/recommendations carefully helps in monitoring them.

For example

In the following, it'll be easier to see if you've done 2 or 3 than to see if you've done 1:

- *'check if course documents include discriminatory language';*
- *'identify any instances where the language used assumes professionals are men';*
- *'identify any instances where the language used assumes all students are white'.*

Here are examples of the sort of words that make it very difficult to measure progress:

- *develop (e.g. skill in using computers);*
- *understand (e.g. how to fire an arrow);*
- *be aware of (e.g. the bones in the leg).*

The above are hard to measure because: 'understand' and 'be aware of' don't indicate to what level; for 'develop' you need to know the starting point. The following are more helpful for checking progress:

- *create a spreadsheet;*
- *fire an arrow;*
- *list the bones in the leg.*

Look at the actions you identified in Section C5. Did you word them in a way that helps you measure progress? If not, could you reword them?

Amending actions

To meet your targets, you may need to be flexible and amend actions you originally identified, if they're not working out well.

This means you need to plan enough in advance to be able to change tack (see Chapter 15 'Handling time and pressure'). You could also look at Chapter 16 'Solving problems and making decisions' to help you review your actions and think about how to amend them.

Example

If your team has to do a presentation and the only member with the necessary computer skills lets you down, what do you do? Find someone else to do it or present the information in a different way? Either of these actions will take longer than originally planned (this is why you need to build in extra time when first making a plan). Monitoring would be important: if looking for somebody else to help you is taking too long, you may need to use a different presentation method.

Providing evidence

Helpful wording makes it easier to identify evidence of your actions and how well they went. It's easy to show, for example, that you've created a spreadsheet (show one you made). Showing you'd 'developed your computer skills' would be harder; you'd need to show your starting point so you could prove your development. See Chapter 7 'Finding, using and analysing information and evidence'.

C11 Putting it into practice

You might need to make all sorts of plans (e.g. project plan; group/team work plan; Personal Development Plan; Individual Learning Plan; career management plan).

To follow are examples you could use to help you plan the main actions and resources, and monitor how you're doing. The Final Review helps you reflect on the process.

Action Plan

Aim (e.g. learning aim):		Deadline	
Main target (e.g. learning target):		Deadline to meet target:	
Actions (What will you do to achieve the target?)	Resources; support (What will help you carry out the action?)	start date	end date

Monitoring

	Review Points		
	1. date:	2. date:	3. date:
What's going well?			
What's not going well?			
What needs to happen now?			

Final Review. Date:

How well did you manage the process of achieving your target?	
What were your main successes?	
What would be useful to improve?	
Any other thoughts (e.g. any feedback; things to remember for next time)?	

C12 Reviewing and improving what you do

How can you improve your skills in identifying actions or recommendations?

Question	Notes	This is what I'll do differently
Are your actions/ recommendations SMART?		
Do your actions/ recommendations relate to aims and targets?		
Have you identified any risks and how they might be dealt with?		
Do they allow for what is needed to carry them out?		
Do they allow for what might happen if they are carried out?		
Do they include ones that are short/medium and long term?		
Are they valid in relation to the information gathered (e.g. evaluations)?		
Can you monitor progress and amend them?		
Can you present evidence for them?		

ENHANCED SKILLS

E1 What do you most want to achieve and what actions are needed for this?

Actions follow on from aims. If you look at what actually happens (i.e. actions) this can say a lot about what somebody's aims really are. Sometimes what you do and the effort you put in indicates what's really important to you. If there's a mismatch between your actions and your aims, or between your aims and what you see as important, you may have a problem.

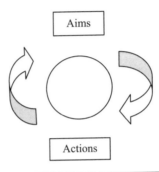

What do you want from the future? Jot down the first things that come into your head.		
	What are you doing at the moment (main actions)?	**How do these tie in with what you want from the future?**
On a course		
At work		
Socially		
In other areas of your life		
Do you need to rethink what you want from the future or to rethink what you're doing now (e.g. do you need to change the balance of what you're doing)?		

E2 Responsibility and initiative

E2.1 Responsibility

Who's responsible for identifying actions?

There are two key issues here: accepting responsibility and identifying the limits of your responsibility.

People probably only identify actions if they accept that they're responsible for doing so (as opposed to thinking it's somebody else's responsibility to tell them what to do). Accepting responsibility is key in identifying and taking actions. However, there may be situations where it isn't your responsibility to identify actions needed. You could end up with too much work or offending someone.

So, what are you responsible for and what are you not responsible for?

Who's responsible for …?	Your notes: person/people	Your notes on the implications for action planning
your own learning.		
other people's learning.		
your own success on a course.		
other people's success on a course.		
current work you have to do on a course/at work (e.g. a project).		
a group or team activity.		
your use of time on the course.		

Who's responsible for ...?	Your notes: person/people	Your notes on the implications for action planning
your use of time at work.		
your use of time socially.		
your use of time domestically.		
your happiness.		
other people's happiness.		
What else?		

What if it isn't clear whose responsibility it is?

Examples of situations where responsibilities are confused may be:

- your work depends on somebody else doing it, but they don't;
- somebody else should take responsibility, but they don't or can't;
- you share responsibility with somebody;
- roles are blurred;
- the work might take you beyond your remit/boundaries.

How can you decide what you should take action on, in complicated or uncertain situations? Possibilities include:

- asking others what they think they're responsible for;

- agreeing with others who will 'stand in' if somebody isn't available;

- considering the risks of not taking action versus the risk of taking responsibility that isn't really yours;

- asking tutors or managers to clarify what you are responsible for.

Beware: in teams (e.g. at work) it isn't very helpful to use 'it's not my responsibility' as an excuse for not acting in a crisis or urgent situation; this could cause antagonism.

When do you need to get approval for actions you wish to take?

This is difficult, as the answer is 'it depends' (e.g. on the level you're operating at; on the situation). You could check with your tutor/manager/client what sort of actions they need to approve and what you can do without approval.

The following is a rough guide:

- On a course, where you can decide your own direction (e.g. a project; dissertation), check with your tutor if you're on the right lines. If you're doing set work, your tutor may leave it to you to decide on actions.

- At work, generally, you won't need approval for routine actions. If you're doing something non-routine or new, you'll probably need approval from someone (e.g. your manager).

The bottom line is, 'is the action risky or might it get somebody in trouble if it goes wrong?' If the answer is 'yes', then it's best to check it out.

E2.2 Using initiative

Using initiative is part of taking action. A dictionary definition of 'initiative' includes things like 'doing things unprompted' and 'being the first to take action'. This is seen as a very important ability, especially at work. Why?

If you're responsible for others (e.g. their tutor or manager), it's very time consuming and frustrating if people continually ask you what to do. Most high level activities (in HE or work) depend on people getting on with things without too much guidance.

Situations requiring new developments or creativity depend on people initiating and taking action. Think of famous entrepreneurs! The more an organisation thrives on new ideas the more it wants people with initiative.

Who's got initiative? If people take action without being told to, they're seen as having it; if they wait for instructions, they're seen as not having it. There may be reasons for not initiating actions (e.g. lacking confidence, skill, time), but you may be judged on what you do/don't do rather than on reasons for this. It may be unfair, but it happens.

If you aren't taking initiative, why and what could you do to help you to do so?

Why I don't take initiative	Actions I could take to help me do so

When might it be best not to take initiative?

Such situations might include:

- putting yourself or others in danger or at risk;
- where it's really somebody else's responsibility and you might antagonise them;
- where you might get the credit for something that should rightfully be somebody else's.

In the near future:

... where I could take initiative	... here I won't take initiative

E3 Developing actions that are appropriate for you

What might make actions appropriate for you?

- You may have preferred ways of doing things (e.g. if you're lost, do you ask the way or look at a street map?).
- Your situation may affect how you do things (e.g. if you don't have a home computer it may influence how and when you do work for a course).
- People have differing motivations (e.g. some are more competitive than others).

- People have different needs (e.g. you may have a disability; need financial support).

- Could you move out of your comfort zone and try new ways to extend your abilities?

- You may come up against difficulties that mean you can't take actions you intended.

- Unexpected opportunities may arise (e.g. somebody describing an easier approach).

For an activity/target you need to do soon, what actions will be appropriate for you?

What's the activity or target?

What actions could you take that would allow for....?

your preferred ways of doing things

the situation and its elements or features

your motivations

your needs

you to try new things or develop new knowledge or skills

any difficulties that might crop up

any opportunities that might crop up

You could go through a similar process in relation to recommendations or actions you're suggesting others should take.

E4 What if you're leading or managing others?

You may need to identify actions for others to take (i.e. 'delegating') or to encourage others to identify their own actions. This might be if you're involved in a team activity or if you're managing others (e.g. in a course/voluntary/sporting activity or at work).

If you have to do this, then you may want to consider:

- if they have the relevant skills and knowledge;

- how they could develop the skills and knowledge;

- if they can do it in the time allowed, given other demands on their time;

- if it's a reasonable thing to ask them to do;

- if it involves any risks for them and if so, how you'll allow for them;

- if they have the resources needed to do it;

- what you wish others would consider when they ask you to do things.

You'll need to make it clear what they have to do; put it in writing so they can refer to it later. You'll also need their commitment, or they may not do it or not do it very well. You could:

- consider the issues indicated above when you allocate activities to people;

- explain why the action is important; discuss and share ideas;

- trust them to do it;

- monitor how they're doing it in a supportive way.

What actions do you need others to take and who are they?

What do you need to consider in allocating actions to them?

How will you get their commitment to what they have to do?

You might also want to encourage people to come up with their own actions

This may be the case whether or not you're in a formal leadership role (e.g. if you're part of a group/team and are trying to make the work go well). What encourages/ discourages you to come up with your own actions? Others may be encouraged/ discouraged by similar things.

You may want to consider:

- being positive about others' ideas for actions;

- giving them time/space to come up with their own ideas for actions;

- keeping quiet about your ideas for actions;

- allocating roles to them in which it's their responsibility to identify and carry out actions;

- making clear the support or resources available for any actions;

- encouraging them to be motivated towards the aims and targets;

- building in set times for monitoring and discussing progress.

What will you do to encourage others to identify actions to take?

E5 Following through

What ultimately matters is not identifying useful actions but actually carrying them out.

Which of the following apply to you?

	✓
I always complete an action even if it becomes clear the action isn't very helpful.	
I complete actions I like but not ones I don't like.	
I complete important actions.	
I start a lot of actions but leave them half finished.	
I identify actions to take but have difficulty getting started with them.	
I complete actions well ahead of a deadline.	
I complete actions on the deadline.	
I leave actions right till the last minute.	
I miss deadlines.	
What else?	

Are you happy with how you answered those questions or would you like to change things? Why do you do what you do? What's the effect of what you do?

It might help to talk to others about this. If you find it hard to complete things, you may assume people who are good at this just enjoy it. This may not be the case: they might not like the 'grind' either, but it might be important to them to achieve the aims. See Chapter 15 'Handling time and pressure' for ideas on how to stick with actions and avoid distractions.

Is there anything about the actions that makes them hard to do? Are you setting yourself (or others) targets that are too high or unrealistic? Look again at Section C6. Are the actions you identify appropriate for you? See Section E3. Are you spending time on things you really don't want to do? See Chapter 18 Personal/Professional Development Planning.

What will you do to improve how you 'follow through' on actions?

E6 Review and developing further

How effective are you at identifying useful actions (or recommendations) and using them as part of a plan to get things done?

In the following, 'actions' also refers to recommendations

Question	Notes on what you do	Notes on what you could do differently
Are the actions you identify 'do-able'?		
Do you find it easy or difficult to identify useful actions?		
Once you've identified actions, can you then make an effective plan to carry them out?		
Are the actions actually taken?		
What outcomes do they have?		
Are they taking you in the direction you want to go in?		
What feedback have you had about your ability to plan and carry out actions?		
What does this feedback suggest you could do instead of what you currently do?		

What needs to happen for you to do things differently?

Notes on anything I need to change in how I see things or clarifying what I want	Notes on skills or techniques I need to develop	Notes on support I need and from whom

15
HANDLING TIME AND PRESSURE

HOW THIS CHAPTER CAN HELP YOU

The 'crucial' skills part of this chapter aims to help you:

- identify how managing your time and dealing with pressure can help improve your performance;
- identify what you need to do and factors that might affect your time management;
- identify sources of pressure (and stress) and your own reactions to it;
- find and choose ways of managing your time and handling pressure or stress;
- develop a plan to manage time and pressure, using relevant support, feedback and resources;
- carry out, monitor and revise your plans as necessary;
- draw conclusions about how effective you were in managing time and pressure and consider whether other strategies could have been more effective;
- identify ways to improve and develop your skills.

The 'enhanced' skills part of this chapter is shorter: it helps you operate to a higher level. As well as the 'crucial' skills' outcomes, you'll be able to:

- identify opportunities for using and developing your skills in managing time and pressure, clearly identifying what you want to achieve;
- plan to use time over an extended period;
- manage time and pressure effectively to meet deadlines and unexpected demands in unpredictable and complex situations;
- develop reasoned plans (including SMART targets, methods and resources), using methods and tools that suit your personal style and take into account your preferences, motivation, needs, circumstances and constraints;
- evaluate your strategies and their effectiveness, including your use of information, ideas, resources and feedback, and how your decisions and other factors affected the result;
- identify how you can further develop your skills in this area.

CRUCIAL SKILLS

C1 Why is this chapter important and how can it help you?

In higher education (HE):

- you may be on a course with modules, where each one must be completed in a semester (12 weeks to get to grips with the topic). You may need to start assessed work before you've had all the classes, to complete it on time. You need to plan your time well;

- you may be doing several modules at once, all with a similar deadline, leading to bunching of work. If you don't plan for this you can end up under pressure;

- if you leave it too late to look for essential resources, they may not be available: advance planning is as essential as the resources;

- if you're doing paid work while studying, you need to fit it all together;

- many students have domestic responsibilities to fit in with course work;

- you'll want (and need) a social life too;

- you may be doing paid work, have domestic responsibilities and have a social life, all of which need to be fitted together (phew!).

In graduate-level jobs:

- you may face conflicting demands at work and between work and the rest of your life;

- some jobs have long working hours (e.g. when starting a new job; trying to establish yourself; working for promotion);

- the more responsibility you have, the more you have to manage not only your own time and pressure but that of others too.

You may feel under pressure for reasons other than time: being away from home (perhaps in a foreign country); setting yourself high targets (e.g. for academic achievement); concerns about what to do next (e.g. in relation to your career); unanticipated problems (e.g. relationships; health; money).

This is starting to sound a bit like 'doom and gloom'! These issues are, of course, just part of exciting experiences where you're learning new things, going in new directions and forging new relationships and friendships. The better you're able to handle time and pressure, the more energy you'll have for all the good things and the more successful you'll be.

This chapter aims to help you identify how to handle time in the situation facing you at the moment and to either anticipate, avoid or deal with pressure.

C2 Other chapters you need to use together with this one

This chapter will help you with the topics in *all* the other chapters. Everything you do at university/college/work involves managing time and everything has the potential to be pressurising, if you let it. We suggest you look at this chapter in relation to each of the others. However, there are three chapters that will specifically help you with this one.

Chapter	Title	How it relates to this chapter	Page
16	Solving problems and making decisions.	When you are handling time and pressure, you'll come across problems and will need to make decisions (e.g. how do you use your limited time?).	357
14	Action planning: identifying actions and recommendations.	Identifying what you need to do is a key element of handling time and pressure.	301
13	Dealing with other people.	Handling time and pressure often means saying 'no' to and being assertive with other people.	275

C3 What's expected of you?

Have you recently arrived in HE?

Whether you've come directly from school or college or are a mature student, you'll probably find a big difference between your previous educational experience and this one.

In HE you're expected to work with little direction from tutors. You may be given assignment instructions, a deadline, a programme of class activities and a reading list or set of resources: the rest is up to you. There may or may not be an attendance register. Nobody will chase you to see if you've started work and your tutor may not know how you're getting on until they see your work at the end of the semester.

Does that sound harsh? It's not intended to be. It's based on the view that HE students are adults who want to learn and it's their responsibility to do so. In schools, teachers act in *'locum parentis'*; that is, they 'stand in for' your parents while you're on school premises. In HE this no longer applies. It's up to you.

If you're a mature student who has worked or had a family, you may assume that HE is like your memory of school, where you weren't responsible for yourself. It isn't.

Have you been in HE for some time and/or are you working?

If so, by now you'll know it's up to you. You may have experienced the effects of leaving work till the last minute. You're likely to have faced time and resource pressures. You may realise it's your responsibility, but need some help in seeing how to cope effectively.

What's expected?

At the start of any course or module you need to:

- get the programme of class sessions;
- get information about assessment (e.g. the task; deadlines);
- look at learning outcomes and assessment criteria to see what's important (if there aren't any, ask your tutor what's needed to pass or get a good mark).

The same thing applies in any situation: find out what's needed, by when and on what basis it'll be judged.

C4 What do you need to do this semester (or term or month)?

It helps to make a list of what you have to do by when. You can use the following three formats.

1 For work required on courses (e.g. current assessed work and deadlines)

If the work is divided into parts, put in the deadlines for those too (i.e. any interim deadlines).

Assessment			
Module title	Assessment task(s) to be completed	Any interim deadline	Final deadline

2 What you do on a regular basis each week

Include: classes (e.g. lectures; workshops; labs; tutorials; seminars); any paid work; any voluntary; social or family activities (e.g. pub; club; sports; films); domestic tasks (shopping; cooking; cleaning). Give the time of day when you do each thing.

Example of a weekly timetable				
Day of the week	Taught sessions	Paid work	Voluntary work/ leisure/social activities	Domestic things
Monday				
Tuesday				
Wednesday				
Thursday				
Friday				
Saturday				
Sunday				

3 Where are the spaces for work for your course?

What does 1 above indicate about what you need to do and when does 2 above indicate you have time or space to do it? This might be any work outside class; for example, assignments; revision.

Example of a weekly timetable for studying out of class: include work for your assessment			
Day of the week	Morning	Afternoon	Evening
Monday			
Tuesday			
Wednesday			
Thursday			
Friday			
Saturday			
Sunday			

How much time should you allow for study?

The national HE 'tariff' is 1 credit = 10 learning hours, so a 10 credit module is 100 learning hours, including taught sessions and assessment. So, 3×20 credit modules in one semester is 600 learning hours. If there are 30 hours of sessions per module (90 hours), you'll have about 500 hours for work on your own. That's about 40 hours a week for 12 weeks.

This is where you cry 'impossible' (though it's similar to paid work where 37.5 is a standard full week but many people do 50 hours). These are estimates; some students spend more time and others just can't fit in that number of hours because of other commitments. However, it gives an idea of the time needed each day to get through the work.

C5 Prioritising, efficiency and things that might affect my time management

You've now got some idea of the size of the task facing you. Consider the following questions:

- What can I drop in order to give me more time for what I must do?

- What activities would I really like to keep?

- How could I do things more efficiently to release more time?

- What might get in the way of doing what I need to do?

- On a 'to do' list, could I give: 1 to what's essential; 2 to things I'll do if possible; 3 to things I can drop?

1 What must I do or could I drop?

Question	✓	Notes
Which activities must I do?		
Which activities do I not need to do at all?		
Which activities could I do less often?		
Which activities could I do to a lower standard?		
What else?		

2 What should I keep?

...in addition to what you really have to do, this might include activities for own sanity, health and happiness.

Question	✓	Notes
Which activities would I like to continue, if possible?		
What will I do to keep fit?		
What will I do to eat healthily?		
How much rest/sleep will I get?		
What will I do to maintain relationships?		
What will I do for fun?		
What else?		

3 What could I do more efficiently?

Question	✓	Notes
Could I share things with somebody (e.g. domestic tasks)?		
Could I combine small activities into one larger one (e.g. food shopping once a week)?		
Could I reduce travelling time (e.g. study in the library/learning centre on days I have classes)?		
Could I do things to a lower standard (e.g. iron fewer clothes)?		
Could I make fewer or shorter phone calls?		
Could I be more efficient in doing work for the course? See the chapters in this book for ideas.		

Question	✓	Notes
Could I check what is most important to focus on?		
Could I spend less so I need to work less to earn money?		
What else?		

4 What might get in the way of doing what you must do?

The following identifies some things that might stop you doing what you must do and gives a series of suggestions to try, to help deal with them. Which might work for you?

People interrupting you while you're studying

	✓
Turn off your phone.	
Let the answerphone/voicemail take messages and answer them all together.	
Ask people to ring or visit between 6–7.	
Put 'do not interrupt' on the door or don't answer it.	
Mean what you say; i.e. if you say only call after 8, don't accept calls before then.	
Just say no.	
See Section C5 in Chapter 13 'Dealing with other people' for how to be assertive.	
Tell yourself that real friends will appreciate your need to study and won't be offended.	
What else?	

Not being well organised

	✓
Have well-organised notes (see Chapter 9 'Making notes').	
Make plans and use them (see Section C6).	
Use a diary (see Section C6).	
Be tidy/put things away (it is quicker to find them).	
Don't leave things till the last minute (you won't do it as well and you'll feel stressed).	
Get to places on time and allow enough time to get there (you'll feel less stressed).	
Make lists (so you don't forget; ticking items off makes you feel better).	
If others mock you for being organised, see Section C5 in Chapter 13 'Dealing with other people' for how to be assertive.	
What else?	

Getting distracted

	✓
Set yourself small targets.	
Give yourself rewards (e.g. 'in half an hour I'll have a coffee').	
Make notes while you're reading (to help you concentrate).	
Don't allow yourself to do x until you have done y.	
Ask friends/family for support (e.g. so they don't distract you).	
Keep your plan (see Section C6) on the wall so you can see what you have to do.	
Keep the target or question you're addressing on the wall to help you keep focused.	
Just say no (Section C5, Chapter 13 'Dealing with other people' covers assertiveness).	
What else?	

Saving money

	✓
Walk rather than using the bus/driving.	
Take advantage of student cards/discounts.	
Buy 'real' food instead of ready meals.	
Have one less drink, drink cheaper drinks, drink water in between drinks.	
Buy things (e.g. toilet rolls) in bulk with friends; buy 'own brand'.	
Look at websites on saving money.	
What else?	

Reviewing what you do

You could look again at your answers in Section C4 and perhaps amend them. If you have difficulty in deciding what to drop or change, you may need to consider what really matters to you (see Chapters 18 'Personal/Professional Development Planning' and 16 'Solving problems and making decisions').

C6 Planning

If you look at other chapters in this book you'll see many references to planning work. This is essential, especially if you have a lot on.

Note that an assessment deadline doesn't indicate when you should be doing the work but when it must be finished. There's nothing wrong with finishing it in advance.

Using a diary

It is a good idea to get used to using a diary. Most people in professional jobs see their diary as an extension of themselves (if they lose it, it's a disaster!). If you put in regular weekly activities, you can see where to allocate time for other things (e.g. study; socialising).

A basic planning technique

- Identify your deadline.

- Set yourself a new deadline for a few days earlier, to allow for checking work and for things to go wrong.

- Divide what you have to do into manageable tasks.

- Work out what resources you need for each task.

- Work out how long each task will take, including time to obtain and use the resources.

- Add half on again (most people underestimate how long something will take).

- Build in some time for unexpected things happening (e.g. see Section C7).

- Identify those tasks needing to be done before others.

- Identify any tasks needing the help of others (start them early, to allow for cooperation not being forthcoming).

- Identify the order of doing the tasks.

- Work back from your deadline: identify when each task must be finished so you meet the deadline (interim deadlines); consider how long each task will take to see when to start it.

- What if there's too much to do in the time? Could you amend your aim so you don't have to do as much? Could you miss out or combine any tasks? Could you do anything more efficiently or less well? Have you misunderstood what's needed (check with the tutor)?

You need a plan that's do-able. One way to think about plans is to see if they are SMART.

- **S**pecific; that is, it's clear what has to be done.

- **M**easurable; that is, you'll know when it is done.

- **A**chievable; that is, it's possible to do it.

- **R**ealistic; that is, you'll be able to do it in the time and with your resources.

- **T**imebound; that is, you have a final deadline and interim deadlines.

Use your plan as a working tool, to remind you what has to be done and check progress. You may need to amend your plan if things don't work out as anticipated.

Example of a plan

End objective		Deadline	
Give a presentation.		31 October (my deadline 29 Oct).	
Task	**Resources needed**	**Interim deadline**	**Progress**
Find information.	Learning Centre. Books, journals.	10 Oct	Took longer than expected – finished 15 Oct.
Make sure room has resources needed.	Computer, digital projector.	12 Oct	Has resources needed – checked 10 Oct.
Prepare structure/content of presentation.	My notes from information search.	20 Oct	Back on target – done by 20 Oct.
Produce electronic slides.	Electronic presentation package.	25 Oct	Computer fault, not done till 27 Oct.
Rehearse presentation.	Electronic slides and speakers notes.	28 Oct	Done. Need to revise slides – took too long.

You could make your own plan using a similar format. You could also consider producing a timeline, a visual representation of what you need to do. See below.

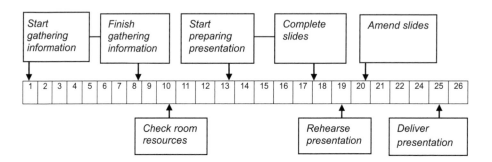

C7 Anticipating or avoiding pressure and stress

Sections C3 to C6 are about managing time. The better you plan time and the more efficient you are, the greater your chance of avoiding pressure: if you don't manage time well, you'll be under pressure, usually when you least need it (e.g. at the point of assessment).

Time, however, isn't alone in causing pressure. Some things cause stress in most people (e.g. relationship breakdowns). For other things, people react differently. What matters is that you're clear about what creates stress in **you**, so you can see how to deal with it.

You might ask yourself the following questions.

- What could happen during this semester/term/month?
- Which of those things might you find pressurising or stressful?
- Which are unavoidable?
- Which could be avoided?

Whether you can avoid something may depend on how important it is to you. What you find stressful may depend on what else is going on. You might cope with something at one point in your life that, at another point, would be over the top. For one person who has too much going on, avoiding social activities might be the thing to do. For another, social activities may help them relax. It's important to know how you react to decide what you need, and not to worry about whether you react the same as or differently from others (see Section C5 in Chapter 13 'Dealing with other people' on assertiveness).

Here are some things that might be pressurising. Might any of them apply to you in the near future? Could you avoid any? Could you plan for any (see Section C8)?

Issue	Why this is an issue for me – my notes	✓	How to avoid – my notes	How to plan for – my notes
Marks/grades on my course.				
Subjects/topics I find hard.				
Money problems.				
Illness (mine).				
Illness (others).				
Developing new friendships or Relationships.				

Issue	Why this is an issue for me – my notes	✓	How to avoid – my notes	How to plan for – my notes
Ending friendships or relationships.				
Arguments.				
Moving where I live.				
Transport problems.				
Children/parents/ partner.				
Work.				
Losing a job.				
Trying to find a job.				
Supporting other people.				
What else?				

How could you build 'avoiding' and 'planning for' into your time management?

You could go back to Sections C4, C5 and C6. Can you amend the notes you made to include any realisations you now have? For example:

- do you need to add actions like 'find a job' and 'visit the careers service'?

- if you want to develop friendships, what actions would help and how can you plan this?

- could changing how you travel to university/college/work or where you live save time?

C8 Dealing with pressure

Some things can't be avoided. You may just find that you're faced with a pressurising situation and you have to deal with it.

Often, with a response to pressure there's both a good side and an unhelpful one. For example, when under pressure you may keep going and try to get everything under control: the result might be you achieve a lot but you get overwrought. In this case, you could either decide to let some things go or to take care of yourself better (e.g. more sleep).

What do you normally do when under pressure?	
What's helpful about that?	**What's unhelpful about it?**
How can you make good use of this?	**How can you allow for this?**

The following gives some possible techniques you could try, if you're under pressure.

Be assertive

- Identify what you really want in the situation.

- What's your bottom line?

- Use assertiveness (see Section C5 in Chapter 13 'Dealing with other people).

Identify help

- Who could help you?

- How? By doing something or by listening to you?

- What could help you? Do you need to find some resources?

- Would professional help be useful (e.g. university/colleges services for study help, counselling, careers; your doctor; at work, Human Resources or your Trade Union)?

Write about it

- Write why you are concerned about it.

- Write down the opposite of what it might be.

- Write the worst thing that could happen (is it so bad?).

- Write down what you would ideally like and what you would have to do to get that.

Keep fit/healthy

- Exercise is a good antidote to pressure/stress and reduces depression. Walk rather than go by bus; walk up stairs rather than take the lift; join a gym; swim; dance.

- Eat properly.

- Sleep enough.

- Drink and drugs make things worse. Drinking a lot increases depression.

Relaxation techniques

- Breathe in to a count of 5 and out to a count of 5, 10 times.

- Tense and relax your muscles in turn, starting with your feet.

- Visualise a scene or setting that makes you feel good.

Stopping yourself going over and over ideas in your head

- Count backwards from 500.

- Talk aloud to yourself about something completely different (it needs to be aloud and it may take 15 minutes before you switch off from your original topic).

- Ask yourself what you are afraid of (this can stop you going over the detail).

Not being able to sleep

- Tell yourself what you're pleased about or have enjoyed that day.

- Keep a notepad by the bed; write down what you're thinking about (so you can let it go).

- Listen to talking on the radio (not music).

- Get up and make a hot drink (to break your chain of thought).

- Have a milky drink (the calcium helps you sleep).

- Avoid alcohol (it makes you sleepy at first but you're likely to wake up later on).

What situation(s) are you facing that are creating pressure or stress?
Which of the above techniques will you try?

C9 Putting it into practice

What will help you put your plans into action and to try out new methods? You could:

- identify electronic tools to help (e.g. computer diaries, a personal organiser);

- use planning tools (e.g. diary; wall chart; lists); set aside time each day to check progress;

- start recording and noting progress, daily (use your plan, diary or journal);

- make notes of what does or doesn't work for you;

- get feedback on how you manage time and pressure (e.g. from tutors; family; friends);

- ask others how they manage time and pressure, to get ideas.

If you aren't doing anything differently, why?

Possible reason	Your notes on implications/what to do
Is the end result of handling time and pressure better not really important to you?	
Is something else important instead?	
Do you not know how to do things differently?	
What/who could help you see how to do things differently?	
Is it a matter of self discipline?	
If so, what you help you stick to your plans?	
What other reasons do you have?	

C10 Review: improving how you handle time and pressure

What have you done in managing time and pressure that worked well?	What have you done in managing time and pressure that did not work?

What will you do the same or differently in future, to improve handling time and pressure?

Activity	This is what I'll repeat/ do the same in future	This is what I'll do differently
Identifying what I have to do.		
Prioritising what I have to do.		
Being more efficient.		
Allowing for things that get in the way of using time well.		

Activity	This is what I'll repeat/ do the same in future	This is what I'll do differently
Planning.		
Anticipating pressure/stress.		
Avoiding pressure/stress.		
Coping with pressure/stress.		

ENHANCED SKILLS

E1 Identifying what you want to achieve

How you spend your time relates to what you see as important. Are you spending your time doing what you want to do or in a way that will get you where you want to be? We may do things because it's expected of us or because we're used to doing things that way.

Choices or preferences may lead to certain consequences. If you want a good degree you'll have to spend a lot of time studying; if you spend most of your time partying you may not get a good degree; if you're ambitious at work you may have to put in a lot of effort (e.g. move house to where the jobs are; work long hours; do further training).

How do you currently spend your time?

After sleeping 8 hours, you'll have 16 waking hours left. How does your day divide up into 2-hour blocks? Over a day, it might add up to 2 hours cooking/eating, 2 hours class-sessions, and so on. If you look at this over a week, you may be surprised by how you spend your time.

	2hrs	2hrs	2hrs	2hrs	2hrs	2hrs	2hrs	2hrs
Mon								
Tues								
Wed								
Thurs								
Fri								
Sat								
Sun								

What does this analysis tell you?

What does the way you spent your time suggest about what's important to you?

Is that what you want to be important to you?

If you continue to spend your time in that way, what's likely to be the outcome?
Is that the outcome you want?
Is the way you're using time making you happy or unhappy or under pressure?

E2 How might you use your time to get what you'd like?

If you're spending time in a way that lines up with what's important to you, that's fine. If not, why not? Look again at Section C9. Doing what you don't want to do can be a source of pressure.

Are there any changes that could shift you towards what's important or what you want to achieve. Here are some thoughts.

- If you have responsibilities taking up much of your time, how long will this go on for? Can you plan now for using your time differently in the future?

- Does your analysis of how you spent your week make clear changes you could make?

- What could you change to give more time for what's important (see Section C)?

- If you were spending your time exactly as you pleased, what would you be doing?

How will you use your time in a way that reflects what's important to you, what you want to achieve or what makes you happy?

What will you do less of or drop?

What will you do more of?

What will you do differently?

E3 Planning over an extended period or in complex or unpredictable situations

Planning for an extended time

What's different about planning over a longer period? You may have a project lasting a whole year, for example, or you may have a long term target. Some key differences are:

- if the timescale is long it may be because the task is large or complex;

- over a longer timescale, the unexpected is more likely to happen. It's simply more difficult to anticipate what could happen in a years' time;

- the longer the timescale, the more difficult it can be to stay on target and keep motivated; things that crop up may seem immediately more important than the original task.

Planning for short-term activities that are complex or unpredictable

It may be that, even though your timescale is short, you are trying to achieve something where complexities and uncertainties are involved.

How can you allow for these issues?

Firstly, what might create uncertainty or complexity for you?

Item	✓	Your notes on what you face or might occur
The issue has many facets.		
Lots of different tasks involved.		
Need for specialist resources.		
Need for funding.		
My own uncertainty about what I want.		
My work depends on cooperation from others.		
Work depends on information that may be difficult to find or access.		
Health issues in myself.		
Conflicting pressures from other sources (e.g. from my personal life).		
Major shifts in my situation.		

Here are some strategies to consider in allowing for the unexpected and the uncertain in relation to your plan (Section C6).

- Estimate the risks of things happening (1 for low risk; 2 for medium risk; 3 for high risk) to see if you need to rethink what you are doing.

- Estimate what might happen and make contingency plans; have fall-back positions.

- Make good use of planning tools (e.g. diaries; plans; electronic aids) to monitor if things start to go adrift, so you can act quickly.

- Make good use of Chapter 16 'Solving problems and making decisions'.

- If others are involved, spend time early on making sure they're committed to the work (see Chapters 12 'Working in a group or team' and 13 'Dealing with other people').

- Build in a lot of time for unexpected things to happen.

- Never work 'to the wire', that is, to the last minute.

- Be flexible and prepared to change things.

- Keep well and fit so you can handle short bursts of intense activity.

- Keep working on your techniques to handle pressure and stress, so you can react positively to problems and periods of intense activity.

- What else in your life might need to be moved or adapted, temporarily or permanently?

- Be prepared to give up, if it's the right thing to do.

E4 Planning that works for you

There's no point in trying to use suggestions for planning ahead if they won't work for you. You need to consider your personal style (e.g. formal/informal; tidy/untidy; considered/spontaneous); preferences; motivations; needs; constraints.

For example

Somebody who likes things organised and to know what they're doing in advance	Somebody who likes to see how things go, leave things open, be spontaneous, not be tied down to something
Implications for handling time and pressure You'll get a lot done but may find it difficult to change what you plan, react to the unexpected or give up. You may get tired. You may get frustrated with those who operate differently (see next column.)	*Implications for handling time and pressure* You may get less done, do things at the last minute, miss opportunities or create difficulties for others in group/team work. You may get frustrated with those who operate differently (see previous column.)
Possible actions Build in more time for the unexpected than your instinct suggests. Set half the targets you initially thought of. Monitor plans. If you resist change, ask yourself why. Agree with others how you'll allow for your differences (e.g. one person is in charge one day, the other the next day; agree which tasks you'll do separately).	*Possible actions* Do more short term planning and use tools to help (e.g. mobile phones). Review progress frequently as you may need to do 'fire fighting'. Either accept that you'll do less or use new strategies (e.g. set aside an hour each day to organise yourself). If you let others do all the organising, they'll get fed up, so agree to do some of it.

Your notes

Your personal style; preferences; motivations; needs; circumstances; constraints
Implications for handling time and pressure
Possible actions

What methods, resources and tools would suit you, to help in planning and handling time and pressure?

Possibilities

	✓		✓
Paper diary.		Landline phone.	
Electronic diary.		Mobile phone.	
Electronic personal organiser.		Email.	
Lap top.		Hard/bound/paper files and notes.	
Home computer.		Computer files and notes.	
Computers at university/college.		Programs to help you produce work.	

	✓		✓
Internet access at university/college.		Develop your computer skills (e.g. a typing course).	
Internet access at home.		See Chapter 16 'Solving problems and making decisions' for suggestions.	
Printer at university/college/work.		Flow charts to show when to do what in which order.	
Printer at home.		Lists.	
Other ideas?			

E5 Coping with pressure/stress that works for you

Your personal style, preferences, motivations, needs, circumstances and constraints will affect how you handle pressure/stress. You need to find methods that work for you and be open to new ones. Section C8 covers basic methods but here are more suggestions.

Methods	Suggested activities within these
Getting other ideas.	There are books on how to handle pressure and stress. Look at the popular psychology or 'help yourself' books section of any good bookshop.
Get help from professionals.	Counsellors; doctors; people who teach relaxation techniques; and so on
Join a group or class.	A yoga/relaxation/meditation or exercise class.
Write it down.	Keep a journal to monitor areas you'd like to give attention to.
Talk it over.	Friends/family/tutors/colleagues/managers.
Look good.	If you make an effort with your appearance, you'll feel better.
Improve your posture.	You'll feel better and others take you more seriously.
Be physical.	Reduce stress by exercise or sport.
Find time for yourself.	Lock the door; have a relaxing bath; go for a walk.
Do things you enjoy.	

E6 Review: improving things for the future

What are your key issues in handling time or pressure? What are you really good at and what are your main issues? How do you know that? What's your evidence? Who says?

Key things I do well	Key things I need to improve	Evidence for these claims

How might you improve the aspects we've identified as 'enhanced'?

Aspect	This is what I'll repeat/do the same in future	This is what I'll do differently and how
Identifying what I really want to achieve and how I want to use my time.		
How to get what I want to achieve.		
Planning over an extended period or in complex or unpredictable situations.		

Aspect	This is what I'll repeat/do the same in future	This is what I'll do differently and how
Planning in a way that works well for me.		
Coping with pressure/stress in a way that works for me.		

16
SOLVING PROBLEMS AND MAKING DECISIONS

HOW THIS CHAPTER CAN HELP YOU

The 'crucial' skills part of this chapter aims to help you:

- recognise, identify and accurately describe the problem or need for a decision;
- use different methods to analyse the problem/issue;
- agree or check with others how you'll know the solution/decision is appropriate;
- select and use a range of methods to solve the problem/make the decision;
- compare each approach and justify the method you decide to use;
- plan your chosen way to solve the problem/make the decision;
- put your plan into action, decide on and use support, use feedback, check progress and amend plans;
- identify and apply methods for checking your solution/decision;
- evaluate your strategy and what affected the result and consider if other approaches might have been more effective;
- plan to improve for the future.

The 'enhanced' skills part of this chapter is shorter: it helps you operate to a higher level. As well as the 'crucial skills' outcomes, you'll be able to:

- identify opportunities for using and developing your solving problem/ decision making skills in complex and unpredictable contexts, clearly identifying what you want to achieve;
- explore complex problems/issues to establish their critical features;
- plan an implementation strategy, using relevant methods, identifying opportunities and constraints and allowing for unpredictable events;
- bring together, justify and present evidence for your solution/decision;
- identify good practice in solving problems and making decisions in your subject area;
- identify how to further develop your skills in solving problems/making decisions.

CRUCIAL SKILLS

C1 Why is this chapter important and how can it help you?

This chapter refers to higher education (HE) tasks that are explicitly about solving problems and to any situations (work or others) where you're faced with a problem or with a diagnosis or decision to make, large or small (e.g. which tasks to prioritise; which job to apply for).

The dictionary defines a problem as a 'doubtful or difficult matter requiring a solution', a decision as 'the settlement of a question' and a diagnosis as 'the identification of a disease or a mechanical fault'.

You could see most HE (or work) tasks as problems to be solved or questions to be answered. In the later stages of your course (or with more work responsibilities), the more complex the problems or questions become and the more you're expected to deal with them on your own. The guidance you get at the start of undergraduate courses (or at the start of a career) reduces as you go up the levels: you're expected to have developed ways of solving problems and making decisions for yourself.

Some subject areas (e.g. operations management; sciences) have specific ways of addressing problems. This chapter looks, rather, at processes that might be helpful across subject areas and for a range of types of problems, questions or situations.

C2 Other chapters you need to use together with this one

Other chapters will be useful to look at alongside this one. The first three below will support your problem solving and decision making. Solving problems and making decisions are an important basis for the topics of the remaining chapters referred to below.

Chapter	Title	How it relates to this chapter	Page
15	Handling time and pressure.	Dealing with problems and decisions involves managing time and pressure.	327
14	Action planning: identifying actions; recommendations.	In solving problems and making decisions you need to identify actions to take and may need to make recommendations at the end of the process.	301
13	Dealing with other people.	You may need to negotiate with others.	275
5	Doing a project.	Projects are likely to involve solving problems and making important decisions.	97
12	Working in a group or team.	Much team working is about solving problems and agreeing decisions.	253

Chapter	Title	How it relates to this chapter	Page
7	Finding, using and analysing information and evidence.	Most problem-solving and decision-making starts with gathering information about it.	147
	Any other chapter.	Most work in HE or the workplace involves solving problems and making decisions.	

C3 A first step

A first step is to identify what the problem or question is. It helps to phrase any task as a problem to be considered or a question to be answered. You could add words like 'how', 'why', 'when', 'what' to the beginning of the task and add to it what you think is needed (e.g. 'Discuss the role of the fool in *King Lear*' might become 'What role does the fool play in *King Lear* and why is it important?'; 'Design a semi detached house' might become 'What features are important in the design of a semi detached house and does my design address them?').

You then need to identify the key aspects making it a problem or an issue; that is, analyse it. In practice, this analysis may not be the first thing you do: you may plunge into trying to solve it and then go back to think about the essence of it. As you go along, you may see different aspects of the problem and, like peeling the layers of an onion, the heart of the matter will emerge.

However, the sooner you get to that 'heart of the matter' the better. If you don't, you may be trying to solve the wrong thing; for example, 'improving people's diet': your solution here may depend on what you see as the key aspect of the problem. The following shows how different views on this may lead to different solutions.

The essence (key aspect) of the problem	Solution
People don't know what a good diet is or why it's important.	An education campaign explaining about diet and its effects.
People don't know how to cook from scratch.	An education campaign teaching people how to cook from raw materials.
People don't have time to cook from scratch.	An education campaign teaching people what can be cooked quickly.
People don't have the money to buy good food.	Increase the minimum wage and state benefits.
People prefer the sort of food that's bad for them.	Either – accept that people have free choice, or – ban shops from selling such food.
There are many more possibilities.	

In HE, you must be able to justify (give reasons with evidence) why you see something as 'the essence' of a problem or issue, so most problem solving starts with gathering information (see Chapter 7 'Finding, using and analysing information and evidence'). You can't just pick something as being the essence of the problem because it appeals to you; you have to give proof. Often, the analysis may be the largest part of the problem-solving process, as once you've identified the key aspects, the solution or process needed to solve it may be obvious.

A problem or issue may not have one key aspect but several, impacting on each other: you may need to prioritise the most important ones or see how aspects are connected. Problems may have 'value' dimensions; decisions may be made on the basis of logic or on the basis of values and feelings. Which solutions in the diet example above have values or political (with a small 'p') stances attached? The solutions you dislike may imply values or political stances that you dislike.

The following gives sets of questions to consider that might help you analyse a problem or issue. Look at them in relation to a problem you face now or a decision you have to make.

The essence	Your notes
Why is it a problem?	
To whom is it a problem?	
What effect does it have?	
On whom or what does it have that effect?	
At what point did it become a problem?	

The aspects or elements	Your notes
What are the different elements of the problem or situation?	
Which have the greatest effect on it, using a rating scale where 1 = least and 3 = most?	
Is there a common thread running through all these elements?	
Do any elements depend on any others?	

Values or feelings	Your notes
Are feelings involved? Which and whose?	
Do any assumptions need to be questioned?	
Are any values involved? Which and whose?	
Are any ideologies relevant (e.g. political)? Whose? How?	

Evidence and justification	Your notes
Who says it's a problem?	
What's the evidence that it's a problem?	
What's the evidence for the elements/aspects you've identified?	
What's your evidence for the values you think are involved?	
How do you know assumptions are being made?	

How can you consider and investigate your problem or question in order to answer questions like those listed previously? Here are some possibilities.

- Look at the wording of your task for clues about the nature of the problem or issue.

- Look at the assessment criteria for clues.

- Look for specific information about your problem or issue (see Chapter 7 'Finding, using and analysing information and evidence').

- Look for general information on your topic (it may reveal aspects you hadn't considered).

- Brainstorm: write down as many ideas as possible about your problem/issue in 5 minutes (without exploring them), then review them to see what to keep. Could friends help?

- Sketch or doodle.

- Discuss it with others (e.g. tutor; students; library/learning centre staff; support or technical staff; employer; colleagues; specialists).

- Look at the web. Put a key term into a search engine (e.g. Google; Google Scholar).

- Look at it from the opposite point of view.

- Look at it from as many points of view as possible (e.g. academics; employers; the public; customers; young; old; women; men; ethnic groups).

- Draw a map or diagram to show the elements and how they link (e.g. a mind map; a flow diagram. See below).

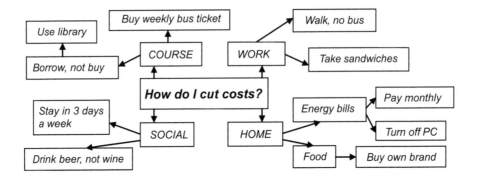

C4 How will you know if you've solved it or if your solution/decision is a 'good' one?

'Good' is in inverted commas as what makes a solution or decision good may vary and there may be no one correct one, just one that's the 'best fit'.

Who judges if it is a 'good' solution or decision?

Person judging	Implications
You?	Work out what will make it a good solution or decision for you, in the situation you're facing.
Another person: your tutor; your employer; an assessor?	Find out, as soon as possible, against which criteria they'll judge your solution/decision (note: they may assess process too).
Are you working with someone else on this problem/issue (see Chapter 12 'Working in a group or team')?	Negotiate how you'll all judge if your solution/decision is 'good' (see Section C5 in Chapter 13 'Dealing with other people').
Is it the person/people who'll be on the receiving end of the solution or decision?	Identify what matters to them (e.g. 'Should a new runway be built at an airport?': the solution may matter to local residents, passengers, air carriers, environmental groups, etc.).

Below are some possible criteria against which you might judge the success of a solution or decision, with space for your notes. Could you reword these criteria to fit your situation? For example, if you need to choose a car:

- 'it works effectively' might become 'it is mechanically reliable';

- 'It meets the needs of the situation' might be 'it'll hold 4 people and a lot of luggage';

- 'it's good enough, given constraints' might be 'it's the best option within my budget'.

Criterion	✓	Reword this for your situation
It works effectively.		
It meets the needs of the situation.		
If it's 'fit for purpose'.		
It's 'good enough', given constraints.		
It's the cheapest/best value for money.		
It's the most attractive.		
It's possible in the time available.		

Criterion	✓	Reword this for your situation
It appeals to relevant people		
It answers the main question.		
It's consistent with what matters to me.		
It's in my best interest.		
It's in the best interest of someone else.		
It'll cause least distress.		
It's the most pleasing one.		
Others?		

Being clear about the criteria for judging if a solution or decision is 'good' can make the solution or decision obvious. For example, if you're choosing a holiday that costs less than £250, is within 3 hours' travelling time, is in February, involves shopping and allows you to speak French, Paris is looking a good option.

For a problem or issue facing you...

who'll judge whether it's a 'good' solution/decision?	against which criteria will they judge the success of your solution/decision? What are they looking for?

C5 How will you solve the problem or explore the issue needing a decision?

There are many methods you could use and which ones are appropriate will depend on the type of problem or issue, any constraints you have and your own skills, preferences and knowledge. This section gives some ideas to get you started.

What **constraints** do you have that might affect the methods you use? Possibilities include:

- time;
- money/cost;
- resources or facilities available;
- regulations or requirements (e.g. cheating; plagiarism; health and safety rules);
- the people with whom you work.

What's **the nature of the problem** or issue? Possibilities include:

- a practical one, or one with a practical outcome;
- an intellectual one, or one with an idea as an outcome;
- a creative one, or one with a creative outcome;
- a social or emotional one, involving relationships or peoples' feelings;
- a physical one, requiring a construction or object as an outcome.

What **skills or knowledge** do you have that are relevant to the topic? Possibilities include:

- knowledge of the subject, the situation or context, the people or the methods;
- people skills;
- technical or professional skills;
- abilities with numeracy, or language;
- creativity.

Overleaf are **possible methods**. Some may overlap (e.g. testing models may be part of experimentation).

Method	Examples, suggestions and thoughts
Finding and analysing information about the situation and the problem.	It may be that this is enough in itself and that identifying the key aspects of the problem makes the solution obvious.
Make a list of the pros and cons.	List all positives and negatives about a possible solution or decision, against the criteria for judging its success.
Critical incident.	You can analyse a situation by identifying the events/activities that have a critical effect.
Experimentation. You may set up an experiment to test a hypothesis.	This may involve having a control group, so you can see if there's cause and effect.
Testing solutions.	This may be different from experimentation (e.g. testing audience reactions to adverts or if a machine works).
Trial and error, trying different solutions to see which one works.	This can take a long time and requires persistence. It's what many of us do without considering other options.
Making physical models.	You can see if they're appropriate in relation to your criteria or test them to see if they work.
Modelling of ideas and concepts.	This means creating a mental model (or framework or process) and seeing if it applies to your situation(s).
Making diagrams, sketches.	This is a way of visualising ideas.
Making plans or maps.	For example, to see if items will fit into a given space.
Brainstorming.	This means thinking up ideas without making judgements about their worth, to free up your thinking.
Blue sky thinking.	What might be possible if you had no constraints? You might then be able to adapt the ideas to allow for any constraints.
Acting out.	You could role play situations or put yourself in somebody else's position to help identify their needs.
Creative use of materials.	You could make shapes with play dough to help develop ideas, or use objects to represent ideas and move them around in relation to each other.
Keep notes.	So you don't lose ideas or information or the results of experiments or of trial and error.
Write.	Write letters to yourself or write creatively about the situation; write down what the opposite situation would be or the opposite of how people feel.

Now think about the situation or issue you're currently facing. What methods might be appropriate for the nature of your problem or issue, that allow for any constraints you have, that have benefits and where you can allow for any difficulties or risks involved?

Question	Your notes
What sort of problem or issue is it?	
What constraints do you have?	
What methods could you try to use to identify possible solutions or decisions?	
What are the benefits of using those methods for your situation or issue?	
What are the difficulties or risks in using those methods for this situation or issue?	

How do you actually decide?

It may depend on the problem or issue. Some decisions (e.g. about creative issues) are made on the basis of taste, itself made up of experience and knowledge of the area and personal preferences. Some are based on values or feelings.

However, most HE or work decisions need to meet certain criteria (see Section C4) and to be justified with evidence for why they're appropriate. You could list your criteria and then make an assessment of how far each possible choice meets it.

Using the car buying example, each criterion is rated (3 is good, 2 is OK and 1 is poor). The highest score might be the best fit. You could use a similar model for your decisions.

Example

Criterion	Model 1	Model 2	Model 3	Model 4	Evidence
Mechanically reliable.	3	3	2	1	Consumer advice magazine
It holds 4 people and a lot of luggage.	1	2	1	3	Specifications for models.
Value for money.	1	2	1	3	Current prices.

There are two models with the same score. Now what? You could consider:

- is any criterion more important than the others (if reliability is more important, then it would swing it for model 2)?

- if the criteria are all about equal, you could add further criteria to see if they change the balance (such as: colour of the car; length of warranty; cost of servicing).

How do you usually make decisions? Do you make them on a different basis in different situations? What works well? You could ask others what they do and what works for them.

Do you find making the final decision difficult?

Some people feel better once a decision is reached; others feel uncomfortable (in case they've closed off options or made the wrong choice).

If you feel better after making a decision, are you in danger of making it too quickly, before you've investigated all possibilities?

If you feel uncomfortable after reaching your decision, you may put off making it, or keep going back over it, or use unnecessary effort investigating every possibility. You may need to steel yourself and have a cut-off point for deciding. Stop yourself when you start going over it again. Here are some thoughts that might help.

- What's the worst that could happen if the decision is wrong?

- In HE, is your tutor really bothered about the solution or are they more interested in the process you used? Even if your solution or decision isn't 'the best', they may be happy if you know what's wrong with it. It may be the evaluation that matters.

- Making a decision can be about coming to terms with giving up what you decided against.

- Being perfect is hard work, and beating yourself up for not being perfect is hard too.

C6 Making a plan

You'll find two other chapters helpful here. Chapter 14 'Action planning: identifying actions and recommendations' helps in identifying useful actions and making recommendations, which may be needed at the end of a problem solving process. Chapter 15 'Handling time and pressure' helps you plan time to meet a deadline and to handle the pressure that can arise when faced with problems or decisions.

By when must you have your solution or decision? You need to plan to meet this deadline. In making such plans, you need to: work backwards from the deadline;

allow more time than you expect for each stage or task (it always take longer); build in time for things going wrong.

Organisations that commission people to do problem solving work, commonly ask those putting forward proposals for 'risk assessments'. This means anticipating what might go wrong, how likely this is and what you'll do to avoid it or deal with it. Here's a common format that you could use.

The rating scale here is 1 = low risk, 2 = medium risk, 3 = high risk. The higher your total score, the riskier your plans. Risks may relate to the situation or issue, your methods, actions needed or any constraints (e.g. if you're working with others, might they become ill?).

In relation to your problem or issue:

Risk	Rating 1–3	Actions to be taken to reduce or deal with the risk

You may need to build the actions you identify to reduce or deal with risks into your plans.

Making a plan

Below is a format you could use.

In the 'Actions' column you could include, for example, getting permission (e.g. to use information; for people's involvement); finding out about regulations or procedures (e.g. ethics committee approval; health and safety training before using equipment); methods to solve the problem.

In the following, a 'milestone' is an outcome that tells you a task has been completed. A milestone can act as a useful review point, as on the due date for achieving it you can see how far you've got and if you need to amend your plan.

Example plan

Example: problem 'should a new runway be built for X airport?'

Task/action	By (deadline)	Resources needed	Milestone	Progress notes
Check amount of current air traffic.	*30 Sept*	*Data from Dept of Transport and from airport we site for last 10 years.*	*Table of data.*	*Awaiting final information, 28 Sept.*
Estimate rise in air traffic.	*3 October*	*Table of data for last 10 years to identify trend.*	*Graph showing rise.*	

For more on plans, see Chapters 14 'Action planning; identifying actions; making recommendations' and 15 'Handling time and pressure'.

C7 Putting your plan into action

You need to make good use of your plan. Look at it each day to check if you're on target. If things aren't going as you anticipate, you need to amend your plan.

You may find your problem changes and is no longer the one you started with; a new one may arise that has to do with your method. For example, if you were relying on somebody to provide expertise and they let you down, you have a new problem. You may then need to go through the problem solving approaches suggested in the sections above to find a solution.

What support and help do you need to put your plan into action? How can you find support and make the best use of help? For ideas, look at Chapter 13 'Dealing with other people'.

How are you going to monitor your plan? Will you:

- check if you've reached your milestones?
- check how well you're meeting the criteria for judging the success of your solution or decision?
- use feedback (e.g. from: a tutor; an employer; friends; other students; colleagues)?

C8 Evaluating your solution or decision

A 'good' solution or decision is one that meets the criteria for the situation: see Section C4.

How will you know if it's met the criteria? Possible methods to evaluate the success or appropriateness of your solution/decision include the following.

- Observation (e.g. observing your solution being used).

- Checking or inspecting (e.g. is it fit for its purpose?).

- Testing (e.g. does it work; does it work over time; does it work accurately?).

- Measuring (e.g. how well does it work; how much can it produce?).

- Sampling (e.g. if you can't see how appropriate it is in all situations, you could try it out in a sample situation or situations).

- Using a specialist (e.g. what does an architect think of your design or a physiotherapist think of your diagnosis?).

- Asking the users (e.g. do they like it, does it meet their needs?).

In HE, tutors may be more concerned about the process used, your approach and your evaluation than about the solution or decision. This is because their purpose in setting problem solving tasks is to help you develop problem solving skills. They're unlikely to want to see solutions or decisions without evidence of how you got there (just as in maths you need to show 'workings' as well as the 'answer'). You may be asked to provide different versions of your solutions to show the line of progress (this often happens in design courses); if so, make clear the order of the versions and how they changed.

If you need to evaluate your methods and your plan, you may be expected to identify:

- what went well or worked well;

- what didn't go well or work well;

- how the methods you used affected the result (positively and negatively);

- how using other methods might have improved or changed the result;

- what methods you'd use in future or how you'd adapt the methods you used;

- which of the methods and approaches you'd use again.

For more help, see Chapter 17 'Reflecting on your learning and experience (including feedback)'.

Things rarely work perfectly and your tutor will expect you to be critical about what you did. You may lose marks for saying everything was OK if it wasn't and gain marks for being perceptive about what didn't go well, why and how you could change that.

C9 Review: improving things for next time

What will you do the same or differently next time?

Activity	This is what I'll repeat/do the same in future	This is what I'll do differently
Analyse the problem or issue.		
Identify how I'll judge if the solution or decision is 'good'.		
Choose and use methods to explore the problem or issue.		
Make a plan.		
Put my plan into action, monitor and amend it.		
Evaluate my solution or decision/methods used.		

ENHANCED SKILLS

E1 Identifying what you want to achieve and how?

As you go up through the levels of HE (or at work), you'll come up against more complex and uncertain situations. By the end of undergraduate courses, in postgraduate studies and in professional jobs, you're expected to make sense of topics yourself and to make your own decisions about what you think. At PhD level, you'll be the ones creating new knowledge.

This means you increasingly encounter problems to be solved and decisions to be made. How much you like this sort of activity may determine whether you decide to go on to postgraduate study or what sort of job you do.

Here are some thoughts to help you identify what you want to achieve and how. Working this out is a decision making exercise in itself.

What do you want?	✓	Ideas and suggestions
Do you want problem solving to be a main part of future work?		Any work involving research has problem solving as an essential aspect, as do management roles.
Do you want it to have some part of your future work?		For most graduate level work it'll be an important element. Those who can do it well may be those who are given more responsibility.
Would you like to avoid it?		This is pretty difficult to do but you could reduce the need to use these skills (e.g. avoid work that has significant management responsibilities).
Would you like it to use your skills in this area to help others?		As well as paid work, some voluntary need such skills (e.g. Citizen's Advice; local politics).
Would you like to identify leisure interests using such skills?		You could brainstorm ideas with others here (chess; bridge; orienteering).
Could you use these skills to manage your life better?		How could you better manage your finances or fit course/work/leisure activities together? Do you need to improve in making personal decisions?
What if you can't achieve what you hope for (e.g. finding a job)?		You could see identifying fall back positions and plans for them as a problem solving activity.

If you have ideas about how you could use such skills in the future, you could then consider how to use your course or current work in a way that puts you in a good position to do so (e.g. by developing areas of expertise). You could see this as a problem to solve and use the 'critical skills section' above to help you solve it.

E2 Exploring complex problems and making complex decisions

Is your problem or issue more complicated than Section C3 suggests? For our example 'should a new runway be built for an airport', there may be conflicting needs from different groups (e.g. air carriers as opposed to environmental groups; passengers as opposed to local residents.) The essence of your problem might actually be 'how can a compromise be found for all these groups'?

One technique is to simplify the problem. For complex situations where there are ambiguities and uncertainties, you can get bogged down in detail. It helps to step back and work out the key issue or question and to look at your detail in relation to that. Using the example 'should a new runway be built for an airport', perhaps a first, simple question is 'who wants or doesn't want it built and why?' This would give a framework within which to think about it.

What if you find it hard to see the key aspects, given all the complex information? Would consulting a specialist help? Could you find recent articles on the topic so you can see what they identified as key points?

If faced with confusing information, try asking the following questions.

- What assumptions underpin each bit of information?
- Is anything misleading?
- Are there any vested interests that might bias the information?
- Are there any ambiguities or contradictions (i.e. could the situation be interpreted in more than one way, or do any aspects of the situation suggest different things)?

Look at the 'Enhanced skills' section of Chapter 7 'Finding, using and analysing information and evidence' for more on being critical.

When finding solutions or making decisions in complex situations, you may need to prioritise. If you can't meet all needs or all criteria, you must decide which are the most important to meet. Sometimes making any decision is better than not making one at all. People talk about 'elegant' solutions or decisions, meaning something simple that accounts for all (or most) eventualities (Einstein's $E = MC^2$ is an example). Could you use some of the methods suggested in Section C5 to identify an 'elegant' solution or decision?

E3 Planning revisited

Sections C6 and C7 covered some key techniques for planning and implementing your plan. How could you further develop these?

You could look at literature on planning techniques or identify suitable computer software (university/college/work ICT support could help). See literature on 'project management' as well as on research or evaluation methods, or journal articles that indicate the methods used to explore something.

You could try 'critical path analysis', where you identify the tasks or outcomes/ milestones that are absolutely critical for your plan to succeed. You could adapt the plan suggested in Section C6 to have both critical milestones and subsidiary ones.

Another technique is to draw a timeline, indicating dates. The end point may or may not be the solution or decision; it could be your evaluation or the result of the solution/ decision (e.g. in health areas, the end point may not be the diagnosis but the cure). You plot actions, milestones or critical points on the line. Seeing it visually helps you identify if you've allowed enough time, if there's a bunching of items that may create difficulties and if you've over complicated it (e.g. too many actions or milestones). See the example in Section C6 of Chapter 15 'Handling time and pressure'.

You might consider the following in relation to yourself and possible impacts on your plan.

Possible personal issues	Your notes
What do I feel confident/ unconfident about and how might that affect what happens?	
How comfortable am I with risk? Do I like to take risks or would I like to minimise them?	
What new skills/techniques would I like to develop? Will the time available allow for this? If there's only time to develop one, what would it be?	
How do I react when unpredictable things happen? What could I do to react in a helpful way?	

E4 Pulling together and presenting your evidence

Section C8 considers this in relation to evaluating your solution/decision and your process to achieve it.

At higher levels in HE, presenting evidence of your process becomes increasingly important. In your 'product' (e.g. work you hand in) you may need a section on the methods you used and an 'audit trail'; that is, to show proof of what you did. Assessors may want to know about the influences on you and on what you did. At work, you may need to justify your solutions (e.g. think of financial or scientific solutions/decisions).

Usually, your 'product' (e.g. report, thesis/dissertation; poster; presentation; viva; observed process) will include a summary of your methods, relevant aspects of information you collected, the solution or decision and an evaluation of what you did and of the solution/decision. Details of what you did might go in an appendix (for written work) or a handout (e.g. for a presentation); here you need key details or examples (e.g. examples of: notes; a research 'instrument'; raw data). If you have an appendix, then in the main body of your work you must refer the reader to it (or they won't bother looking at the appendix).

You may have to produce a journal/diary that records what you did or a portfolio showing successive versions of your solutions: see Chapter 3 'Producing portfolios and journals (including diaries, blogs, etc.)'.

E5 Identifying good practice in your field

Section C8 looks at evaluating what you did. At higher levels of courses and at work you may need to take this further and identify good practice in carrying out similar processes and addressing similar situations. For example, whilst doing the work you may have discovered new approaches or techniques that are in use.

You may need to make recommendations about what would be good practice in further situations. If in doubt, check with a tutor or manager.

E6 Review: improving things for the future

How comfortable are you with the crucial skills in solving problems or making decisions (including diagnoses)? Have another look at Section C9.

How might you improve the aspects we have identified as 'enhanced'?

Aspect	This is what I'll repeat/do the same in future	This is what I'll do differently and how
Being clear how to use problem solving and decision making skills.		
Exploring complex problems and issues; dealing with uncertainty and ambiguity.		
Using appropriate planning techniques and software.		
Pulling together and presenting evidence.		
Identifying good practice in solving problems/making decisions in my subject.		

17
REFLECTING ON YOUR LEARNING AND EXPERIENCE (INCLUDING FEEDBACK)

HOW THIS CHAPTER CAN HELP YOU

The 'crucial' skills part of this chapter aims to help you:

- identify the main features of reflecting and how the process can help you learn;
- think about the effectiveness of your own performance and your attitude and approach to reflection and learning;
- recognise opportunities to reflect on and take responsibility for identifying your strengths, weaknesses, needs and wants and developing your skills, knowledge and understanding;
- consider different ways of reflecting and learning, identifying things that affect your own reflections and learning;
- identify and choose ways to help you reflect and learn and plan to use methods that best suit you and your situation;
- make and implement your plans;
- seek and use feedback from a range of sources;
- identify how you could improve your skills in reflecting.

The 'enhanced' skills part of this chapter is shorter: it helps you operate to a higher level. As well as the 'crucial' skills' outcomes, you'll be able to:

- work out what you most want to achieve; reflect on and appraise your skills/experience in identifying and meeting your own needs/wants;
- identify opportunities for using and developing your skills in reflecting and learning, to achieve your aims in a range of situations;
- adapt what you do to achieve your aims, trying different ways of reflection and learning to meet new demands and address difficulties;
- critically reflect on your approaches and their effectiveness;
- plan your further development.

CRUCIAL SKILLS

C1 Why is this chapter important and how can it help you?

Dictionary definitions of 'reflection' aren't very helpful here, as the word is used in education in a specific way. Many courses include reflective activities (also called 'evaluations' or 'self evaluations' or 'self assessments') and reflection is a key aspect of Personal/Professional Development Planning (see Chapter 18). This is because, over recent years, a view of how people learn has developed that sees 'reflection' as absolutely key to learning.

The 'constructivist' theory of learning is that we learn by making our own sense of what we encounter. This is very different from a view that sees us as repeating existing knowledge. Constructivists believe we acquire knowledge through doing something with it; for example:

- thinking it through to make connections with what you already know;

- physically doing something, like making notes;

- using knowledge to solve a problem;

- talking about it.

Even physically 'doing something' involves thinking about what you're doing (e.g. why does this work in one situation but not in another? what would happen if I did that instead?).

The process of thinking about what you're learning/doing, in order to make sense of it, is 'reflection'. If we do something repeatedly without changing it, it may be because we haven't thought about the effect it has and what we could do differently.

Reflection isn't only seen as a key activity in higher education (HE). Most professional bodies and many employers have Continuing Professional Development (CPD) schemes where it's essential. These usually include appraisals and keeping a professional portfolio.

Reflecting on something afterwards ('reflection **on** action', Schon, 1987) helps you identify what you've learnt for similar situations in future. Practising 'reflection on action' helps you develop the ability to think about and adapt something while it's actually happening ('reflection **in** action', Schon 1987). Highly skilled people do this (e.g. comedians think on their feet when dealing with an audience; surgeons adapt their approach if faced with a crisis).

Reflection could be seen as a process of asking yourself questions (e.g. Why did I do that? What effect did it have?). This is similar to the process of being critical, outlined in Chapter 7 'Finding, using and analysing information and evidence'. There is, however, a difference. In HE, 'being critical' is often related to situations and information outside yourself, whilst 'reflection' is often related to what you do. Evaluating what you've learnt, done or thought is part of reflection.

Where courses (or CPD schemes) require reflective activities (or evaluations, self-evaluations or self-assessments), they want something quite specific. They don't want a lot of unconnected thoughts about something but for you to be able to describe or explain:

- what you've learnt;

- what something that you did or thought or experienced 'means';

- what was effective and what evidence you have for this;

- what wasn't effective and what evidence you have for this;

- what you can build on or repeat;

- what you need to improve;

- how you plan to improve it and what specific actions you'll take.

Only if you do all of that will you be seen to have reflected effectively and this chapter looks at how you can do this.

C2 Other chapters you need to use together with this one

This chapter is **the basis for** some other chapters and it is very important to use it as such.

Chapter	Title	Why 'reflection' is essential for this chapter	Page
18	Personal/Professional Development Planning (PDP).	Reflecting on your needs, wants, experiences, learning and performance is the basis for the PDP process.	401
14	Action planning: identifying actions and recommendations.	Action planning is an essential aspect of the reflection process and of the PDP process.	301
15	Handling time and pressure.	This covers planning to meet your development needs as part of PDP, and you won't know what they are without reflection.	327
3	Producing portfolios and journals (including diaries, blogs etc).	Most portfolios and journals rely on the process of reflection for you to identify what to include.	49

This chapter is valuable to use with any of the other chapters, as it will help you evaluate your own performance and make decisions about what to do to improve or develop.

C3 Ways of reflecting

Reflection is a crucial skill for any situation (e.g. in HE, at work, socially). You're already doing it: if you play football and think about the match afterwards, you're reflecting on what you did and what you could have done; you may think about things you said to somebody; you may leave an exam thinking about the questions you did well (or not). We all do it.

So if we all do it, why do we need this chapter? We may reflect on some things more than others. We may reflect unhelpfully (just going over what you did wrong isn't much use if you don't work out what to do instead). We may not do it in the form required in HE or for CPD.

What's your usual practice?	Your notes
What do you normally do when you reflect on something?	
What works well about this?	
What does not work very well about this?	

Here are some possible ways of reflecting.

- Talk to somebody about it. Hearing yourself describe it can help you think it through. How the other person reacts might help too. Do their reactions annoy or please you? Why? Are they helpful? Why?

- Write about it. Put your writing aside for a day, then review it. What do you think now? This helps you see a situation as somebody else might. You could write about it in a structured way (see Section C4 for a possible process).

- Keep a diary or journal, not only of what has happened but also of your feelings and reactions. You might see patterns or progress.

- Pretend you're somebody else talking to yourself. Sit opposite your jumper or jacket. Tell 'yourself' what happened or how you felt. This can be powerful (do it in private, though!).

- Record it and play it back at a later stage, to see what you now think.

- Pay attention to your gut reactions. If somebody makes a suggestion and your reaction is uncomfortable, ask yourself why: it might be telling you what you really think. This can work well if you have a decision to make.

- Make diagrams or charts (e.g. to show connections).

- Draw your learning or your feelings or events and their impact.

An important way of reflecting is to look at evidence. What does it indicate about what you learnt, did, said or thought? This merits a section of its own, as if you have to present your reflections for assessment, your tutors will want evidence for what you claim.

C4 Using evidence (including feedback)

C4.1 Feedback

One important form of evidence for what you've learnt, done, said or thought is feedback.

We get feedback all the time. Here are some examples:

- people's facial expressions or body language in reaction to what you say or do;

- people's casual comments about you ('that's a nice jacket') or your views ('why on earth do you think that film was good?');

- people who seek (or avoid) your company;

- tutors' or other students' responses to your comments in class;

- things that work (or not) when you create or repair them.

Feedback is anything that gives you information about the effectiveness of what you did, said or thought. Research suggests (Sheffield Hallam University, 2007) that students only see feedback from tutors as 'legitimate' if it is written, but in reality we all receive it in different forms all the time.

One issue is what we do with feedback. Some may be hurtful or blatantly incorrect. Some of us 'hear' all the negative things rather than the positives.

When you get feedback, think about the following, to help make judgements about its value.

- Who gave it? What do they know (e.g. are they experts/experienced? How important are they to you? Might they have a vested interest or some sort of bias?).

- When did they give it? Immediate feedback is good. After time, memory may be faulty.

- Does it make clear what was effective (or not) about what you did, said or thought?

- What's the evidence for their views? Why do they think what they think?

- What's the weight of evidence? If one person says x and others say y, who's right (of course, the person saying x may know more)? Are they generalising from one incident that's uncharacteristic of you?

Think about some recent feedback you've had

Which aspects are valid or helpful?	Which aspects are not valid or unhelpful?	Which aspects will you do something about?

Seeking feedback

If you'd like feedback, who might offer a valid or relevant view (e.g. a member of a group you've worked in; an expert in the topic)? It's a good idea to:

- ask for feedback as soon after the event as possible;

- ask specific questions ('How well did x work?'; 'What effect did it have when I did y?');

- ask for clarification (e.g. if people look puzzled, ask them why). If they make judgemental statements (e.g. 'That was good'), ask what they mean;

- check if they meant what you think they meant ('Did you mean my writing was illegible?');

- thank them.

Your aim is to get feedback, not justify yourself. It's not a good idea to argue or defend: they'll be wary of giving you feedback again and if you asked for feedback, it's ungracious to then grumble about it. Just because you thank them, doesn't mean you agree with them.

Giving feedback to others

The reverse is the case for giving feedback. You may need to do this for course activities or at work (e.g. peer assessment; appraisals).

- Give the feedback as soon after the event as possible.

- Give specific information ('X worked well'). Don't make judgemental statements that people can't do anything about (e.g. 'It was rubbish'). Help them see what to do in future.

- Give evidence for what you think.

- Avoid uncomfortable discussions by being assertive (see Chapter 13 'Dealing with other people'): 'That's my feedback, do feel free to use it or not'.

C4.2 Other evidence

In order to reflect on what you've learnt, done, said or thought, you could start with the evidence and see what it suggests about you (see Sections C5 and C6).

What evidence might you have and what might it reveal? 'Good' evidence is:

- relevant and valid for the claim (i.e. it needs to prove what you say it proves);

- sufficient (i.e. doing something once may not be proof that you could do it again);

- current (i.e. occurring at the time you are referring to);

- authentic (i.e. directly relating to you, not somebody else).

In the 'notes' column overleaf you could record evidence you already have or how you might gather it. What opportunities could you take to get such evidence?

Evidence	Examples of what it might show	Your notes
Written assignments.	Skills in: writing; being critical; using information; developing arguments; managing time. Knowledge.	
Projects.	As above, plus: being able to work autonomously; initiative; problem solving.	
Group or team work activities.	Skills in: communicating; negotiating; cooperating; doing what you say.	
Doing presentations.	Skills in: communicating verbally and visually; structuring information. Knowledge of the topic.	
Workshop activities.	Willingness to participate; interpersonal skills. Knowledge of the topic.	
Lab activities.	Accuracy; operating safely; being rigorous; being careful. Knowledge of the topic.	
Friendships.	Interpersonal skills; being trustworthy/reliable; good listener. Knowledge of people.	
Family relationships.	As above, plus: tolerance; flexibility.	
Leisure interests.	Shows what you value. Different activities develop different skills/knowledge.	
Social activities.	Shows what you value. Interpersonal skills. Knowledge of people.	
Sporting activities.	Shows what you value. Persistence. Competitiveness. Team working. Determination.	
Photographs.	Records of what you've done, people you've known.	
Images you have created.	Your creativity and its development; influences on your work; use of technical skills.	
Part time or temporary jobs.	Knowledge of working practices (e.g. timekeeping, attendance), plus skills/abilities the job needed.	
Full time or permanent jobs.	As above. How many jobs you've had may show your stability; jobs and job changes may show motivations.	
Travel.	Get up and go; interest in world around you; independence. Knowledge of the world.	
Voluntary activities.	Shows what you value. Altruism, 'social conscience'. Different activities develop different skills/knowledge.	
Political activities.	Shows what you value. Political knowledge. Communication and organisational skills.	
Student union activities.	Different activities develop different skills/knowledge. Communication and organisational skills.	
How you spend your time.	Shows what you value.	
What else?		

C5 How effective is your performance?

This is a key question for a reflective activity. You'll need to identify what you're good at, what you're less good at, what you'll do to build on the good and what you'll do to improve.

Here, identify something you recently did (perhaps something you are being required to reflect on as part of your course).

You can consider the following questions in relation to this. Look again at Section C3 for ways of thinking about this and Section C4 to help you identify evidence for your judgements.

Questions	Your notes, including evidence you have for your views
What did you do (or say or think) well?	
What effect did this have?	
What did you not do (or say or think) very well?	
What effect did this have?	
Did anything have an influence of what you do/say/think? What? How?	
What would you do/say/think in future that's the same?	
What would you not do/say/think in the future?	
What skills, techniques or knowledge do you need for the future, in relation to this?	
Do you need to amend your attitude at all?	
What support/information do you need to help you for the future (including other chapters)?	

C6 What does your experience 'mean'?

Reflection is not just about identifying what's effective and what isn't. It's also about interpreting evidence. What does the evidence say about you? Here are some examples.

Examples

Scenario	Possible interpretation	But on the basis of more information...
A spends every evening in the pub and B spends every evening watching TV.	A is sociable and B isn't. B is passive and A is active.	What if A drinks alone in the pub? What if B watches TV with friends?
A is a frequent contributor to class discussions. B never contributes.	A is interested in the topic and B isn't. A is willing to cooperate and B isn't.	What if A's comments are irrelevant or unreasoned? What if B is quietly listening and making sense of it all? What if A is stopping B speaking by talking too much?

The above examples show how the same situation can be interpreted differently and how this might depend on the information available. The interpretations above consider individuals' interests (in the topic), attitudes (active or passive), skills or abilities (cooperating) and ways of learning (speaking or listening).

Why is it important to interpret your experiences to work out what they indicate about your abilities, preferences, values and learning?

- You're the best-placed person to know what evidence about you really 'means'. You may need feedback from others, but you're the one with the most complete picture.

- When you present reflective work you need to organise it so others can make sense of it and to tell them what it shows about you.

- When you present yourself in other contexts (e.g. in a CV; interview; e-portfolio), you need to tell others what you're like, with evidence and examples.

- Having a clear idea of 'who you are' at a particular point in time can help you work out what you want to build on and what you'd like to be different.

Go back to the start of Section C5, where you identified an experience and considered questions in relation to it. You could now consider the following questions about the same experience.

Questions about the experience	Your notes, including evidence for your views
What does it suggest about what interests you?	
What does it suggest about what you value or what's important to you?	
What sort of attitudes does it suggest you have?	
What does it suggest about skills, abilities or knowledge you have: your strengths?	
What does it suggest about skills, abilities or knowledge you don't have: your weaknesses?	
What connections does it have with other situations? Is what you did here different or similar?	
What would somebody who doesn't know you conclude from what happened/ what you did or said or thought?	

C7 How do you learn?

On a course and at work you'll continue to learn: thinking about **how** you do so is important.

- In reflective work required for courses, tutors want to know not just what you learnt, but how and what was (or wasn't) effective about your method of learning.

- You may be limiting yourself to familiar methods of learning. Could you try new ones?

How you learn will depend on several things, for example:

- what you think you're supposed to be learning (e.g. factual information or principles/concepts) and what's required (e.g. as indicated by the assessment criteria);

- what sort of thing it is you're learning (e.g. the subject or topic);

- your own mix of skills, abilities, preferences and habits.

You'll probably use different methods to learn different things in different situations. If you always do the same thing you may have a problem; what works in one situation may not work in another. As a general rule, the more ways of learning at your disposal, the more you'll be able to learn in a range of situations.

You may have heard of 'learning styles'. There are misunderstandings here. Theory (Kolb, 1984) doesn't say we should accept that an individual has one learning style they prefer to use, but rather that in order to learn effectively s/he must develop all the styles, not just the preferred one. There are different views, too. One (held by the authors) is that people learn in different ways depending on what they're learning and the situation.

Thinking explicitly about how you learn helps you identify what's useful, what isn't and what else you could try.

In the following, in each column, tick ways of learning you use in the situation given. While doing this, think about the advantages and disadvantages of the way of learning for that situation and you.

Example of thoughts you might have

Way of learning	When using information	When working with other people	When doing practical things
Trial and error.	I don't use trial and error. I work out in advance what I need and plan to find it.	I plunge in and sometimes it works and sometimes I offend people.	I try different ways. This works well for me but can take quite a long time.

Way of learning	When using information	When working with other people	When doing practical things
	✓	✓	✓
Trial and error.			
Planning what to do in advance.			
Thinking about it while I'm doing it.			
Thinking about it afterwards.			
Talking about it.			
Getting advice from others.			
Watching what others do/say.			
Learning it by heart.			
Questioning it.			

Way of learning	When using information	When working with other people	When doing practical things
	✓	✓	✓
Keeping records of what happened.			
Surfing the web.			
Watching films, programmes, DVDs about it.			
Seeing how it relates to theory.			

So, what works for you and when?

What's working well for you in how you learn, and in what situations?	What's not working very well for you in how you learn, in what situations?	What else can you try?

C8 Planning actions based on your reflections

The whole point of reflecting is to then plan to take action to build on strengths and improve or change where there are limitations.

Planning is a topic in its own right and is covered in separate chapters. **It's very important that you look now at Chapter 14 'Action Planning: identifying actions; making recommendations'**. Any assessed reflective work is likely to require it. You'll also find Chapter 15 'Handling time and pressure' very useful.

C9 How will you record or present your reflections?

How can you record your reflections and the evidence for them?

Recording method	Our notes	Your notes on how you might use this
Reflective log/blog/ diary.	A narrative often with personal thoughts. Who'll see it? Others (assessor)? If so, be more careful about contents than if it's just for you. See Chapters: 3 'Producing portfolios and journals; 10 'Presenting your work; making it look good'.	
Portfolio of evidence with reflective notes or summaries.	See Chapters: 3 'Producing portfolios and journals (including diaries, blogs etc)'; 10 'Presenting your work; making it look good'.	
Reflective writing/ video/ audio.	This is 'free' form (no specified structure). How you organise/ select items is important: think about the audience and what you want to achieve. See Chapter 10 'Presenting your work; making it look good'	

Recording method	Our notes	Your notes on how you might use this
Stories.	See previous page. Your reflections may be creative pieces (written; audio; film). This helps you see it as others might. Structure/order/ key points are important. Many films/novels are based on true stories; see them for ideas	
Web pages/ Wiki.	A communal/collaborative web page(s) to which you contribute thoughts/ideas/feelings/responses etc. can be used for collaborative learning with reflective elements (e.g. on placements; design courses).	
CD/DVD.	This is a recording format and in considering the implications, look at the above items. See Chapter 10 'Presenting your work; making it look good'.	
Critical incidents.	Select and describe what you see as critical events; pick incidents that truly demonstrate what you want to show; use this chapter to help you 'make sense' of them.	
Placement report.	Check (with an assessor) how important it is to describe what happened and how important it is to make sense of that. What should the balance be between the two? Use Chapter 2 'Writing reports'.	

Why do you need to record your reflections and evidence? How will this affect what you do?

Possible purposes of the reflection records	Implications: our thoughts/ suggestions	Your notes: implications for what you need to do
I'm required to present records in a specified way (e.g. for assessment or for CPD).	Check requirements and assessment criteria. You may be given a format, but there may be scope within it for your own approach.	
I have to present records to others but I can choose how to do so. *or* For others to use as it stands.	Make clear what you want the user to see/understand. Methods include: contents list; sections; frequent summaries; well-selected evidence; its appearance will matter.	
As a repository of information for my own use, from which I will draw things when I need them (e.g. to make a CV).	May be better to keep too much than find later that something is missing. Must be well organised to find things. Needs storing where you won't lose it (e.g. if electronic, backed up).	
To help me monitor and plan my development.	Create sections according to the aspects you want to concentrate on. Find a way of highlighting progress, to build your confidence.	

Presenting reflective work to others

It's likely that you'll have to:

- indicate what you learnt;
- interpret what you did/said/thought to indicate what it shows about you/ your learning;
- indicate what was effective, with evidence for it;
- indicate what wasn't effective, with evidence for it;
- indicate what can you build on or repeat;
- indicate what you need to improve or change;
- indicate how you plan to improve or develop and what specific actions will you take.

For assessed reflective work in HE it will **not** matter how well you did the original activity; what matters is how good you are at reflecting on it (doing what the previous 7 bullet points say). Basically, it is how you present it that will matter.

There's an exception to this. If you need to tell others how good you are, then how well you did the original activity does matter (e.g. in CVs/application forms; in interviews; in some portfolios).

You need evidence for what you claim (see Section C4) and to organise the evidence so the reader/user understands what it says about you. The statements you make and words you use also do this. See Chapters 18 'Personal/Professional Development Planning (PDP)', 3 'Producing portfolios and journals (including diaries, blogs, etc.)' and 10 'Presenting your work; making it look good'.

C10 Improving your skills in reflection

Reflection is a difficult skill because it involves thought processes that are hard to describe. Use the following to think about how well you reflect.

Aspect	This is what I'll repeat/do the same in future	This is what I'll do differently
Being clear about what reflection is, in an HE or CPD context.		
Identifying appropriate evidence.		
Getting and using feedback.		
Giving feedback.		
Identifying my strengths and areas I need to improve.		
Interpreting evidence to draw some conclusions about my experience.		
Identifying how I learn and what's effective or not.		
Recording and presenting my reflections.		

ENHANCED SKILLS

E1 What do you most want to achieve from reflection?

What you want from reflection may have implications for how you go about it (e.g. if you want to use it to help you do well on a course/at work, you'll need to find out what's needed to do well). What do you aim to get from reflection and what are the implications for you?

Possible aims	✓	Notes: implications for what you need to do
To develop skills for lifelong use; to continue to update and improve my ability as a professional.		
To help me think about what I want from my life and how to get it.		
To use it to ensure I do as well as I possibly can in my course/current job.		
To use it to think about more personal things (e.g. relationships).		
To help me think about something that's really bothering me at the moment.		
I just want to meet whatever requirements there are for assessment or CPD?		
What else?		

E2 How could I achieve my aims in relation to reflection?

Looking at your responses to E1, what do you need to help you?

Possible issue	Examples and suggestions	Your notes
Do you need to acquire or develop any skills?	e.g. skills of: analysis; interpretation; action planning; recording evidence; presentation.	
Do you need to develop any knowledge?	e.g. theory on reflection; learning theory; planning methods; use of critical incidents.	
What sources of information or support might there be?	e.g. learning centre/library; the web; tutor; workplace mentor; professional body; employer; family; careers adviser; examples of e-portfolios).	
What opportunities could you seek out or use that would help you?	e.g. short courses you could attend (e.g. on career planning or creating CVs); work shadowing; volunteering.	
Do you know what's needed for reflection or for a CPD process?	Use Section C. Check written requirements (e.g. on professional body websites). Ask: tutors; past students; other professionals.	
Are you trying to use the reflective process in a complex/ uncertain situation?	Follow the approach suggested in Section C to help manage the complexities. See Chapter 16 'Solving problems and making decisions'.	

E3 Improving your learning

The reflective process is essentially about learning. How can you use this chapter to learn in any context (e.g. when facing new demands)?

This book is based on two assumptions.

1.	What makes somebody effective is the ability to analyse what's needed in a situation (and by you), and then to do/say/think what's effective for the situation (and for you).

2.	You need a base of knowledge, skills, techniques and approaches to call on, as appropriate for the situation. It's no use having knowledge or skills if you don't know when to use them.

Hence this book! All the chapters are based on the above assumptions. What could help you see what's needed in a given situation? In the following we give an example to help you.

When you face a new situation...	Our example: when you're having a meeting (e.g. with students or colleagues)	Your notes about what you do (it may help to think of a particular situation or type of situation)
do you start by identifying its key features (however briefly/quickly)?	e.g. the meeting: what's it for; where will it be; how long will it take; who'll be there; what will they want?	
do you start by identifying what you want to get out of it?	e.g. the meeting: to find more out about a topic.	
do you put those two analyses together to work out what you need to do (however briefly/quickly)?	e.g. the meeting: focus on listening/asking key questions of experts; take time to consider your own opinions.	
have you got the skills needed?	e.g. the meeting: listening skills; questioning skills.	
have you got the knowledge needed?	e.g. the meeting: to ask focused questions, do some research on the topic in advance.	
do you reflect 'in action' while it's happening?	e.g. the meeting: X seems to know most; I don't really understand the replies; I'm not sure what they want.	
do you amend what you do on the spot?	e.g. the meeting: address your questions to X; ask for clarification about replies; ask what they want.	
do you reflect 'on action' after the event?	e.g. the meeting: I still need more information; some of my questions worked/some didn't; other people seemed impatient with me.	
do you action plan for the future?	e.g. I need to do more research on the topic in advance, so I'm better prepared next time.	

What's your reaction to the above process/series of questions above?

- Does this process look useful (or not) to you?

- If useful, could you practise it in a situation in the near future?

- If it doesn't seem useful, why? What could you do instead to help you learn better in, and from, experiences?

E4 Reflecting on and improving your reflections

Aspects related to each of reflection	Your notes/evaluation of yourself
What do you think you do well in the reflective process?	
What do you find difficult about it?	
What affects how well you reflect (e.g. you do it when you've enough time but not in a crisis; you do it when you need to focus)?	
In an ideal situation, what would you do to reflect well and improve your learning?	
What feedback have you had about your reflective processes? What would you like feedback about?	
Who could help you develop your reflective processes (e.g. a mentor; a tutor)? How could they help?	

It may be useful to produce a summary of key things you need to improve and how.

What do you need to most develop or improve in your reflective processes?	How will you do that?	What might have an impact or influence what you can do (including constraints)?

You could now look at Chapter 14 'Action Planning; identifying action; making recommendations'

REFERENCES

Kolb, D.A., (1984), *Experiential learning: experience as the source of learning and development*, New Jersey: Prentice-Hall.

Schon, D.A., (1987), *Educating the reflective practitioner*, San Fransisco: Jossey-Bass.

Sheffield Hallam University, (2007), *The FAST project*, last accessed 25 February 2009 at: http://www.open.ac.uk/fast/

18
PERSONAL/PROFESSIONAL DEVELOPMENT PLANNING (PDP)

HOW THIS CHAPTER CAN HELP YOU

The 'crucial' skills part of this chapter aims to help you:

- identify the features of PDP (and CPD) and how it can help you achieve what you want (academic; personal; professional; lifestyle) and improve your performance;
- accept responsibility for your own learning and operate autonomously;
- decide on personal aims and directions for development;
- reflect on own abilities, skills, knowledge, attitudes and approaches in relation to your aims and how to achieve them;
- develop a plan to meet your development aims and needs, considering approaches that suit you;
- identify and find information on ways to achieve what you want and on people and resources who might help;
- identify factors that might affect your plans and your progress;
- review, revise and amend your plan, using feedback and support;
- compile a record;
- use this record for a range of purposes;
- identify how to improve your PDP skills.

The 'enhanced' skills part of this chapter is shorter: it helps you operate to a higher level. As well as the 'crucial' skills' outcomes, you'll be able to:

- identify opportunities for using and developing PDP (and CPD) in complex and unpredictable contexts, clearly identifying what you most want to achieve;
- reflect on and evaluate your ability to identify and meet your needs;
- devise an implementation strategy for PDP, identifying opportunities and constraints and allowing for complex situations and unpredictable events;
- adapt what you do to achieve what you want/need, reflecting on progress and direction and taking into account uncertainties and ambiguities;

- evaluate your PDP strategy and its effectiveness;
- select material to record and adapt your use of it for different purposes;
- identify how you can further use and develop your PDP skills.

CRUCIAL SKILLS

C1 Why is this chapter important and how can it help you?

Your university/college may use other terms for Personal (and/or Professional) Development Planning. Possibilities include: Personal Development Portfolio; Personal Development Record; Personal Development Profile; Progress File; Individual Learning Plan. 'Professional' may replace or be added to 'personal'. If you're in employment, other terms may be: Continuing Professional Development (CPD); Appraisal.

All these refer to a process that helps you develop as a learner and as a professional (or in your chosen lifestyle), whereby you:

- identify what you want to achieve now and in the future;

- review where you currently are in relation to your aims and hopes;

- plan how to get to where you want to be;

- keep a record of the process.

PDP should be a feature of all courses leading to a higher education (HE) award. PDP is 'a structured and supported process undertaken by an individual to reflect upon their own learning, performance and/or achievement and to plan for their personal, educational and career development' (QAA, 2009).

In some courses, PDP (or aspects of it) is a formal part of the course and may be assessed. It may be part of tutorial support and you may be given resources to use.

Implied in the PDP process are some high level skills. You need to 'unpack' the process to see what's actually required; it isn't as straightforward as our summary above suggests.

- You need to decide what you want in the long term and what you need to achieve in the short/medium term to get there (this isn't always easy).

- You need to look at your past and at what it says about you as a learner or a professional or in your chosen lifestyle. It means identifying your strengths and limitations in relation to what you want to achieve (i.e. your skills, attitudes, knowledge, etc.), so you know what to build on and what to develop, improve or change.

- This means being able to use reflection as a skill.

- You need to identify actions to take, develop a plan and follow it through, amending it when things change.

The word 'personal' is used here to relate to the development of you as a person (i.e. your skills, qualities, abilities, knowledge) in order to support your development as a learner or a professional or in your chosen lifestyle. It's only concerned with other issues you might see as 'personal' (i.e. relationships, interests, leisure activities) inasmuch as they impact on this.

You may not follow a 'straight' career. You may decide, for example, to bring up a family; be engaged in political or voluntary activities; be involved in creative activities that may or may not create income. This is what we mean by 'your chosen lifestyle'.

Why is PDP seen as important? It encourages individuals to take responsibility for their learning and development. It formalises, and therefore helps develop, skills and processes needed every day, at a micro level (what do you want to do today and how will you get it done) or a macro level (what do you want to do with your life and how will you do it).

This process needs some thinking about and it needs practice; this chapter aims to help you with it.

C2 Other chapters you need to use together with this one

Some elements of the PDP process are covered in more detail in other chapters and are only briefly referred to in this one, so you **must** look at other chapters for fuller support.

Chapter	Title	How it relates to this chapter	Page
17	Reflecting on your learning and experience (including feedback).	Reflection and reviewing where you are.	379
14	Action planning: identifying actions; making recommendations.	Identifying useful actions to take to achieve what you want; part of the planning process.	301
15	Handling time and pressure.	Developing a plan, within a timescale, to help you achieve what you want.	327
3	Producing portfolios and journals (including diaries, blogs, etc.).	Keeping a record of the process and recording achievement.	49

There are other chapters that will also support the PDP process.

Chapter	Title	How it relates to this chapter	Page
7	Finding, using and analysing information.	You may need to gather information about options open to you (jobs, other courses).	147
16	Solving problems and making decisions.	You'll be making decisions about what to do or what you want.	357
10	Presenting your work: making it look good.	You may need to present a portfolio of evidence (paper-based or electronic).	205

C3 What do you want? Implications for short-, medium- and long-term aims

Some people are clear about what they want out of life: the sort of work they want to do, the level they want to reach and how ambitious they are, where they want to live and how, if they want to be married and have children, if they want to stay in the UK or go overseas, and so on.

Others will know what they want in some of those areas. Others may have vague hopes but not clear aims. Some will have no ideas beyond the end of the course or the year.

Research (Gist et al, 1990) suggests that two things are important: knowing what you want to achieve; being able to implement a plan to get there. It also suggests that the second of those is key. Aims and targets are not much use if you can't 'follow through'.

The following gives five formats/exercises to help you think about what you want. You also need to look at Chapter 17 'Reflecting on your learning and experience (including feedback)' here.

In identifying what you want; go as far ahead in time as you can. If 20 years is too far, don't worry; think ahead to the end of this year (or month!).

Some of the things you may want to consider in relation to the following include: friends; family; colleagues; other students; tutors; leisure/sport; social; money; appearance; politics; power; control; solitary/alone; time; outdoors; fun; caring for others; children; people with specific needs. That's not a complete list; other things may matter to you too!

1 Likes and dislikes	Your notes
What do you enjoy in your life at the moment?	
What have you enjoyed in your life in the past?	
What do you dislike in your life at the moment?	
What have you disliked in your life in the past?	
Which of these things would you like to be part of your life in the future?	
What do you not want to be part of your life in the future?	

2 Important/not important	Your notes
What's important to you in your life now?	
What's been important to you in the past?	
What's not at all important to you now?	
What's not been important to you in the past?	
What does the way you spend your time say about what's important to you?	
Which of the things identified in response to the above would be important to you in the future?	
What of these things would you really like to avoid in future?	

It's particularly important to look at Chapter 17 'Reflecting on your learning and experience (including feedback)' for the following.

3 Strengths and limitations	Your notes
What are your main skills or abilities?	
Which of these would you like to go on using and developing?	
What are your main strengths in relation to your knowledge?	
Which areas of knowledge would you like to go on using and developing?	
What are the skills or abilities where you're really limited or have difficulties?	
Which of these would you like to improve or develop?	
Which of these would you like to avoid or work around?	
What are your main limitations or difficulties in relation to your knowledge?	
Which areas of knowledge would you like to improve or develop?	
Which of these would you like to avoid or work around?	

4 Needs and constraints	Your notes
What's stopping you doing what you want to do now?	
What's stopped you doing what you wanted to do in the past?	
How long will any 'constraints' that you have go on for?	
Can you remove them? Can you work around them? Are you stuck with them?	
What do you need to help you in your current situation?	
What have you needed to help you in the past?	
Will any of the things you need change or stay the same? How can you allow for them?	
What does the above suggest about what's important to you?	
Do you now need to amend boxes 1 and 2 above about likes/dislikes; important/not important?	

Looking at your responses above:

- if you already have aims and targets, do they confirm them or make you question them?

- do they suggest any new or different aims and targets for the future?

What's an aim and what's a target?

Aim: where/how/what you'd like to be/do/end up.

Target: a specific point to reach, that's measurable (i.e. you'll know when you've hit it).

At this stage, your aims and targets may be vague or more specific.

Example

	Vague	*More specific*
Aim	*I'd like to do visually creative work.*	*I'd like to work in a graphics agency.*
Target	*Get relevant vacation or part time or voluntary work.*	*Get vacation work next summer in a graphics agency.*

Aims and targets

What are yours?

Your aims	Your targets that relate to these aims	Your timescale

If you find it difficult to decide on aims and targets, Chapter 16 'Solving problems and making decisions' could help.

C4 How will you get there?

What actions must you take to meet your aims and targets, for example, to get a good degree, to decide on a job and then to get it? What will you need to do?

What help or resources will you need to carry out those actions? Have you got the skills or knowledge to do them? If not, further actions might be needed (e.g. find more information on available jobs; improve your writing skills).

How can you get information about resources/help you need?

- Ask at information points in your university/college (e.g. Learning Centre/ Library; student services; ICT support) or relevant managers/sections at work (e.g. Human Resources).

- Look at the e-learning environment in your university/college. There may be a support section/tab leading you to relevant information.

- Ask in the students union. They may be able to direct you to help.

- Look at the web sites of employers or professional bodies.

- Your university/college careers service has access to a national web site . It covers: types of jobs; how to get into them; guidance on career decision making.

- Internet (but can you trust who's providing the information?).

- Ask others (e.g. friends; relatives; work colleagues; people doing the job you fancy – but think about how 'expert' they are).

- Look at Chapter 7 'Finding, using and analysing information and evidence'.

- Look at other chapters in this book for help in developing skills or ways of doing things.

- Browse in a bookshop; look in a Learning Centre/Library.

It helps to pull together all your thoughts about your aims and how you'll achieve them. You could use a format like the one in the example plan below.

Example plan

Aim (e.g. career aim): I'd like to work in a graphics agency.		Deadline 2013	
Main target (e.g. career target): Get vacation or part time or voluntary graphics work.		Deadline to meet target: May 2010	
Actions (What will you do to achieve the target?)	Resources; support (What will help you carry out the action?)	start date	end date
Create a CV and speculative letter.	See examples in Internet sites. Find relevant job adverts for skills/knowledge/experiences needed. Talk to professionals in agencies.	Jan 2010	March 2010
Identify possible agencies.	Look in Yellow Pages, on Web, talk to professionals I know.	Jan 2010	March 2010
Tailor each letter to suit and send with CV.	Find out about each agency (e.g. from Web pages) to identify their focus. Rewrite my standard letter to suit their focus.	March 2010	May 2010

For further guidance on making plans and setting timescales, **look at both Chapter 14 'Action planning; identifying actions; making recommendations' and Chapter 15 'Handling time and pressure'**

C5 What do you need to allow for? Putting your plan into action

The most important aspect in getting where you want to be is your ability to follow through on your plans. What might affect how you put your plan into practice? It's likely to involve personal change and that's hard. It's easy to slip back into familiar ways and so it's well worth thinking about what might help or hinder you.

Once you've identified what might help or hinder, you've got options: change your aims and targets (see Section C3); change your actions and plans (see Section C4); develop your ability to 'follow though'. The following helps you think about this.

1 Your approach to plans	Your notes
What are you like at making plans? Do you like doing it, or avoid it?	
What effect does this have?	
What you do when planning and why?	
Do you usually follow plans you make? Sometimes? Rarely?	
What effect does this have?	
What do you do when following plans and why?	
What does the above suggest about what's important to you?	
What do you need to do in the future that's the same or different?	

2 Your resources and opportunities	Your notes
Have you got the resources you need to put plans into action?	
What opportunities/situations do you need to carry out your actions and plans?	
For resources and opportunities, are there financial issues? What are they?	
For resources and opportunities, are there time issues, e.g. time? What are they?	
For resources and opportunities, are there requirements (e.g. health and safety; legal)?	
For resources and opportunities, are there location issues (e.g. location of jobs you'd like)?	

3 Personal issues	Your notes
Do you have any health issues that affect your plans (positively or negatively)?	
What could you do about this, if anything?	
If you can't do anything about it, what effect will it have on what you can/can't do?	
Do you have any domestic issues that affect your plans (positively or negatively)?	
What could you do about this, if anything?	
If you can't do anything about it, what effect will it have on what you can/can't do?	
What else?	

4 Motivation	Your notes
How much do you really want your aims and targets?	
Are they important enough to make you deal with any negatives above?	
If not, do you need to adapt your aims and targets or your plans?	

See Chapter 15 'Handling time and pressure' for ideas on following through on plans and actions.

C6 Monitoring progress and amending plans

Where you're trying to develop yourself or to do things in a new way, it's important to monitor progress. You could:

- keep a diary or journal;

- keep a record or evidence of things you've done or achieved;

- note progress on your plan.

How can you make judgements about your progress? You could:

- make targets SMART (**S**pecific; **M**easurable; **A**chievable; **R**ealistic; **T**imebound). See Chapter 14' Action Planning: identifying actions; making recommendations' for help.

- identify your own criteria for seeing if you're performing well enough

- use assessment criteria (e.g. criteria from: your course; professional standards) that relate to the skills/knowledge you want to develop

- use feedback from others; see Chapter 17 'Reflecting on your learning and experience (including feedback)'.

In seeking feedback you could consider:

- who's best placed to give feedback on the required area/topic/skill?

- what do you want to know about your performance? The more specific you are in asking for feedback, the more useful it will be.

You may be able to get support from others in thinking through what you want and how well you're doing (see Chapter 13 'Dealing with other people').Some opportunities for this are:

- in a tutorial on your course (they may or may not use PDP type materials in them);

- in an appraisal meeting at work, to review your progress and development needs (there'll probably be CPD materials to help with this);

- with a mentor.

You'll need to work out in advance what you'd like to get out of meetings like the above, and how they can help you.

What if you're not making progress?

You could use Section C5 to identify the reasons. What if you're not monitoring and recording your progress? You could use Section C5 to consider why.

You'll need to amend your plans on an ongoing basis. If you've made progress, you may want to consider further targets or aims. If you haven't, you may need to revise them, to amend your actions and timescale, or develop new skills or approaches.

What sort of new skills or approaches? In his book about emotional intelligence, Golman (1996) identifies 'delayed gratification' as key to achievement; that is, you need to be able to put off what you'd like immediately, in order to get what you want in the end. Where would you fit on a scale indicating delayed gratification? Do you eat the things you like first or leave them till last? Do you put off work to do something you enjoy? Does it depend what it is that you need to 'defer'? Look at Chapter 15 'Handling time and pressure' for ideas on keeping on target.

Of course, you may decide that you want to live life spontaneously, doing whatever appeals at the moment. That's a valid 'lifestyle' decision. The implication of planning ahead is that you can't always do what you want in the moment. The implication of doing what you want in the moment is that it may stop you planning ahead.

You could also consider changes in circumstances. Has an economic change made certain jobs easier or harder to get? Have you done better or worse in your course/ work and does this open up or close down opportunities? Has your personal situation changed?

C7 Producing a record

You need a record of your aims, targets, plans and progress against them and of evidence of what you've achieved. Why can't you just 'do it'? Why the need for all these records?

There are a number of reasons for keeping a PDP or CPD record.

- It'll help you focus. It's a way of 'making' you do it.

- It's a tool for helping you think things through. Using writing or visual images can help you with what can be a difficult reflective process.

- You can collect material that you can then use as a basis for reflecting (see Chapter 17 'Reflecting on your learning and experience (including feedback').

- If PDP is assessed in some way, you'll need to keep records to prove what you did.

- It may be a CPD requirement of your profession that you keep records.

- A record of your achievements can make you feel good.

- You can use your records for many other purposes (e.g. for: a curriculum vitae (CV); a job/course application; interviews; portfolios of design/ creative work; research funding).

If you need to provide evidence for what you have done, then it needs to be:

- current (done at the time you are referring to);

- sufficient (enough to prove what you want to prove);

- valid (it proves what you say it proves);

- authentic (about you, and not somebody else).

For more on recording evidence and information, see Chapter 3 'Producing portfolios and journals (including diaries, blogs, etc.)', as these are the most likely ways in which you'll have to present PDP evidence.

It's likely you'll need to record:

- action plans;

- progress reviews;

- evidence of what you did;

- personal reflections on what you did and what it 'means';

- feedback received;

- academic, personal and/or professional experiences and achievements;

- skills; qualities; abilities; knowledge;

- approaches to learning and what you've learnt or how you've developed;

- life/non-curricular experiences (e.g. those relevant to your skills/course/job/future aims).

C8 Reviewing and improving what you do

How can you improve your PDP skills?

Element	This is what I'll repeat/do the same in future	This is what I'll do differently
Deciding on my aims and targets.		
Reflection: thinking about what matters to me.		
Reflection: thinking about what I'm good at (or not).		
Producing action plans.		
Putting plans into action.		
Monitoring and amending plans.		
Recording what I do.		
Presenting my records.		

ENHANCED SKILLS

E1 How can the PDP process help you?

The Critical Skills section above considers the processes involved in PDP. In what situations could those processes be really helpful?

They might be particularly helpful at transition points in your life or when you need to make major decisions. These may include:

- changing from one course to another;

- leaving a course;

- committing yourself to or leaving a relationship;

- having children;

- acquiring responsibilities as a carer;

- getting a first professional job;

- changing jobs;

- getting or seeking promotion;

- moving between part time and full time work;

- retiring;

- changing interests or getting involved in new ones;

- involvement in a new social circle.

Such situations are likely to be unpredictable and involve uncertainties or complexities (e.g. a new job could involve: a change of location; domestic issues; finance; a new social circle).

The more complex and uncertain the situation, the more you need to think it through using the processes covered in Section C above (e.g. what's important to you, what do you need, how does it fit into your long term aims, do you have the skills and abilities needed for it?).

Issue	Your notes
What situations face you now, where this PDP process might be useful?	
What's involved in the situations? Are there complexities and uncertainties?	
What situations might you face in the future, where the PDP process might be useful?	
What's involved in the situations? Are there complexities and uncertainties?	

The processes suggested previously in Section C could help you identify what you want from situations and how this relates to your aims and the actions you need to plan for.

This may then suggest you need to amend your aims and targets, or it may help you clarify your long term aims (e.g. career or lifestyle) and the targets you might hit along the way.

Does thinking in this way dismay you?

Does 'PDP thinking' turn you off?	Your notes
Would you rather just 'go with the flow'? In all areas of your life or in just some?	
What are the implications of that?	
Is this OK? Does it tie in with how you want to live your life?	

You could look forward, in order to help you think about the here and now.

A bit gloomy, but...	Your notes
what would you like an obituary about you to say?	
what do you have to do now in order for it to say that then?	

E2 Your skills in the PDP process

How good are you at knowing what you want and need, and then taking action to get that?

Do you dislike that question? Do you see it as selfish? If so, it might be useful to look at Chapter 13 'Dealing with other people' as that considers assertiveness. Assertiveness is about valuing both yourself and others, whereas aggression is seen as getting what you want at the expense of others and passivity as letting others get what they want at your expense.

An assertive approach allows for your needs and those of others to be met. You may, of course, decide you want something so much that you'll go for it regardless (e.g. in competitive situations such as applying for jobs or in sports). Or you may decide something else is more important than your own needs (perhaps you see somebody else's needs as more important in a particular situation).

In both these above cases you're identifying your aim (e.g. to win or to please another person) and are taking appropriate action. However, what if your approach isn't appropriate for your aim? What if you'd like to win but are being passive? What if you are so busy pleasing others you don't think about what you want?

If you are (or aren't) taking action to meet your aims, why? Is this related to your attitude (assertive; aggressive; passive) or is it to do with circumstances, your skills or knowledge?

Issue	Your notes
Are you identifying what you want or need?	
Why or why not?	
Is that OK, or could you take a different approach?	
Are you taking actions to meet your wants and needs?	
Why or why not?	
Do you need to change any attitudes, to take action?	
Do you need to develop skills or techniques, to take action?	
If circumstances are stopping you from acting, could you do anything about them?	
What help or resources do you need?	

E3 Implementing your plans

When considering developing a plan, implementing it, monitoring progress and amending it, it might also help to think about the following.

Issue	Examples and suggestions	Your notes
What opportunities might help you reach your aims and targets? This might include opportunities to develop skills or knowledge.	Your choice of topic for a project/course options. Part time/voluntary work. Leisure activities. Student union or course responsibilities (e.g. course rep). Travel or taking time out.	
Who/what might be able to help?	Work shadowing to see what a job entails. Support staff (e.g. technician). Borrowing equipment (e.g. for filming or recording). Workshop spaces for artists. Sound studios.	

What is it about you that might affect your plans?

Influences on your plans	Benefits/positives/how I can use this	Things I need to improve and how
Your confidence.		
Your skills or techniques.		
Your knowledge.		
What else?		

Look at Chapters 15 'Handling time and pressure' and 16 'Solving problems and making decisions'. Both look at how to avoid or deal with uncertainties and unpredictable events and with complexity.

You might now want to review and amend your plans.

E4 Evaluating and amending what you do

Plans rarely work out exactly. They're a guide rather than a straightjacket and, as with any journey, you might find a better route.

Evaluating what you are doing is a key aspect of amending plans. You may need to change your plans because of changing circumstances, constraints or aims, but you may also want to change them because what you are doing isn't working very well.

Schon (1987) wrote of 'reflection on action' and 'reflection in action'. His view was that the latter is really important; being able to work out while you are in a situation what's working or not so you can amend it on the spot. He thought that getting practice at 'reflection on action', (i.e. after the event), is practice for doing this.

You need to evaluate how effective your PDP process is after the event, so next time you can make it better while it's happening. Below are questions to help you think about how effective you are in using the PDP process.

Questions	Your notes
Which decisions have you made that have been helpful and how?	
Which decisions have you made that have been unhelpful and how?	
Is any lack of decision making on your part having an effect? How?	
What effect is your use of information having on your PDP process?	
Are you using feedback and if so is it helping you? How? Why? Why not?	
What other factors are affecting what is going on? How?	
How helpful is your reflection on your own performance? How? Why?	

Questions	Your notes
Have you made a plan? If not, why not?	
Are you carrying out your plan? If not, why not?	
Are the actions you've identified effective? How? Why?	
What are the main things you need to do differently?	

You might now want to review and amend your plans.

E5 Your records of your PDP process

What are you going to use these records for? This will affect:

- the way you keep them (e.g. paper based; electronic; web pages; blog);
- what you keep (e.g. originals; copies; images; assignments; letters; certificates);
- how you 'catalogue' it (e.g. by topic; year; type of item).

What if the items are big or 3 dimensional, how will you store or record those?

Look at Chapters 3 'Producing portfolios and journals (including diaries, blogs etc)' and 10 'Presenting your work: making it look good'.

Purpose of the records	✓	Implications
They'll be assessed.		Identify the assessment criteria (what will pass/get a good mark?) and meet them. Your tutor may determine the form you present them in. Somebody else must make sense of it, so it has to be clear.
As the basis for my CV or application forms.		Store information in sections that correspond with CV/applications (so you can find it easily). Don't lose it; store it in a safe place. Keep updating (no missing information); keep copies. Store a basic CV/application to adapt for different purposes (never use a standard one for everything). If you're sending images, see Chapters 3 and 10.

Purpose of the records	✓	Implications
To show information at interview.		Artists and designers have always shown examples of their work at interview. If you're from another subject, what work would impress? How will you store such examples? How will you catalogue them so you can find them easily? See Chapters 3 and 10.
As part of Continuing Professional Development (CPD).		Check professional body or employer requirements. Find out how they want you to present the information and devise a record keeping system to allow for this. Make sure you keep it updated and don't lose it (your professional status may depend on it).
For your own personal use to keep track of your development.		How can you organise your records to meet your needs (e.g. by topic; type of skill; things you're good at)? How could you organise it flexibly in case your needs change? How will you easily find items needed? How could you store material so it increases your confidence (e.g. by achievements)? What format will encourage you to use it, not just put it away?

E6 What would help you improve your PDP practice and skills?

Possible issue	Our suggestions	Your notes
Do you need to improve your motivation to engage in PDP?	Identify purposes for it. Identify how it can help you. Identify future problems if you don't do it.	
Do you need to have a clearer view of where you are heading?	Talk it over. Seek professional help (e.g. careers service; counsellor). Read information about possibilities. Keep using Section C above.	
Do you need to improve your decision making?	Use Chapter 16 'Solving problems and making decisions'. Look at other books/ materials on decision making. Ask yourself why you find this so hard.	

Possible issue	Our suggestions	Your notes
Do you need to improve your planning and acting on your plans?	Look at Sections C and E in this chapter.	
Do you need to improve your ability to reflect?	Look at Chapter 17 'Reflecting on your learning and experience (including feedback)'.	
What else?		

REFERENCES

Gist, M.E., Bavetta, A.G., Stevens, C.K., (1990), 'Transfer training method: its influence on skill generalisation, skill repetition and performance level', *Personal Psychology*, vol. 43, 501–523.

Golman, D., (1996), *Emotional intelligence. Why it can matter more than IQ*, London: Bloomsbury.

QAA, (2009), *Policy statement on a progress file for Higher Education*, on-line at http://www.qaa.ac.uk/academicinfrastructure/progressfiles/archive/policystatement/, last accessed 27.1.09.

Schon, D.A., (1987), *Educating the reflective practitioner*, San Fransisco: Jossey-Bass.

If you have found this book useful you may be interested in other titles from Gower

Mastering University
Sheffield Hallam University Enterprises Ltd
CD-ROM: 978-0-566-08708-0

Winning Research Funding
Abby Day Peters
Paperback: 978-0-566-08459-1
e-book: 978-0-7546-8560-9

The Management of a Student Research Project
John A Sharp, John Peters and Keith Howard
Paperback: 978-0-566-08490-4
e-book: 978-0-7546-8548-7

The Interviewer
Sheffield Hallam University Enterprises Ltd
CD-ROM: 978-0-566-08608-3

How to Get Research Published in Journals
Abby Day
Paperback: 978-0-566-08815-5
e-book: 978-0-7546-8894-5

GOWER

Blended Learning and Online Tutoring:
Planning Learner Support and Activity Design
Janet Macdonald
Paperback: 978-0-566-08841-4
e-book: 978-0-7546-9251-5

Informal Learning:
A New Model for Making Sense of Experience
Lloyd Davies
Hardback: 978-0-566-08857-5
e-book: 978-0-566-09199-5

Electronic Performance Support:
Using Digital Technology to Enhance Human Ability
Edited by Philip Barker and Paul van Schaik
Hardback: 978-0-566-08884-1
e-book: 978-0-566-09239-8

An Adventure in Service-Learning:
Developing Knowledge, Values and Responsibility
Anto T. Kerins
Hardback: 978-0-566-08894-0
e-book: 978-1-4094-0190-2

Visit **www.studentskills.org** and